The English Reformation

Crown power and religious change, 1485–1558

Colin Pendrill

Series Editors
Martin Collier
Erica Lewis
Rosemary Rees

Heinemann

Hereford
SIXTH FORM COLLEGE
Learning Resources Centre

HEINEMANN ADVANCED HISTORY

Heinemann Educational Publishers
Halley Court, Jordan Hill, Oxford, OX2 8EJ
a division of Reed Educational & Professional Publishing Ltd
Heinemann is a registered trademark of Reed Educational & Professional Publishing Ltd

OXFORD MELBOURNE AUCKLAND
JOHANNESBURG BLANTYRE GABORONE
IBADAN PORTSMOUTH NH (USA) CHICAGO

First published 2000

ISBN 0 435 32712 7
02 01
10 9 8 7 6 5 4 3 2

Designed and typeset by Wyvern 21 Ltd

Printed and bound in Great Britain by The Bath Press Ltd, Bath

Photographic acknowledgements
The authors and publisher would like to thank the following for permission to reproduce
photographs: Ancient Art & Architecture Collection: p. 101; The Art Archive/Civiche Racc
d'Arte Pavia, Italy/Dagli Orti: p.67; The Art Archive/Galleria degli Uffizi Florence/Dagli
Orti: p. 61; The Art Archive/Museo del Prado, Madrid/Dalger Press: p. 66; Bridgeman Art
Library/V&A Museum: p. 9; Bridgeman Art Library/Berger Collection, Denver: p. 24;
Bridgeman Art Library/Bonhams, London: p. 178; Bridgeman Art Library/City of Bristol
Museum & Art Gallery: p. 46; Bridgeman Art Library/Corpus Christi College, Oxford: p.
154; Bridgeman Art Library/Ipswich Borough Council Museums & Galleries, Suffolk: p.
27; Bridgeman Art Library/Lambeth Palace Library, London: p. 108; Bridgeman Art
Library/Louvre: p. 12; Bridgeman Art Library/National Portrait Gallery, London: p. 194;
Bridgeman Art Library/Palazzo Barerini, Rome: p. 169; Bridgeman Art Library/Philip
Mould Historical Portraits Ltd., London: p. 79; Bridgeman Art Library/Richard Philip,
London: p. 175; Collections/Liz Stares: p. 56; Mary Evans Picture Library: pp. 21, 31, 32,
37, 75, 83, 181; Fotomas: pp. 117, 125; National Portrait Gallery: pp. 95, 123.

Cover photograph: © Fotomas

Written sources acknowledgements
The author and publisher gratefully acknowledge the following publications from which
written sources in the book are drawn. In some sources the wording or sentence has been
simplified.

Dickens, *The English Reformation*, Pennsylvania State University Press 1989; p. 226: Elton,
England under the Tudors, Routledge 1974; p. 227, 229: Fletcher, *Tudor Rebellions*,
Longman 1983; p. 222: Haigh, *English Reformations*, Oxford University Press 1993; p. 229:
Loades, *Revolution in Religion: The English Reformation 1530–70*, University of Wales Press
1992; p, 216: Lockyer and O'Sullivan, *Tudor Britain 1486-1603*, Longman 1997; p.
229–30: Murphy, Keen, Tillbrook and Walsh-Atkins, *England 1485–1603*, Collins 1999; p.
119: Servini, *English Reformation*, Hodder and Stoughton 1997; p. 123.

CONTENTS

HOW TO USE THIS BOOK

This book is divided into two distinct sections. Chapters 1–7 are AS-style sections covering the period 1485–1558. These chapters attempt to explain the interaction of politics and religion in England during this period. The text of this descriptive analysis gives the student in-depth information and some clear analysis. The questions at the end of each chapter will challenge the student to use the information in the chapter to analyse, prioritise and explain the important aspects of the subject. In addition to essay questions, Chapters 5 and 6 also have source questions based on sources quoted in the text, to help students with this type of exam question. In answering these questions, it is hoped that students will acquire a clear understanding of the key features of change and continuity in Church and State during this period. It looks in more depth and detail at the impact of the Reformations, both Protestant and Catholic, during the reigns of Henry VIII, Edward VI and Mary I. There are also source questions at the end of Sections 1 and 2 in the A2 section to help students think through the issues raised.

The A2 section, running from 1533 to 1558, is more analytical in style and principally geared to the requirements of those taking History at A2.

At the end of each of the AS and A2 sections, there is an assessment section. These assessments are based on the requirements of the new AS and A2 specifications provided by the three awarding bodies: Edexcel, AQA and OCR. There are exam-style source and essay questions for each specification. These are followed by detailed guidance on how students might answer the questions, together with sample answers.

Viewpoint and historiography

This book is designed for students studying the period for the first time. As such, it was decided not to spend too long explaining different interpretations of the period by different historians (called historiography) since this may confuse those new to the period. The viewpoint of this book can be described as 'revisionist' (see pages 58–9), but students who wish to explore other viewpoints will find references to other schools of thought in the text, an overview at the beginning of the A2 section, and a full list of other books in the Bibliography.

AS SECTION: POLITICS AND RELIGION 1485–1558

INTRODUCTION

The Wars of the Roses

By 1485, England had been periodically torn apart by civil war for the previous thirty years. These wars were called the Wars of the Roses and were fought between the Houses of York and Lancaster. Although the impact of these conflicts was not as great as used to be thought, the power of the Crown was seriously undermined. Three kings met violent deaths and a series of pitched battles were fought all over the country. In 1461 the Yorkist Edward IV overthrew the Lancastrian Henry VI. In 1483, after a period of stability during the second reign of Edward IV (1471–83), the wars started again. Instead of being York versus Lancaster, it was now York against York. When Edward IV died unexpectedly in 1483, at the age of forty, Edward's young son, Edward V, was violently overthrown and probably murdered by his uncle Richard, Duke of Gloucester, who then became King Richard III. Two years later, in 1485, Richard III was killed at the Battle of Bosworth and was succeeded by his Lancastrian opponent, Henry Tudor, who was crowned as Henry VII. The Wars of the Roses did not end there, but Henry VII did manage to hold on to the Crown until his death in 1509.

Henry VII re-establishes the power of the Crown

Chapters 1–4 of this book examine the ways in which Henry VII managed to strengthen the power of the Crown and show up the importance of the English Church and English churchmen in helping to overcome the political instability of the Wars of the Roses. The English Church in this period was Roman Catholic, part of the universal Catholic Church that was the Christian Church throughout western Europe. Although the English Church owed allegiance to the Pope in Rome, this was not a problem for English kings at this time, as the Pope's authority was seen as mainly spiritual. The English Church was actually run by the king, aided by the Archbishops of Canterbury and York, and Church and State worked well together on the whole. The king's chief ministers were often churchmen who were chosen as bishops by the king and confirmed in their office by the Pope. In the everyday working of the Church, the Pope was a distant and remote figure.

Harmony between Church and State under Henry VIII

When Henry VIII became king in 1509, the power of the monarchy was strengthened further. Unlike his father, Henry VIII won the throne not by battle, but by peaceful succession and he faced no opposition to his kingship. The power of the nobility was temporarily enhanced as they were now seen as fitting companions to the new king in his court. During Henry VII's reign the nobility had been treated with suspicion; now they became a court nobility serving the king as advisers and companions. In 1513 and 1523 Henry VIII launched invasions of France and, diplomatically, England's position as one of the great powers in Europe was established.

Relations between the king and the Church were strengthened too, by the king's decision to make Thomas Wolsey his chief minister after 1515. The king gave Wolsey a bishopric and the Archbishopric of York and later insisted that the Pope make him a cardinal and a papal legate as well. By 1520, then, England was very much at peace with itself and relations between the State and the Church seemed harmonious.

The impact of the Reformation in the 1520s

During the 1520s, some parts of Europe – not very many as it happened – decided to break away from papal control and set up their own Protestant Churches. These Protestants, based mainly in parts of Germany, claimed that they were reforming the Church in line with the teachings of the Bible. Hence these changes have become known as the Reformation.

In England, during the 1520s, it seemed very unlikely that such reforming ideas would catch on. Henry VIII associated the Reformation with rebellion and disorder, and he wrote a book against Luther's religious ideas. Wolsey, as a cardinal and papal legate, was naturally very much opposed to the spread of new religious ideas (known by the Catholic Church as heresy). Moreover, the Catholic Church in England was not widely unpopular in the 1520s.

The Henrician Reformation 1533–8

In Chapters 5 and 6 the book tries to explain why and how Henry VIII moved the English Church in a Protestant direction in the 1530s. During the late 1520s, quite unexpectedly, relations between Henry VIII and the Pope gradually worsened. Henry VIII wanted to divorce his wife, Catherine of Aragon, and the Pope, who had the power to grant divorces, was unable to give his consent. In 1529 Wolsey fell from power as a result of this problem and, during 1533–4, Henry VIII passed a series of laws that cut England off from Rome and declared that the king, not the Pope, was, and always had been, Supreme Head of the English Church.

This was followed by the dissolution of the English monasteries between 1536 and 1540, which was an unprecedented act of theft by the English Crown. Religious institutions that had stood for many centuries were swept away and their lands and wealth were taken by the king. New Articles of Religion and Injunctions on religious practice were introduced at the same time and, in 1538, the king decreed that every parish should have an English Bible. Henry VIII found reformers like Thomas Cranmer and Thomas Cromwell to help him bring about these changes. In some ways, this seemed like a breathtaking revolution in the relationship between Church and State. In another way, the changes were not so wide ranging as they first appeared; they merely confirmed the king's existing power over the Church.

Reformations under Edward VI and Queen Mary 1547–58

Chapter 7 deals with the reigns of Edward VI (1547–53) and Queen Mary (1553–8) and the effects that their reigns had on the English Reformation.

From 1547 to 1553, England was ruled by Edward VI. However, he was only a nine-year-old boy when his father died, therefore power passed to his uncle, Edward Seymour, the Duke of Somerset and later to John Dudley, the Duke of Northumberland. During this period, the Church in England became more Protestant and two English Prayer Books were introduced as well as a set of 42 Articles of Religion.

At the same time there was popular discontent, expressed in two rebellions during 1549, one in the West Country and one in East Anglia. There was also political instability at the centre of government. Seymour seized power as Protector which was against Henry VIII's will. He was overthrown and later executed by Northumberland. The latter met the same end when his attempt to prevent the succession of Princess Mary on Edward's death in 1553 failed rather miserably.

With the accession of Mary, the Protestant Reformation, which had just been gathering pace under Edward VI, was destroyed. Mary was a staunch Catholic and proceeded to reintroduce Catholic worship, abolishing the Royal Supremacy established by her father and bringing back the papal Headship of the Church. The Church of England became the Church in England once again. In some ways the religious history of England had now come full circle!

HEINEMANN ADVANCED HISTORY

CHAPTER 1

1485–1509: How did Henry VII re-establish the power of the Crown during his reign?

KEY POINTS

Despite the weakness of his claim to the throne, Henry VII was able to increase the power of the Crown because:

- he defeated other claimants to the throne
- he worked hard at the business of government and increased the Crown's income
- he chose good advisers
- he exercised rigorous control over the **nobility**, who had undermined the power of the Crown during the so-called **Wars of the Roses**
- he re-established England as a major European power through careful diplomacy, making invasion less likely
- he gained powerful support from the Church.

KEY TERM

The nobility. These were the great titled landowners in England, such as dukes and earls. They were seen as the king's natural advisers and the men who ruled England in his name. Loyal servants of the Crown could receive ennoblement from the king. Those who betrayed him could lose their title and their lives. The nobility had the right to sit in the House of Lords.

KEY ISSUE

The Wars of the Roses. A series of conflicts and battles between the Houses of York and Lancaster during the period 1455–85. The conflict became serious when Richard, Duke of York, claimed to be the true king of England in place of the feeble King Henry VI. Henry VI was descended from the first Duke of Lancaster, which is why his supporters were called Lancastrians. The serious fighting of the wars was concentrated in the periods 1459–61, 1470–1 and 1485.

WEAKNESS OF HENRY VII IN 1485

On an August day in 1485, the last major conflict of the so-called Wars of the Roses took place at Bosworth Field in Leicestershire. King Richard III, who had overthrown his nephew, Edward V, two years before, was killed at the end of the battle. A relatively unknown Welshman, Henry Tudor, who had spent much of his life in exile, was crowned king by his supporters on the battlefield. He took possession of London unopposed and was officially crowned as King Henry VII. He seemed to be in a weak position for several reasons:

- His claim to the throne was rather feeble. On his father's side, he was the son of Henry VI's half-brother. On his mother's side, he was related to the Beaufort family, who were illegitimate descendants of King Edward III (1322–77) and barred from the throne.

- He became king with support from the French, who were traditionally England's main enemy in Europe.
- The political turbulence of the previous thirty years had seriously undermined the power of the English Crown. The Lancastrian king, Henry VI, had been overthrown not once but twice and had been murdered in the Tower of London. The Yorkist claimant, Edward IV, had also been overthrown. His two sons were overthrown and probably murdered in the Tower of London on the orders of their uncle, Richard of Gloucester, who reigned for only two years, as Richard III, before being killed at Bosworth. Against this backdrop of political instability, many may have wondered how long Henry VII would last.

CHALLENGES TO HENRY VII DURING HIS REIGN

In the first part of his reign, Henry VII faced serious challenges from other men who claimed to be the real king of England.

Lambert Simnel. Simnel claimed to be Edward, Earl of Warwick, and was crowned by the king's enemies in Ireland as Edward VI. Although an impostor, he gained support from Edward IV's sister, the dowager Duchess of Burgundy, in the shape of 2000 German mercenaries. With help from Ireland and joined by Richard III's heir, John de la Pole, Earl of Lincoln, the rebels sailed from Ireland, landed in Lancashire and marched towards London. Luckily for Henry, his forces prevailed at the Battle of Stoke in 1487 and the Earl of Lincoln was killed.

Perkin Warbeck. Another impostor and Yorkist claimant, Perkin Warbeck, would trouble Henry for nine years, gathering support from Henry's many enemies at home and abroad. Warbeck claimed that he was Richard, Duke of York, one of the princes in the Tower and younger son of Edward IV. In 1495, Henry had to execute his Chamberlain, Sir William Stanley – the man who had placed the crown on his head at Bosworth – for conspiring

KEY PEOPLE

Lambert Simnel (1475–1525) was the son of an Oxford carpenter and claimed to be Edward, Earl of Warwick (see the Yorkist family tree – page 7). He was crowned in Ireland, but was defeated at the Battle of Stoke in 1487.

Perkin Warbeck (1474–99) was the son of a customs official in Tournai, in the Low Countries. From 1491 he claimed to be Richard, Duke of York, the younger of Edward IV's two sons, and he was recognised as Richard IV by the Emperor Maximilian. He was captured in 1497 and hanged in 1499.

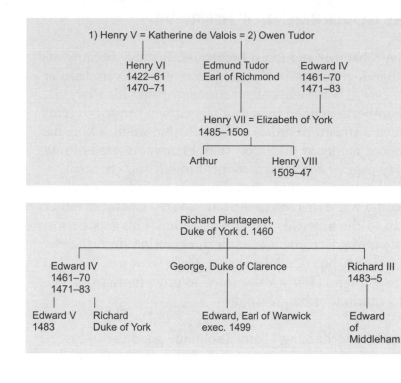

The Lancaster and Tudor family tree (the dates given are the dates of reigns).

1) Henry V = Katherine de Valois = 2) Owen Tudor

- Henry VI
  1422–61
  1470–71
- Edmund Tudor
  Earl of Richmond
- Edward IV
  1461–70
  1471–83

Henry VII = Elizabeth of York
1485–1509

- Arthur
- Henry VIII
  1509–47

The family tree of the House of York (the dates given are the dates of reigns).

Richard Plantagenet,
Duke of York d. 1460

- Edward IV
  1461–70
  1471–83
- George, Duke of Clarence
- Richard III
  1483–5

- Edward V
  1483
- Richard
  Duke of York
- Edward, Earl of Warwick
  exec. 1499
- Edward
  of
  Middleham

with Warbeck. In that same year, Warbeck attempted a landing in Kent. Having failed there, he moved on to Ireland and then Scotland. In 1496 he crossed the border with a Scottish army, but the attempted invasion soon degenerated into serious pillaging and looting instead. In 1497 Perkin's activities sparked off a serious tax revolt in Cornwall, where the local people did not see why they should pay for war against Scotland. They marched unhindered to London, only to be routed and dispersed at Blackheath. Their uprising encouraged Perkin to land in Cornwall in the same year, but then, at last, he was captured. Not until 1499, fourteen years after Henry's accession, was Warbeck finally executed, along with one genuine Yorkist prince, Edward, Earl of Warwick.

Edmund de la Pole. There still remained one serious Yorkist claimant: Edmund de la Pole, Earl of Suffolk. He was in exile in the Low Countries until he was handed over to Henry in 1506. He was not executed until 1513, four years after the king's death. So, for much of his reign, Henry VII's claim to the throne was in doubt and there were serious attempts to remove him, in just the same way as he had removed Richard III.

THE GOVERNMENT OF HENRY VII

Privy Chamber and Royal Exchequer. Possibly because of his weak claim to the throne, Henry worked very hard at the everyday business of government. From his **Privy Chamber**, attended by only a few chosen servants, Henry issued a stream of orders and letters. No English king has worked harder at his papers than Henry. He used to sign every page of the royal accounts himself and check all details of income and expenditure. Increasingly, royal income was delivered to the king's Privy Chamber rather than to the unwieldy **Royal Exchequer**. This very personal system of government was not in operation immediately after 1485, but developed as the reign went on. Interestingly, Henry VII seemed to grow more suspicious and cautious as he grew older.

Royal Council. King Henry also made good use of his Council to help to restore law and order. The Council was made up of men hand-picked by the king to advise him and to run the government. They, with or without the king, could meet as a law court and punish wrongdoers. In 1487, by means of the so-called Star Chamber Act, Henry set up a special council, possibly only a temporary measure, to deal with those guilty of rioting or disorder. Henry's servants remained loyal to him – none more so than the infamous **Empson** and **Dudley**, who ran the **Council Learned in the Law**, which operated after 1498. They acted as royal debt collectors and even invented a number of the debts that they collected!

Henry VII and royal finances

There were several sources of royal revenue for fifteenth-century kings:

- **Crown lands.** These were lands owned by the Crown, which brought in rent or goods. Henry VII owned more lands than some earlier kings, since he inherited both Lancastrian and Yorkist lands.
- **Profits of justice.** Henry VII worked hard, especially in the second half of his reign, to increase his income from fining those, especially the wealthy, who broke the law. After 1498, the Council Learned in the Law was given

The **Privy Chamber** was the king's private room or study. Under Henry VII it became an important part of government, where the king was attended by a few hand-picked servants.

The **Royal Exchequer** was the government department responsible for financial administration. It had become increasingly slow and inefficient.

Richard Empson (1450–1510) was a lawyer and royal debt collector. Arrested and charged with treason by Henry VIII, he was executed in 1510.

Edmund Dudley (1462?–1510) was a lawyer and, like Empson, a royal debt collector in the Council Learned in the Law. Arrested in 1509, on Henry VII's death, he wrote *The Tree of Commonwealth* in the Tower before his execution in 1510.

The **Council Learned in the Law** was set up by Henry VII as an offshoot of the Royal Council. It dealt with the king's financial rights and enforced the financial penalties that he imposed. It became increasingly harsh and unpopular during the last ten years of the reign.

A bust of Henry VII by Pietro Torrigiano.

Parliament was called occasionally by the king. It was made up of two chambers or Houses, as today. The House of Lords was more powerful, as it contained all the titled nobility as well as all the bishops and some abbots. The House of Commons was made up of lesser men, representing the shires (counties) and some towns. Parliament had little power during this period, but it did pass Acts of Parliament (or statutes) at the Crown's bidding and had to agree if the king was to raise parliamentary taxes such as the Fifteenths and Tenths.

the task of exploiting this source of income more effectively.

- **Feudal or prerogative rights.** As king, Henry had special rights that he could exploit for financial gain:
  - *Wardship.* This was the right to control and exploit the lands of children until they came of age. Wardship would also allow the king to arrange and sell a child's marriage.
  - *Taxes on trade.* As king, Henry fixed the levels of taxes or tariffs on the importing and exporting of goods.
  - *Sale of offices.* As king, Henry appointed all the senior officials in Church and State. He exploited this right by frequently selling important posts.
  - *Taxes granted by Parliament.* **Parliament** was called seven times by the king and each one voted him extra taxes. In theory, such taxes were for defending the kingdom from invasion or for launching an invasion of another country. In peacetime the king was meant to run the government from his own income.

The state of royal revenues. As a result of the king's hard work and exploitation of all possible sources of revenue, Henry managed to increase royal revenue and ensure that his expenditure was usually less than his income. At the end of Edward IV's reign, in 1483, yearly royal income was around £90,000. By the end of Henry VII's reign, it had risen to £113,000 per annum. Furthermore, by this time, Henry had also amassed plate and jewels equivalent to two years' income. Nonetheless this achievement should not be exaggerated. The English Crown remained underfunded in Henry's reign. Compared to the kings of Spain and France, the King of England was still the poor relation. Not until Henry VIII's Reformation in the 1530s did the Crown gain access to new and extensive sources of income.

How did Henry control the nobility?

The key to re-establishing the power of the monarchy in England was for the Crown to control the nobility. The Wars of the Roses had begun when Henry VI was unable to control or destroy the most powerful magnate of the day (and heir to the throne), Richard, Duke of York. Henry VII would ensure that none of his nobles amassed such power. At first, he consulted with the nobility in Great

Councils and led them on an expedition to France in 1492. However, the king always remained suspicious of the nobility and this suspicion became more intense after 1495 when his Chamberlain, Sir William Stanley, betrayed him.

Bonds and recognizances. The new king, unlike Henry VI and Edward IV, was very sparing in giving the nobility new titles and patronage, and he enforced the law systematically against errant noblemen, giving them no chance to increase their power. He refined the old system of **bonds and recognizances**, whereby noblemen (or their relatives) would face fines for misbehaviour and massive suspended fines in case of future misbehaviour. Of 67 noble families alive during the reign, no fewer than 36 were under some form of bond or recognizance. One individual, Lord Burgavenny, was fined a total of £70,000 in 1507. As Burgavenny was unable to pay this huge sum straight away, Henry allowed him to pay £500 a year for the next ten years.

Attainders. In addition, many families had their lands confiscated by **Acts of Attainder**. Twenty-eight attainders were passed against those who had fought Henry in 1485. In particular, Henry tried to enforce laws against illegal **retaining of armed men** by the great lords. He even fined John de Vere, a loyal servant, when he assembled rather too many of his men to greet the king on a royal visit! Henry also controlled the marriage market. Marriage between noble families had, in the past, allowed some families and some individuals to build up huge amounts of land. Now the king ensured that this would not happen in future.

Noble support. Henry was also better placed to control the nobility than the two Yorkist kings before him because he did not rely on the support of a great nobleman to become king. The Earl of Warwick had helped Edward IV to the throne and the Duke of Buckingham supported Richard III's seizure of power in 1483. Both Warwick and Buckingham, unhappy with their rewards, later rebelled against the Crown. Henry VII, in contrast, had only limited support from the English nobility before the Battle of Bosworth. The greatest man to fight for him was John

KEY TERMS

Bonds and recognizances were a system of fines and suspended fines imposed on noblemen. These had existed for a long time, but Henry VII used them more systematically than before.

Acts of Attainder were Acts of Parliament which declared that particular individuals were guilty of treason. As a result, the Crown could confiscate their lands.

Retaining of armed men. Noblemen had great households of servants who would wear their badge or livery. These men were retained or maintained by their lords and owed them service and obedience. By this means, some nobles had built up their own private armies during the Wars of the Roses. Henry could not abolish retaining, as he had no standing army and he relied on such retainers for his military power.

de Vere, the Earl of Oxford. He was not in the same league as Warwick or Buckingham in terms of personal power and, anyway, he remained loyal to Henry.

Why was the nobility less of a threat to the Crown after 1485?

Although Henry VII worked very hard to keep his nobility in check, he was fortunate in that there were no great or 'super' nobles for him to contend with.

Henry had no brothers. The king's brothers were always the greatest men in the kingdom. Edward IV's first reign came to an end in 1470 when his brother George, Duke of Clarence teamed up with the Earl Warwick (the Kingmaker) to overthrow him. In 1483 Edward IV's son and heir was overthrown by his other brother, Richard, Duke of Gloucester.

The Yorkists. Most of the great and powerful men who had caused problems for the monarchy in the recent past had been destroyed by the Wars of the Roses, and much of the land that had sustained their opposition had reverted to the Crown. Some of the lands of the Yorkists, Edward IV, George, Duke of Clarence and Richard III were inherited by Henry VII as they were Crown lands. In addition, the next Duke of York would be Henry's second son, the future Henry VIII. Furthermore, the Yorkists had left no powerful heirs. Edward IV's sons had been murdered, George of Clarence's son was safely in the Tower and was later executed, and Richard III's only son had died in infancy before Bosworth.

Other great families. Other great noble families were also in difficulties by or after 1485. The powerful Neville family had lost much of its land as Warwick the Kingmaker had no son and his two daughters married the brothers of Edward IV. The Duke of Buckingham had been executed by Richard III and his son was still a child when Henry Tudor came to the throne. The Duke of Norfolk was killed at Bosworth fighting for Richard III and his son had to show clear loyalty to King Henry in order to regain his family's ducal title. (The dukedom was not regranted to the Howard family until the reign of

Henry VIII.) A final bonus for Henry VII was the violent death of the Earl of Northumberland while collecting taxes in Thirsk in 1489.

So during Henry VII's reign, none of the nobility was powerful enough to cause serious problems. By rewarding noblemen very sparingly, enforcing bonds and recognizances and relying on lesser men to carry out the work of government, Henry ensured that this continued to be the case.

Henry VII's ministers

Henry's government was also strong because he was served by a group of loyal and long-lived ministers. Cardinal John Morton was Archbishop of Canterbury and Lord Chancellor until his death in 1500. **William Warham**, another churchman, took on both positions thereafter. The Earl of Surrey was Treasurer throughout the reign. Henry's mother, Margaret Beaufort, and his uncle, Jasper, Earl of Pembroke, were likewise loyal and effective servants of his government. The historian Diarmaid MacCulloch has pointed out that several of these servants had no heirs other than the king and this may have underpinned their loyalty to the regime. Henry also benefited from a natural desire on the part of most of the nobility not to get involved in further civil war. This was not surprising as, even during the worst phases of the Wars of the Roses, many of the great magnates did not want to get involved. They realised that they had too much to lose if they backed the 'wrong horse'.

How did Henry VII's foreign policy increase his power?

Another reason for Henry VII's success in government was that he did not get involved in wars abroad. English kings could not afford to fund serious continental campaigns. Instead, Henry's foreign policy was essentially defensive. He reacted to events abroad in order to secure his position in England.

Henry neutralised the threat from France. England's traditional enemy was France. In 1453 the Hundred Years War between the two countries came to an end, but the

A portrait of William Warham by Hans Holbein, 1527.

French continued to interfere in English politics. In 1471 the French had helped to bring back Henry VI and, in 1485, they had helped to fund Henry's successful invasion of England. In 1492, Charles VIII of France gave assistance to Perkin Warbeck in his attempt to unseat Henry. So, in the same year, Henry invaded France with 26,000 men, but it was clear that he did not intend to fight. Instead he made peace in the Treaty of Etaples. In this treaty, Henry was granted an annual French pension (another boost for his income), improved terms of trade and an agreement that neither side would help the other's enemies.

So Henry VII used diplomacy and invasion for dynastic ends – that is, to stop foreign powers from supporting Yorkist claimants to the throne. Luckily for Henry, the attention of the kings of France during this period was drawn towards conquest of land in Italy, so they had no real desire or ability to create problems in England.

Henry made peace with Scotland. Scotland, like France, posed a threat to Henry's position. James IV of Scotland gave support to Perkin Warbeck, but in 1497 Henry made a truce with Scotland and he followed this up with a full treaty of peace and alliance in 1499. This was improved upon even more in 1502 when James agreed to marry Henry's sister Margaret. The Scottish threat had been effectively dealt with.

Henry made a new alliance with Spain. The rising power in Europe was Spain, which had recently been united by the marriage of Ferdinand, King of Aragon, and Isabella, Queen of Castile. In 1489 Henry agreed to the Treaty of Medina del Campo. By this agreement, Spain agreed not to support any Yorkist claimants and a marriage alliance between England and Spain was projected. This finally came to fruition in 1501 with a marriage between Henry's eldest son, **Prince Arthur**, and the Spanish princess, **Catherine of Aragon**. Although in theory Spain was a useful ally, in practice it did little to help England. The alliance was forged only after very lengthy negotiations on the basis that both countries feared France. This did not mean that they would fight together.

Good fortune. Overall, Henry VII enjoyed good fortune in foreign affairs. France was busy elsewhere and its great enemy was Spain not England. So during this period England was automatically secure from a major foreign invasion. Scotland shared a common border, but it did not have the military strength to be a serious threat.

How did the Church in England help to strengthen Henry's position?

Background. The English Church was a **Roman Catholic Church**. It owed allegiance to the **Pope** in Rome. During Henry's reign, relations between the king and the Pope were cordial enough, but fairly distant. Great arguments had raged between English kings and the Papacy centuries earlier. During the reign of William Rufus (1087–1100), Archbishop Anselm had been exiled for supporting the Pope rather than the king. Under Henry II (1154–89), there was another serious disagreement between the king and Archbishop Thomas Becket, which resulted in the Archbishop's murder in Canterbury Cathedral. Under King John (1199–1216), the Pope had placed the whole realm under Papal Interdict over an argument about who should be Archbishop of Canterbury.

Loyalty of the Church. By Henry VII's reign, such great arguments were things of the past. In reality it was the king, not the Pope, who ran the Church in England and he needed the Church to buttress his royal power. Great Churchmen held high offices of state. The Lord Chancellor was always a cleric. We have already seen that Cardinal John Morton was Lord Chancellor as well as Archbishop of Canterbury, as was his successor, Archbishop Warham. **Richard Fox**, the Bishop of Winchester, was another effective and valued Crown servant.

The key point is that the Church in England was always loyal to the reigning monarch. It upheld the rule of law and the sanctity of the royal office, especially after the Wars of the Roses. The king appointed the **bishops and archbishops**, and the Pope always confirmed his choices. Henry VII, like his predecessors, chose educated and able men who could help to run government at the centre and

KEY TERMS

The **Roman Catholic Church** was the Christian Church throughout western Europe. Catholic means 'universal' and Christians believed that there could be only one Christian Church.

The **Pope** (*Papa* = Father) was the spiritual head of the Roman Catholic Church and was based in Rome. He claimed to be the spiritual successor to the apostle St Peter, who had come to Rome and was buried there. He was chosen from and elected by the senior clergy in Christendom, known as cardinals. He ruled over a collection of territories in central Italy called the Papal States and served until his death.

KEY PERSON

Richard Fox (1447?–1528) was trained as a lawyer and was secretary to Henry VII while he was in exile in France. He was at Bosworth and then served the king as secretary and diplomat. He was bishop successively of Exeter, Bath and Wells, Durham and finally Winchester, which he reached in 1501.

KEY TERMS

Bishops and archbishops
were the senior clergymen or
clerics in England and Wales.
The two archbishops – of
Canterbury and York – were
the most senior clerics of all.
The bishops and archbishops
were appointed by the king
and confirmed by the Pope.
They served until death or
until moved to a different
diocese or see.

A **diocese** is the
administrative area ruled over
by a bishop. There were 21 of
them in England and Wales
by 1485 (see the map). They
are also referred to as sees or
bishoprics.

in the localities. The archbishops and bishops were
responsible for running the churches in their own **diocese**.
This system of Church government had endured for
centuries, Church and State co-existed in harmony and
there was no indication during Henry VII's reign that the
relationship was about to change.

**English and Welsh
dioceses in 1485.**

ASSESSMENT OF HENRY VII

It is easy to see why historians have often given a favourable assessment of Henry's reign. He secured his position, seeing off other claimants to the throne, and took the business of government seriously. He increased the Crown's income, kept the nobility under control and re-established England's position in Europe with marriage and trade treaties.

Nonetheless it is important not to go too far in praising Henry. There were serious rebellions during his reign, and his government, in the later years, became harsh, unfair and unpopular. In addition, he had good fortune in terms of the reduced power of the nobility and the less threatening situation abroad. In many ways, the monarchy under Henry VII remained weak. He was not very wealthy compared to the kings of France and Spain (or compared to his greatest subjects), he had no standing army, and local government remained in the hands of unpaid officials.

Although the Wars of the Roses had unseated three kings, the Crown itself remained well respected. Henry VII took advantage of this and, through hard work and determination, increased the power of the monarchy. However, his success depended upon a monarch who was serious about government. He did not invent new institutions of government that would ensure stability when a less determined or less gifted administrator wore the crown.

SUMMARY QUESTIONS

1 Describe the methods used by Henry VII to end the instability of the Wars of the Roses.

2 In what ways and to what extent did Henry VII succeed in controlling the nobility?

CHAPTER 2

1509–15: How great were the changes in government and foreign policy brought about by the accession of Henry VIII?

KEY POINTS

The early years of Henry VIII's reign saw important changes in central government and foreign policy.

- The accession of a new king brought calls for reform that went largely unheeded.
- The early years of the reign witnessed conflict between the nobility, who were anxious to regain power denied them under Henry VII, and Henry VII's old counsellors, who hoped to maintain Henry VII's strict methods of government.
- Henry VIII did not wish to devote his energies to government and administration in the way his father had done.
- Henry VIII adopted an aggressive foreign policy, which had a serious impact on government.

ACCESSION OF HENRY VIII

Henry VII had married Edward IV's daughter, Elizabeth of York (see the family tree on p. 7). In this way, he reunited the families of Lancaster and York. He invented the Tudor rose, white within and red without (combining the white rose of York and the red rose of Lancaster), as a powerful symbol of England's new-found unity. By the time of his death in 1509, Henry VII had provided England with an adult male heir – the first time this had happened since 1413. Although his eldest son, Prince Arthur, had died in Ludlow in 1502, Henry VII had a second son, another Henry, who could succeed peacefully to the throne.

The old king's hopes of creating a new Arthurian Age had been dashed, but there is no doubting the scale of his achievement. By the end of his reign, the Wars of the Roses and the political instability that came with them were no more. England enjoyed peace at home and was well respected abroad. The monarchy as an institution was stronger and financially secure. The nobility had been tamed and the Church was strong, unchallenged and loyal.

Hopes of change and reform

New Learning. The accession of the young King Henry, aged only seventeen, was widely welcomed. In place of the old, cautious, hard-working and miserly 'control freak', Henry VII, England acquired a young, athletic and intellectual monarch hailed as *stupor mundi* – the wonder of the world. It was a time of new ideas and **New Learning**, and scholars like Sir Thomas More hailed the new king as a monarch who would usher in an age of learning and reform. Corruption would be swept away and England, they thought, would enjoy a Golden Age.

Reform of the Church. At the same time, many humanists, good Catholics to a man, were hoping that the Roman Catholic Church might be reformed. In particular, they hoped for a more educated and committed lower clergy and high churchmen who would abandon or curtail the pomp and circumstance and the political power that went with their jobs. The humanists wanted reform but not **Reformation**. In the early days of the new regime, hopes were high, but the reformers were doomed to disappointment. In sixteenth-century England, reform was unlikely as the political nation – the landowners who governed the realm at the centre and in the localities – were conservative by nature. They feared that reform of Church and State would lead to chaos and anarchy. Outside the circle of humanist scholars and thinkers, men clung to the older medieval idea of an unchanging world.

KEY TERMS

New Learning was advocated by many leading scholars – or humanists, as they were known. They believed that much could be learnt from the study of ancient Latin and Greek texts. Some applied their scholarship to the study of the Bible in Greek and Hebrew.

Reformation means a wholesale change in the Church and came to mean breaking away from the Catholic Church to form Protestant churches. These churches refused to accept the Pope as head of the Church and introduced alternative beliefs or doctrines to those put forward by the Catholics.

KEY ISSUE

Reform of the Catholic Church. There had long been demands from Catholic scholars and some Catholic clergy that the Catholic Church should be changed or reformed. The aim was to improve the Church's spiritual well-being, but not to create a new or different Church.

HOW DID HENRY VIII CHANGE METHODS OF GOVERNMENT DURING THE YEARS 1509–15?

Although the hopes of the humanists would be dashed, the accession of Henry VIII did change the way in which England was governed. Increasingly since 1495, Henry VII had ruled England on his own. He had made little attempt to consult or involve the nobility and Parliament. Instead he governed the kingdom from his Privy (i.e. private) Chamber via a body of personal and loyal servants. They were often gentlemen who wore the king's uniform, including a chain of office, and they carried out the king's orders. With the new king, this all changed.

Henry VIII and the nobility

Henry VII's death was kept secret for two days. Empson and Dudley, Henry VII's royal debt collectors, were quickly arrested and, in a grizzly foretaste of what was to come, were executed. One hundred and seventy-five bonds and recognizances were then cancelled. Many noblemen made sure that they attended the first meeting of the new King's Council. With Henry VII dead, the nobility seized the chance to regain the influence and power that had been denied them in the previous reign.

The young king, who had led a very sheltered life up to now, revelled in his new power and his new friends. He liked to joust and to hunt. He loved splendour and pageantry. He needed blue-blooded aristocrats to act as fitting companions in a splendid Renaissance court. His glory would be enhanced by their power. A newly powerful group of nobles would strengthen their new sovereign's position.

How did foreign policy change after the accession of Henry VIII?

War with France. In particular, the nobility would be needed for Henry's main project – the renewal of the Hundred Years War against France. The real sport of kings was war and Henry VIII, unlike his father, was determined to fulfil his kingly role in this area. He would make England great and powerful once again by making war on the traditional enemy. He would reunite his dispirited people by launching a new crusade. He would be another Henry V, finding everlasting glory on a foreign field.

Henry VI had lost the English empire in France in 1453. Edward IV and Henry VII had invaded France, but for both it had been something of a defensive measure to prevent France from interfering in English affairs. Both expeditions had seen no fighting and both had ended with peace and a French pension. Henry VIII would not be bought off in that way. He would regain lost territory. If the best came to the best, he would be King of France as well as England. Had not one of his predecessors, Henry VI, been crowned King of France less than a century before?

Problems in seeking war with France. There were, however, several initial problems with Henry's anti-French policy:

- Henry thought he would need an ally against the French. After all, France was a much larger country than England in terms of land, population and wealth. Gaining an ally was the easy bit. All he had to do was to marry Catherine of Aragon, who, happily, was still at the English court after the premature death of her first husband, Prince Arthur. With Catherine as his wife, Henry would have Catherine's father, Ferdinand of Aragon, who had claims on French territory in the Pyrenees, as his ally.
- A more serious problem for Henry's war policy was that the French had given no cause for invasion. Since 1494, they had been more interested in the spoils to be gained in Italy rather than in provoking England.
- Many of Henry VII's old counsellors, men like Archbishop Warham and Bishop Fox, advised caution. They urged the new king not to waste his country's limited wealth on a foolish adventure of this kind, which could end only in disappointment. Even if territory were captured, the impoverished English Crown would not be able to afford the cost of defending it. For a while, the king was undecided, caught between the nobility urging him forward, in order to cement their own power and influence with the new king, and his father's counsellors urging caution.

The campaign of 1513 taken from a contemporary engraving.

Defeat of France and Scotland 1513. It was not until 1513, four years after his accession, that Henry at last led his great expedition into France. It was a huge affair, with some 30,000 troops, and it achieved some success. The towns of Therouanne and Tournai were captured and a French force was defeated – or rather, after an initial skirmish, they decided to flee. The French spurred their horses away with such speed that the English christened the encounter 'the Battle of the Spurs'. In the same year, 1513, the English achieved a more serious victory. The Earl of Surrey routed the Scots, France's traditional ally, at Flodden Field and, to add to England's joy, the Scottish king, James IV, was killed. This left the regency for James V in the hands of his mother, who happened to be Henry's sister Margaret.

Impact of war and an active foreign policy. These victories had a serious impact on the way in which Henry VIII approached the business of government:

- The victories came with an enormous price tag that England could not really afford. Henry VII's treasure, accumulated over many years, was quickly being spent. Not only was there the cost of the expeditions themselves but, in the case of the French adventure, there was the cost of maintaining two towns to keep them safe from recapture.
- Henry's success also meant that he would continue to look to foreign policy as his top priority. The great invasion set the tone for the foreign policy of the next

fifteen years of the reign. The king demanded a foreign policy that was expensive and flamboyant. Even in peacetime he wanted to make his mark in Europe, so he ordered expensive pageants and parades to impress his fellow kings.

- The 1513 expedition against France also changed the way in which England was governed. At first, the successes against France and Scotland seemed to enhance the position and power of the nobility, just as they had hoped it would. After the victories, Charles Brandon was made Duke of Suffolk while the Earl of Surrey, Thomas Howard, recovered the Dukedom of Norfolk, which had been lost by his father when he ended up on the wrong side at Bosworth Field. Sir Charles Beaufort, commander at Tournai, was made Earl of Worcester and Sir Edward Stanley was made Lord Mounteagle. It was the greatest series of creations for some fifty years and it seemed to cement the power of these men around the king.

- However, the triumph of the nobility was short lived, as the expedition of 1513 also threw up an administrator of genius, a man of lowly origins who would outstrip the nobility in terms of power and influence. He would dominate affairs in a way that no adviser to an English king had ever done and he would do so for some fourteen years. He became known as 'alter Rex' or the other king. His name was Thomas Wolsey.

Why did Wolsey rise to power?

Wolsey as almoner. Wolsey was the son of an Ipswich butcher. An able boy, he had been sent to Oxford and became bursar of his college. He left under a cloud when he overspent the college's money and his career seemed to be in decline until he got a place on Henry VIII's Council as almoner. This was a junior official who looked after the distribution of food and money to the poor, who waited patiently at the king's door. From this position, Wolsey became more prominent because some of the older counsellors, like Fox and Warham, wanted to retire to their bishoprics.

Wolsey organises the French expedition. In 1513 came Wolsey's big break. The nobles around the king were fine for sport and parties and going to war against the French, but now the king needed someone who could get the expeditionary forces assembled, well fed and well supplied. Wolsey, who at first had actually advised against the war, saw his opportunity. If the king really wanted war then his loyal servant would deliver that war. Wolsey was a tireless worker, a natural **bureaucrat** and a marvellous speaker. He soon found out how to win Henry over and the king was grateful to have someone reliable to organise the great expedition.

Wolsey establishes his authority. When the fighting was over Wolsey, like the nobility, received his rewards. In 1514 he was made Bishop of Lincoln, Bishop of Tournai and Archbishop of York. The next year, two more plums fell into his lap. He was made Lord Chancellor of England and, at Henry's insistence, a cardinal. In 1524, again after more lobbying of the Pope by the king, the great Cardinal was made *Legate a Latere* – the Pope's special envoy – for life. Wolsey thus outranked the Archbishop of Canterbury, William Warham, and it was only the latter's longevity that prevented Wolsey from acquiring his office as well! Wolsey thus became the greatest man in the kingdom.

Henry's attitude to government. Wolsey's meteoric rise and acquisition of such wide powers came about not just because he was ambitious and able, which he was, but because the king wanted it. Henry VIII was very different from his father in terms of his attitude to government. Henry VII was a usurper – he had become king through battle and needed to work very hard to hold on to his crown. Henry VIII had succeeded peacefully to a well-ordered country, which was at peace at home and abroad. He, like the noble friends with whom he spent his time, was not, and did not wish to be, an administrator like his father.

Some of the nobility did hold important government posts. The Duke of Norfolk, for example, was Lord Treasurer. However, such posts were largely honorary. These men were not expected to dirty their hands in the day-to-day business of government. On the other hand, Wolsey displayed an enormous appetite for such work. He gloried in being in charge of nearly everything and the king

A portrait of Henry VIII aged about 18. It was painted around 1509 by an unknown artist.

was naturally delighted that the wearisome business of government – sitting down to listen to serious-minded counsellors – which he had endured during the first few years of the reign, was now a thing of the past. Wolsey, it seemed, could do everything.

This new system of government – employing a chief minister – allowed the king to act out his own role of kingship, which was very different from his father's. In

Justices of the Peace were local government officials appointed by the Crown in every shire. They were usually landowners of gentry status and were unpaid. They oversaw the enforcement of law and order in their area and were known as JPs.

many areas of government, there was little need for Henry's input anyway. The daily routines and rhythms of governing the kingdom and administering justice could go on as they always had. No one really expected the king to introduce reforms in government. Local government, which had most impact on most people, was left happily in the hands of the local rulers – nobles, gentry, **Justices of the Peace** and the like.

A new pattern of government

In domestic affairs and central government, Henry was happy to give Wolsey a free hand to reform or not as he chose. What concerned Henry VIII was foreign policy, relations with other countries and other princes, questions of peace and war – these were the matters to concern great kings. Wolsey was very important in this area too, but the king took charge and dictated the main lines of policy. In foreign policy, Wolsey would remain very much the servant, offering advice but deferring to his master's wishes.

So a new pattern of government emerged after 1513. The nobility, who had regained power in 1509, were left on the sidelines, playing a part at court, in attendance on the king, but exercising only limited power. Wolsey, like Henry VII, continued the work of government, while Henry VIII indulged his passions but retained ultimate control. It was a system of government that worked well for over fifteen years.

SUMMARY QUESTIONS

1 Describe the main changes in domestic policy brought about by the accession of Henry VIII.

2 Explain why Henry VIII reversed Henry VII's defensive foreign policy.

3 Account for Wolsey's rise to power between 1509 and 1514.

CHAPTER 3

1515–29: What were the main achievements of Cardinal Wolsey's ministry?

OVERVIEW

Thomas Wolsey worked very hard indeed. He had a tremendous capacity for work. He dominated the government of both Church and State for some fifteen years, which was particularly impressive given that his master was the moody and changeable Henry VIII. No Englishman below the rank of king had ever wielded so much power for so long. Under Henry VII, John Morton was Chancellor, Cardinal and Archbishop of Canterbury, but he did not dominate the age in the way Wolsey did.

Wolsey upheld law and order and governed with a firm hand, but without the arbitrary and oppressive harshness of Henry VII. During the Cardinal's ministry, there were no serious internal problems or rebellions, such as those that had dogged England from 1455 to 1499. Of course, there were still many problems and tensions in English society. Taxes were high and the poor remained poor. Wolsey also made mistakes and was a vain and arrogant man. Yet if we look at Wolsey's career as a whole, and appreciate the problems and opposition that faced him, we cannot but marvel at the scale of his achievement. Wolsey got things done.

KEY POINTS

Wolsey's achievements fall into a number of areas.

- He took a serious interest in upholding law and order, acting as a judge in central law courts.

A portrait of Cardinal Wolsey by an unknown artist.

- He attempted reforms in financial policy, which proved insufficient to keep pace with the king's increasing demands for money.
- He attempted to curb the illegal enclosure of land.
- He implemented Henry VIII's foreign policy in peace and war with some assurance and not a little ingenuity.

WOLSEY'S ACHIEVEMENTS IN THE LAW COURTS

The Court of Chancery

Unlike Henry VIII, Wolsey showed a genuine concern for how the people were governed. As **Lord Chancellor**, he presided as judge in the Court of Chancery. This was not a common law court, which was fortunate as Wolsey had little or no legal training. Instead, the court operated according to the law of 'equity', where the Chancellor could give his own judgement according to his own sense of justice. It dealt with cases where common law did not apply or was uncertain.

Chancery was a civil not a criminal court, and dealt with matters of property, wills, trusts and such like. The office of Lord Chancellor was thus not especially glorious for the ambitious power-seeker. It involved a lot of work and sittings (during the legal terms) and Wolsey could often be seen involving himself in fairly trivial cases. He did not reform the system, nor did the number of cases before the court increase significantly. Critics have claimed that Wolsey's vanity was fed by his ability to give judgements, but many of these were not in high-profile cases.

The Court of Star Chamber

In addition to Chancery, Wolsey revived the Court of Star Chamber. This was where members of the **King's Council** sat as a law court. Medieval legal theory proclaimed that the king was the fountain of justice. Star Chamber was a natural extension of this principle, with the King's Councillors acting as deputies for their master. This is clear from the court's official title: 'The Lords of the Council in the Star Chamber at Westminster'. The name 'Star Chamber' was used because there were gold stars painted on the blue ceiling in the room where the court met.

Unlike Chancery, this was a criminal court. It used to be thought that Wolsey used Star Chamber to humble members of the nobility, making them bend to the will of the low-born butcher's son from Ipswich. Naturally, some of those convicted in the court were from the upper classes. The Earl of Northumberland, Sir Robert Sheffield and Sir William Bulmer were all found wanting and were punished by Wolsey. However, this was hardly a campaign against the rich and famous. What these cases do show is that Wolsey would enforce the law impartially against high and low. Wolsey fined three Surrey JPs for corruption; the law enforcers, above all, must act according to the law.

In fact, most of the cases heard in Star Chamber were brought by the **litigants**, not by the king or Wolsey.

KEY TERM

The **King's Council** was a group of officers of state and other officials appointed by the king. They offered advice on matters of policy and government. It was not a fixed body in terms of personnel and did not yet have fixed meeting times.

KEY TERM

Litigants is the official term for those bringing legal cases.

If Wolsey's social origins do not explain his zeal as a judge, perhaps they do explain his concern with poor men's cases. Hearing these cases was very worthy, since there was no glory or political advantage to be won here. Under Wolsey, the number of such cases heard each year in Star Chamber may have increased by as much as tenfold, from 12 to 120.

Assessment

Wolsey's involvement in the law led to a real revival and reinvigoration of the courts concerned. Historians used to say that this revival upset the common lawyers in the common law courts and that Wolsey deliberately tried to undermine these common law courts by taking cases from them, having them heard instead in Chancery or Star Chamber. This view is largely bogus. The volume of cases appearing in Wolsey's courts was indeed increasing, but this trend had been evident before Wolsey appeared on the scene. Star Chamber and Chancery had a simpler procedure that was attractive to litigants and there were clear boundaries between the areas of jurisdiction of the different courts. The old idea that common lawyers became increasingly hostile to Wolsey and joined a chorus of opposition to the Cardinal is now largely discredited. John Guy, for example, has argued that all these law courts were seen as complementary, not competitive.

As the volume of cases increased and as his other commitments multiplied, so Wolsey had to set up semi-permanent committees to deal with the backlog of cases. This was typical of Wolsey's pragmatic approach to problems. It did not impress the historian G. R. Elton, who wanted to compare Wolsey unfavourably to his hero, Thomas Cromwell, 'chief minister' in the 1530s. But it should impress the impartial observer. With all his other duties, it was surprising that Wolsey took his legal work so seriously. Furthermore, the energy and commitment he brought to his work as Chancellor compares more than favourably with the work of his clerical predecessor, William Warham, and his lay successor, **Sir Thomas More**.

KEY PERSON

Sir Thomas More
(1478–1535) was a leading lawyer and humanist who became Lord Chancellor in 1529. He opposed the king's divorce from Catherine of Aragon and was executed in 1535.

WOLSEY AND FINANCE

No one likes a tax man. As the king's chief minister and therefore the man who made Henry's dreams of diplomatic triumphs come true, Wolsey had to take on the role of tax man. He did this with some success. The English Crown had never been very wealthy – just about able to pay for the government of the country without going into debt, provided it did not engage in active or aggressive foreign policy. As Henry VIII clearly wished to 'cut a dash' in Europe, Wolsey would need to give the taxes a lift.

Subsidies

Wolsey is credited with introducing a new parliamentary tax, the **subsidy**. Until now, Parliament had been called upon to grant taxes only on special occasions, usually for war. The parliamentary grant of money was called the **Fifteenths and Tenths**. The problem with this tax was that the amount granted was fixed during a time of rising prices and each shire had to find the amount as best it could. In 1513, to meet the expenses of war, Wolsey brought in his new tax, the subsidy. This was a tax based on income: the more you earned, the more you paid – it was all terribly modern! The subsidy was used once more in 1523, when war was again declared on France.

Forced loans

Another option open to Wolsey and the king in order to raise extra revenue was the tried-and-trusted **forced loan**. These loans, which the king could ask for periodically, were not usually repaid. In 1522, Wolsey launched a major inquiry into England's financial and military capacity. The military side of the inquiry came to little, although it demonstrated the nation's military weakness, but the information about financial matters could now be used to help with future loans. In 1522–3, Wolsey collected one such forced loan from the wealthy.

The Amicable Grant

During March to April 1525 Wolsey tried for a further loan, euphemistically known as the Amicable Grant. With high levels of extraordinary taxation having been levied earlier in the 1520s, the announcement of this friendly

The **subsidy** was the main direct tax under the Tudors, imposed occasionally with the agreement of Parliament either on land or on goods.

Fifteenths and Tenths had been the main parliamentary tax since the fourteenth century. It was granted occasionally and was based on landed property. Towns represented in Parliament paid a tenth of the value of their property; the rest paid a fifteenth. By Henry VII's reign the amount of the tax was fixed and fairly low.

A **forced loan** was an occasional tax that could be demanded without Parliament's consent. Although it was supposedly a loan, it was not usually repaid and was therefore always more unpopular than parliamentary taxes.

donation, which did not have parliamentary approval, was greeted with hostility, as Source 1, written anonymously in 1525, indicates.

A portrait of Thomas Howard, third Duke of Norfolk, painted by Hans Holbein.

Source 1

In 1525 King Henry, claiming that he was about to invade France at the invitation of the Emperor, desired of his subjects a tax, which he called an amicable grant. But the commons pleaded their poverty, saying that they had no money. They said that they would not give anything by Royal letters but only by Act of Parliament, which King Henry took unkindly. The **Dukes of Norfolk and Suffolk** wrote to Cardinal Wolsey that the commons laid all the blame on him and that, if insurrection should follow, the quarrel would be against him. The Cardinal wrote back to them that it is the custom of the people, when anything misconrenteth them, to blame those that be near about the king. When they dare not use their tongues against their king, they will not fail to give evil language against his chief adviser.

Adapted from a letter written anonymously in 1525.

Interestingly, Source 1 indicates that the initiative for the tax came from the king, not Wolsey. Nonetheless, Norfolk and friends, jealous of Wolsey's power, clearly hoped that Wolsey would be in trouble and they were right. The subsidy granted by Parliament in 1523 was still being collected and now the king was demanding more money. In Suffolk, Wolsey's home county, there was serious opposition, with some 10,000 men gathering around Lavenham.

In the end, the king decided to withdraw the tax and to use Wolsey as scapegoat for the popular hostility towards it. The leaders of the uprising in Suffolk were brought before Wolsey and he had to ask for their pardon and pay the expenses incurred during their imprisonment. While Wolsey had clearly miscalculated, it should be remembered that the demand for money came from the king, who needed extra funds for the war he was contemplating against France. This plan was later dropped, so the tax was not needed.

Wolsey's financial achievement

As chief tax-gatherer, Wolsey was unlikely to be a popular figure. However, in the fifteen years of his authority, he had brought in a more effective parliamentary tax, the subsidy, and had maintained higher levels of taxation for longer than normal without provoking serious unrest. If the Crown remained short of money, this was because of Henry VIII's unwillingness to cut down on his expenditure. As a Renaissance prince, he wanted to be at the centre of a cultured court, to be a builder of great palaces and to be respected on the European stage. He would not be a miser like his father. One of Wolsey's most important achievements was his funding of Henry's dream.

A portrait of Charles Brandon, Duke of Suffolk.

Some have argued that Wolsey was too arrogant and demanding in his handling of Parliament and thus missed the chance to gain further taxation. The truth is, however, that Parliament still believed that the king should govern the country from his own resources and should resort to Parliament for extra taxes only when the realm was threatened with invasion. Wolsey did not manage a wholesale reform of Crown finances, but it is hard to see how anyone, except the king himself, could have achieved more. Ultimately, Henry was not interested in the means by which money was acquired, only in spending it!

WOLSEY AND ENCLOSURES

The problem of illegal enclosures

An impressive feature of the Cardinal's work was the range of activities with which he concerned himself. As well as legal and financial matters, he took an interest in economic problems facing the realm in general and the poor in particular. He launched a campaign against the illegal enclosure of land by landowners. This was not a huge problem at the time, but it was believed that enclosing landlords acted against the interests of tenant farmers by destroying common land, increasing rents and dismissing tenants to bring in sheep.

'Utopia' was a book written in 1516 by the humanist scholar Thomas More. Utopia is a fictional island meaning 'no place', but the book is actually a critique of aspects of contemporary society.

Sir Thomas More made reference to this problem in his famous book of 1516, *Utopia*. This book highlighted many problems and evils in contemporary society. More claimed that sheep had 'turned into man-eaters', by which he meant that men were being driven off the land and into poverty by landowners who changed from arable to sheep farming.

Commissions of inquiry

Statutes passed through Parliament in 1489 and 1514–15 attacked enclosures and prohibited new ones. In 1517, 1518 and 1526, Wolsey appointed commissioners to inquire into illegal enclosures and these reports resulted in a couple of hundred successful prosecutions. Once again, this was Wolsey the innovator, acting against wrongdoing and corruption. He was well meaning and, if he failed to tackle the underlying social and economic problems of the day, that is because such problems were by their nature insoluble. In addition, Wolsey, like the rest of the 'political nation', recognised that the rights of property owners were of great importance.

HOW SERIOUS WAS THE OPPOSITION TO WOLSEY?

If Wolsey made enemies, we should not be surprised. All powerful men make enemies. All decisions by chief ministers will leave groups disgruntled about what is happening and about what they fear will happen. Reformers in the 1530s and some historians since have often exaggerated Wolsey's unpopularity because they wanted to see it as a major cause of the Reformation after Wolsey's death. It is important, however, to realise that Wolsey contributed enormously to more than a decade of internal peace and stability, and that the opposition to Wolsey never came close to removing him from office because he retained the king's favour. The Amicable Grant episode humiliated him, but it could not unseat him. Henry knew when he was on to a good thing.

What were Wolsey's aims in foreign policy?

Although the government and administration of the realm took up much of Wolsey's time, his real passion, as for Henry himself, was foreign affairs. Here he could bestride the European stage and he could play out the role of peacemaker, statesman and honest broker in the company of the most powerful men in the world. For example, in 1521, when **Francis I** and **Charles V** were falling out, as they often did, it was Wolsey who met up personally with both men and tried to patch up peace. Wolsey, it seemed, could shape the fate of nations. Of course, Wolsey was an arrogant man and he enjoyed this role hugely, but the crucial thing is that, behind the pomp and circumstance, Wolsey's main aim was to stop England from going to war in Europe.

Wolsey was concerned that England should have an active foreign policy, but one that stopped short of warfare. Ultimately, the hostility between France and Spain meant that England had no fears of invasion and every chance of being treated with respect, possibly even deference, by both sides as they looked for an ally. The French were desperately worried by the fact that, after his election as Emperor of Germany in 1519, Charles V's territory seemed to encircle France. Meanwhile, the Emperor was very worried about French expansion in Italy.

Under these circumstances, Wolsey hoped to win peace and glory for England. He was partially successful in this endeavour. After its success in France in 1513, England did play a prominent part in European affairs in a way that was quite different from the defensive days of Henry VII. England was now a power to be reckoned with.

Relations with France after 1514

In 1514, England made peace with France, and Henry seemed bent on peaceful coexistence with the old enemy. To seal the new friendship, Henry's younger sister, Mary, was married to Louis XII of France. However, in 1515 the ageing bridegroom died and a new, young and ambitious man, Francis I, became King of France. This event

KEY PEOPLE

Francis I (1494–1547) was the Valois King of France from 1515 to 1547. There was intense personal rivalry between him and Henry VIII. His foreign policy was increasingly concerned with conquests in Italy in order to prevent France being surrounded by Hapsburg territory.

Charles V (1500–57) was the Hapsburg King of Spain from 1516 and elected as Holy Roman Emperor (ruler of Germany) in 1519. He also ruled over the Low Countries and was seen as a natural ally by Henry VIII. He was also the nephew of Henry's wife, Catherine of Aragon.

HEINEMANN ADVANCED HISTORY

England's place in European diplomacy.

The map shows dates of conquest including: 1483, SCOTLAND, IRELAND, WALES, ENGLAND, NORWAY, SWEDEN, DENMARK, North Sea, Atlantic Ocean, NETHERLANDS, Holstein 1460, Brandenburg, HOLY ROMAN EMPIRE, Saxony, Silesia, To Habsburgs 1477, Palatine, Bohemia, 1477, Lorraine, To Habsburgs 1493, Bavaria, Moravia, Brittany, Burgundy, Bourbon, La Marche, Austria, Swiss Cantons, Tyrol, Auvergne, Savoy, MILAN, Republic of Venice, Provence, Republic of Florence, FRANCE, 1481, Republic of Genoa, Papal States, Navarre, Republic of Siena, Naples, Aragon United 1479, ROUSSILLON To Spain 1493, PORTUGAL, Castile, SPAIN, Sardinia To Aragon 1295, Granada 1492, Mediterranean Sea, Sicily To Aragon 1283

undermined England's new peace policy, as Francis was keen to strengthen his position as king by avenging the English invasion of his country in 1513.

Francis started with the usual French trick of stirring up the Scots against the English. Henry VIII naturally began to think in terms of a new English invasion of France, but Wolsey persuaded him that the time was not ripe for such a venture. He pointed out that England now had no credible ally to divert French attention elsewhere. The wily Ferdinand of Aragon, who had double-crossed Henry so often in the past, was dead but his successor Charles (the future Emperor Charles V) was too busy establishing himself in his new and foreign kingdom of Spain. The **Emperor Maximilian** was usually impoverished and not a great commander by any means, so he too was unlikely to prove a useful ally.

The **Emperor Maximilian** was the Hapsburg Emperor of Germany 1493–1519. Luther's protest against the Catholic Church began while he was Emperor. He was Charles V's grandfather.

The Treaty of London 1518

So, instead of war, Wolsey devised a brilliant peace plan that would still bring Henry the glory he craved. In 1518, with great imagination and a little diplomatic daring, Wolsey hijacked a papal call for a crusade against the Turks and turned it to England's advantage. After many twists and turns in the complex world of European diplomacy, he brought together the great powers of Europe – including England, France, Spain and the Holy Roman Empire – to sign up to the Treaty of London.

This was a 'universal and perpetual' peace deal, complete with **collective security**. Long-term peace would be secured with France by the return of Tournai to France for 600,000 crowns and by a proposed marriage between Francis' son and Henry's infant daughter, **Princess Mary**. England was at the centre of affairs and it was Wolsey's triumph. This was duly noted by the Venetian ambassador. 'Nothing', he said of Wolsey, 'pleases him more than to be called the arbiter of Christendom.'

The Field of the Cloth of Gold 1520

Two years after the Treaty of London, Wolsey triumphed again. Once again it was peace with glory for England. In June 1520, Henry VIII led a huge expedition to France, but this time he was not going to war. He met Francis I in person amid two splendid entourages in a field near Calais, which, of course, England still owned. The venue became known as the Field of the Cloth of Gold because of all the magnificent pavilions and pageantry on display. It was all highly impressive and hugely expensive. There were feasts and revels and games, and peace broke out again between the ancient enemies. The episode has been seen as an empty Renaissance folly but, in Wolsey's eyes, it was better than being at war.

Renewal of hostility to France 1523

Not surprisingly, peace between Henry and Francis could not last, but Wolsey had done well to keep England out of war for ten years. War with France came again in 1523. In that year, France suddenly seemed weak and vulnerable, and it was too good an opportunity for Henry to miss.

An engraving of the Field of the Cloth of Gold, by an unknown artist.

Charles de Bourbon, who was the Constable of France and leader of the French army, had rebelled against his king in alliance with Charles V. In addition, the main French army was pinned down in Italy, far from home, and French influence in Scotland was close to collapse, so there was no danger of interference from that quarter. It was too tempting for Henry. Late in the campaigning season, Suffolk was sent off to France. Boulogne was taken and the English force headed purposefully towards Paris. However, the expedition ran into bad weather and experienced serious supply problems as it moved further from the coast. In the end, it was forced to turn back in disarray.

Peace maintained 1524–7

Henry hoped for a further expedition the next year, but Wolsey managed to deflect him from that course. The king was again tempted to invade the year after that, in 1525, when the Emperor's forces routed Francis' army at Pavia in Italy. Francis himself had been captured at the battle and taken off to captivity in Spain. Surely now an English assault on France would lead to an English conquest. Henry would soon be King of France! He proposed that if Charles helped him in this endeavour, then he could marry Henry's only daughter Mary and later inherit France and England for himself. Sadly, Charles showed no interest in the scheme and indeed opposed an English conquest of France.

Enraged by the unexpected rebuff, the king, with Wolsey in close attendance, now sought to return to peace with France in order to embarrass the Emperor. In 1525 the peace between England and France was signed. It had proved an exciting twelve years of constant and complex diplomacy. Henry had achieved little and learnt the hard way that England could not renew the Hundred Years War and reconquer France. Wolsey, by contrast, had achieved much. He personally was a key player in European diplomacy and, except for the brief and fruitless campaign of 1523, he had kept England out of war.

WOLSEY'S ACHIEVEMENT IN DOMESTIC AFFAIRS AND FOREIGN POLICY

The successes of Wolsey

Taken together, the many successes of Wolsey in domestic affairs and foreign policy are clear. It was a tremendous achievement to wield power in so many spheres for so long. He made sensible innovations in some areas, but stopped short of sweeping reforms that might have caused trouble. He ruled England with a steady hand, displaying neither cruelty nor vindictiveness, and he helped to enhance the nation's reputation abroad.

Of course, some traits of his character may seem rather offensive. He clearly enjoyed the exercise of power, not stepping out of doors without making it into a grand procession. He was always very well attended and he was at the centre of a household that rivalled the king's in terms of numbers and splendour. But perhaps we should excuse the butcher's son a certain pride and arrogance in his achievements and remember that pageantry and splendour were expected from such a powerful man. No minister had ever ruled the kingdom in the way he had. He exercised justice with equity, taking an interest in poor men's cases; he raised revenue as required by the king's expensive foreign policy; and he managed the difficult and temperamental Henry VIII with a tact and diplomacy that none could match. The historian David Starkey suggests that this was because they were both big men!

Criticisms of Wolsey

Wolsey had enemies, such as the king's **minions** and some of the nobility, but there was little by way of the serious faction fighting that would disfigure the politics of the post-Wolsey court. Nobles like Norfolk and Suffolk might enjoy seeing the Cardinal embarrassed, as happened over the Amicable Grant, but they were not queuing up to bring him down, as they knew that he enjoyed the king's favour. The poet John Skelton might satirise Wolsey's power and arrogance, but his 1522 poem 'Why come ye not to court?' did nothing to undermine the Cardinal. The language and claims were so exaggerated that no one could take it seriously. Among other charges against Wolsey, Skelton claimed that the Cardinal had used black magic in order to win influence over the king.

So the Cardinal's position remained unchallenged. More sustained criticism of Wolsey would come later, but that was at the time of his fall from power or after his death when reformers, who had now found favour with the king, found him an easy target. Wolsey has been criticised because Henry VIII eventually dismissed him from office. However, Wolsey fell because of the king's frustration at being unable to annul his marriage with Catherine of Aragon. This was an utterly unique problem in the annals of English history and one that Wolsey was powerless to solve. In other words, Wolsey fell not because he was corrupt, not because he had failed in some way, but because the king suddenly asked the impossible.

SUMMARY QUESTIONS

1 Describe the problems Wolsey faced in dealing with enclosures and royal finances.

2 How successful was Wolsey's foreign policy?

CHAPTER 4

How corrupt and unpopular was the English Church before the Reformation?

ARGUMENT

The state of the English Church before the Reformation, which began in the 1530s, has been a crucial question much debated by historians. It used to be claimed that a Reformation, involving widespread and serious changes to the Church, would have happened only if the English Church was in serious need of reform. If it was in serious need of reform, then it must have been unpopular and the object of considerable criticism.

Revisionist historians have countered this by claiming that the old view read history backwards. In other words, because historians concentrated on opposition to the Church and criticism of its personnel, such historians naturally exaggerated the scale of the problems. In doing this, they also ignored all the Church's good points and, by careful selection of evidence, arrived at a seemingly convincing but actually erroneous conclusion.

The revisionist argument depends on the claim that the Reformation in England was not a great or wide-ranging set of changes at all, so the selective searching for opposition to the Church before the 1530s is not necessary. They claim that if the Church is looked at in a balanced way, we see that it was actually doing quite well. The Church was a great and many-sided institution, central to the lives of most people. As such, it was bound to have its share of problems and critics, but that should not be taken to mean that it was in danger of collapse or that it was universally unpopular. Though there was criticism, no one at the time realised that a Reformation was about to occur.

HOW SERIOUS AND WIDE-RANGING WAS CRITICISM OF THE CHURCH BEFORE 1529?

Opposition to the Church operated at four main levels in the 1520s.

- **Anticlericalism.** There was criticism of the personnel of the Church both high and low, from village priests to Roman cardinals; criticism of lifestyles; and criticism of clergy seen as not fully committed to or measuring up to Christian ideals. This type of criticism is called anti-clericalism.
- **Antipapalism.** In addition, there were disputes about who had ultimate authority over the Church in England. Antipapalism took the view that the Pope was not, as he claimed, the head of the Church with full powers over it.
- **Erastianism.** The flip side of the antipapal coin was the claim that the king or prince was the Supreme Head or protector of the Church rather than the Pope in Rome. Those who took this view supported the idea of Erastianism.
- **Heresy.** Lastly, there were those individuals and groups who questioned some of the Catholic Church's main teachings or doctrines. Such people were called heretics. For long periods, heresy was not a major threat to the Church, but in the 1520s, in parts of Germany and Switzerland, heretical groups sprang up which would successfully break away from allegiance to the Catholic Church. Such groups of heretics are called Protestants.

All these strands of criticism and threat were of long standing in England as elsewhere in Europe. Anticlericalism, antipapalism and heresy posed little real threat to the English Church in the 1520s. Erastianism usually operated to uphold the Church and its powers, but in the late 1520s, because of a peculiar set of circumstances, it would be the main force that brought about Reformation.

ANTICLERICALISM

Colet's sermon 1511

If we study criticism of the clergy, we can see that open or recorded criticism was very limited before 1530. In 1511, **John Colet**, a humanist scholar and Dean of St Paul's, preached a sermon that historians have made famous. In his sermon before the assembled clergy in **Convocation**, he attacked what he saw as the major problems and abuses within the Church. His criticisms were aimed at the clergy. He claimed that too many of the clergy who served the Church were unduly ambitious. As they strove to move up the ecclesiastical hierarchy, in search of greater powers, they were often guilty of moral laxity. They were greedy and covetous, and took too much interest in worldly affairs.

But this sermon did not mean that the Church was about to be radically reformed. Colet's criticism was generalised, traditional and exaggerated. Such attacks could be made of any set of clergy at any time, since it is in the nature of Christianity to set high standards of behaviour that some will be unable to live up to. It was also the kind of sermon that Convocation might expect to hear, one churchman preaching to other churchmen. It would have been more worrying for the Church if Colet had been a layman. In addition, Colet wanted to make an impact on his audience, but the strength of his critique may have helped to ensure that no serious reform of the clergy was attempted. The impact of criticism is usually more significant than the existence of criticism, and Colet seems to be something of a lone voice. In another way, however, this sermon does show that the Church contained, as always, reforming spirits who wanted to see change.

Impact of Colet's sermon. The main point to bear in mind when considering the impact of such criticism is that the secular Church was very much of this world. The **secular clergy** were expected to minister to laymen and it has always been a difficulty for even the most committed churchmen to decide how to work in the secular and fallen world without being tainted by it. That dilemma, after all, was the one that produced monasticism – the attempt to

John Colet (1466/7–1519) was Dean of St Paul's and founder of St Paul's School. He was a humanist and friend of Erasmus. He adopted a very simple lifestyle and gave many sermons against corruption in the Church.

Convocation was a solemn and official meeting of the clergy of the province of Canterbury (Southern Convocation) or of York (Northern Convocation). Convocations usually met when Parliament was called.

The **secular clergy** were those from Archbishops down to parish priests who ministered to their congregations, attempting to bring the consolations of the Church to laymen.

Regular clergy, by contrast, were monks, nuns and friars, and the like. They were called 'regular' because they lived by the rule (in Latin, *regula*) of their founder. Originally, such people had set themselves apart from the world in order to avoid its corruption and to devote themselves entirely to the service of God. But not all monks lived in remote places. Monasteries were often major landowners and major employers, and some monks acted as vicars in parish churches or were appointed as bishops.

withdraw from the world and devote oneself to a truly spiritual life of devotion, contemplation and prayer.

The impact of Colet's sermon should also be put into the context of the realities of the English Church in the 1510s and 1520s. The Church in England was dominated by the power and person of the king. The king appointed the top churchmen or prelates – both secular and regular – bishops and archbishops, abbots and priors, and he used the Church, with its great (and probably growing) wealth and lands, as a rich source of patronage. It was not the Church's fault if the king appointed men who were educated and able administrators, rather than educated and especially spiritual. Very often the king expected the bishops to work for him in central government, rather than busying themselves in their dioceses. Thus three further strands of criticism of the clergy should be added to the mix, but all of them were caused by royal control of Church appointments.

Absenteeism

Many English bishops did not reside in their diocese. Wolsey did not visit York Minster until his fall from power fourteen years after his appointment as Archbishop. Richard Fox, Bishop of Exeter and then Winchester under Henry VII and Henry VIII, was often absent on state business in the King's Council. Even worse was the case of the see of Worcester, which was 'not occupied' by four Italians in succession between 1497 and 1534. However, absenteeism did not mean that the faithful were unattended. On the contrary, there was often an army of Church officials and clergy who got on with the daily business of ministering to the flock and overseeing every feature of Church life from services to land management. Absent bishops would appoint suffragan bishops as deputies to carry out their episcopal functions. Each bishopric would have archdeacons and deans. Each bishop would have his own chancellor and other clerical officials. This was how the Church was run.

Of course, not all bishops were absentees all the time. Bishop Fox and Archbishop Warham, for example, decided to retire from court to concentrate on **episcopal** matters. In

1517 Fox wrote to Wolsey that he was turning his back on 'meddling with worldly matters, especially concerning the war or anything appertaining to it'. Absenteeism of bishops was a normal feature of Church life in western Europe and there were no signs that it was getting worse in the first three decades of the sixteenth century.

Pluralism

A further so-called abuse often associated with absenteeism, and one also targeted by Dean Colet, was pluralism. Many clergy, but probably not most, held a number of Church offices at the same time. Thomas Magnus provides a useful example of this. He was Archdeacon of the East Riding of Yorkshire and acquired canonries at Lincoln and Windsor at the same time. He was also Master of St Leonard's Hospital in York, Master of the College of St Sepulchre and of Sibthorpe College, vicar of Kendal and rector of Kirkby, Bedale and Sessay. In each case, however, the work was fairly nominal or was done by a deputy. This did not mean that Magnus sat around allowing his various incomes to flood in. He was a devoted servant to Henry VII and Henry VIII, working at times in the King's Privy Council and the **Council of the North**.

Wolsey, too, was a notable pluralist, holding several bishoprics and abbeys at the same time. Yet Wolsey and Magnus were the exceptions not the rule and we must not think that ecclesiastical tasks went undone because benefice holders were pluralists. Indeed, there were a large number of officials in sixteenth-century England and there was no shortage of recruits. A Church living represented a steady job with the chance of advancement. This was not true of most jobs.

Simony

The way in which the Church was so closely linked to the government, both central and local, meant that there were always complaints of clergy having bought their office. Buying and selling of such offices – simony – had always been an offence, but it was very hard to legislate against. In an age of patronage, those selected for high office in the Church might surely be expected to pay for the privilege. We do not know how widespread the practice was; all we

The **Council of the North** came into being in the reign of Richard III in order to govern the turbulent northern region of England, which was so far from London. It was based in York and was usually run by a nobleman or bishop who was not local.

can say is that the higher clergy in England were, on the whole, respectable and well respected. Most of the bishops of the period were civil lawyers, some were canon lawyers, but few were trained theologians. Most were good administrators and there were no notable scandals associated with the bishops apart from Wolsey's pluralism and illegitimate children. If none, except perhaps **John Fisher**, were men of European rank in terms of scholarship and reputation, most were diligent and hard working.

The state of the parish clergy

Some anticlericalism was also directed at the parish clergy. These men, who worked cheek by jowl with their parishioners, were a very diverse group and we get only brief and fleeting insights into their lives and characters. As always, generalisations need to be treated with caution. Many parish clergy were relatively poor and it was no wonder that educated men avoided such positions. Consequently, many parish priests had only limited education and many had no real understanding of Latin, the language of the scriptures. At the other end of the scale, in wealthier parishes, the priest might be more educated – perhaps the product of one of the growing number of colleges in Oxford and Cambridge.

The state of the monasteries

Heresy. The author of the Lutheran heresy in Germany was an Augustinian monk, **Martin Luther**. In England, however, there was very little evidence of heresy spreading among the regular clergy. Robert Barnes, who was burnt as a Lutheran in 1540, was admittedly an Augustinian friar, but he was very much the exception. The regular clergy – monks, nuns, friars – were a conservative group, whose existence depended on tradition. Most lived according to a rule that set out a daily routine centring on prayer, contemplation and education. There may have been around 12,000 regulars in the 1520s, 2000 of whom would have been nuns. The size of the houses varied enormously. Some had over a hundred inmates, but the average number was around ten to twelve.

Corruption. If the monasteries were unlikely to be hotbeds of heresy, had they become so corrupt that they caused

A painting of Luther by Cranach the Elder (1472–1553), one of Luther's friends.

fierce anticlerical outbursts? After all, the monasteries were to be one of the main victims of Henry VIII's Reformation – so did they deserve their fate? The answer to this is, very clearly, no. Visitations made before the Reformation show many of them to have been in good order. They had some shortcomings, naturally, but often these were fairly trivial. The Franciscans, Carthusians and Brigettines were always seen as retaining spiritual and moral purity, while other houses had perhaps become too comfortable, with too many servants. But such criticism was far from new and it was not becoming more vociferous on the eve of the Reformation.

Secularisation. Some have claimed that the monasteries played too great a role in secular affairs, instead of withdrawing from the corruption of the world, which was the original monastic ideal. Yet monasteries could not withdraw from the world. Most houses were major landowners, employing servants and tenants to cultivate their land. They often supplied priests to churches and so were drawn into the daily life of parishioners.

Popularity. In addition, it is now clear that the monasteries were not in decline in terms of their numbers or their

KEY TERM

The **Pilgrimage of Grace** in 1536 was a rebellion caused mainly by the changes in religion, particularly the dissolution of the monasteries, introduced by Henry VIII. It was based in the north of England.

spiritual well-being. They retained a degree of popularity as charitable institutions and centres of religious veneration. Hailes Abbey was said to own some of Christ's blood and was the centre of pilgrimage. The great **Pilgrimage of Grace** in 1536 was a vast demonstration of popular support for the monasteries as they were threatened with destruction. In the 1520s, opposition to the monasteries was very limited.

How serious were the anticlerical outbursts before 1529?

Colet and Melton. We have outlined a number of criticisms of the Church and have noted that an institution as large and diverse as the Church is usually in the process of reform, often from within. So how serious were the actual outbursts of anticlericalism in the half-century before the Henrician Reformation? During the reign of Henry VII, it is hard to find any serious complaints about the Church. The accession of Henry VIII, of course, brought with it demands for reform, but these were surprisingly few and far between. Dean Colet's sermon of 1511 has already been noted. A year before, there appeared a *Sermo Exhortatorius* (an Exhortation) by William Melton, who was chancellor of York Minster. Here he complained that too many priests were rude and ignorant.

The Hunne case 1514. Richard Hunne was a merchant tailor and freeman of the City of London. In December 1514 he was found dead in a church cell in Lollard's Tower in Old St Paul's. He was in gaol under suspicion of heresy, as some heretical books had been found at his home. One clergyman and two gaolers were accused of murdering Hunne, who had been in dispute with his local church on and off for the past three years. The three men were never brought to trial and this was widely seen as the Church protecting its own. Meanwhile, Hunne's body was burnt at Smithfield as the body of a heretic even though he had not been convicted of heresy. This case has always been seen as a major example of popular anticlericalism in London in the early part of Henry's reign. In fact, it is nothing of the sort. There were no riots or demonstrations against the Church on Hunne's behalf at the time or afterwards.

Thomas More and the humanists. If there was widespread popular anticlericalism before the Reformation, we would expect to see rather more, and more explosive, anticlerical incidents than that concerning Hunne. There were, of course, a number of legal cases involving tithes, especially in London, but that was not unusual. The important point is that tithes continued to be paid to the Church without serious dispute. In fact, anticlericalism was not a major force in this period.

The career of Sir Thomas More demonstrates quite well that, although there were critics of the Church, their hopes of achieving radical reform were extremely limited. More was a humanist scholar and friend of **Erasmus of Rotterdam**, the most famous critic of the Church in his day. In the 1520s More was Henry's humanist favourite at court. Henry regarded him as good company and, as a man of international reputation, More added a certain lustre to the Henrician court. He did not become important until he replaced Wolsey as Chancellor in 1529. By then the king was in dispute with the Church over his marriage to Catherine of Aragon and he gave reformers their head. But humanists like More were horrified by the attack on the Church which was to come. They supported reform not reformation. Before 1529, anticlericalism and the cries for reform of the Church were largely an irrelevance.

KEY PERSON

Erasmus of Rotterdam (1469?–1536) was the most famous humanist of his day. He lectured at Cambridge and advocated a broader education, including the study of 'Pagan' authors. He wrote the most famous satire on the Church of his day, *The Praise of Folly*, published in 1511.

ANTIPAPALISM

The strength of antipapal views in Germany and England

In Germany, the Reformation was stimulated by a widespread feeling of antipapalism and German nationalism. Many German princes and city-states felt that the Pope and papal agents were exploiting them. Luther referred to the Pope's supporters as 'Romists' and his first big step in establishing a separate Lutheran Church, distinct from the Catholic Church, was not so much new doctrines – they came later – but the claim that the Pope was not the spiritual head of the Christian Church.

According to Luther, the Pope was merely the Bishop of Rome and thus could have no authority over Germany.

In England, such antipapalism is hard to detect. This was because the Church in England was not so much papal as royal. Major disputes between the king and the Pope were things of the past and English kings had emerged as the victors. Papal interference in the English Church was minimal. The Duke of Suffolk, Henry's brother-in-law, once famously claimed that 'it was never merry in England while we had cardinals amongst us'. This can hardly be used to show that the English were about to renounce the papal headship of the Church. In England, unlike Germany, the Pope was a remote and powerless figure. Furthermore, there was no dramatic sense of English nationalism that might fuel such antipapalism. The German states were disunited, weak and vulnerable; England, by contrast, had been united for centuries and had experienced strong central government since the Wars of the Roses.

KEY TERM

The **papal legate** was a churchman who acted as the Pope's special representative or envoy in a particular country. The Pope made appointments personally and such legates were the most powerful men in the Catholic Church, ranking above archbishops.

Did Wolsey cause antipapalism?

Wolsey as papal legate. At Henry VIII's insistence, Wolsey was made a **papal legate** in 1518 and the office was, unusually, granted to him for life in 1524. It meant that he was superior to the Archbishop of Canterbury, William Warham. It has thus been argued that opposition to Wolsey meant opposition to the Pope, and therefore antipapalism was more pronounced in the 1520s than before. However, this argument is far from convincing. In many ways, Wolsey's legateship may have helped to engender a greater sense of unity among the bishops.

The aged and feeble Warham was hardly an inspiring leader of the English Church. As legate, Wolsey could grant licences and dispensations that were usually granted by the Pope, so he could speed up such cases, which would not need to go to Rome. The legate could also take charge in matters of wills and the granting of probate; this right he usually sold back to the bishops.

Opposition to Wolsey as legate was limited. Warham did not make difficulties and Wolsey had useful patronage at his disposal to keep people deferential. The bishops appointed during Wolsey's legateship – Tunstall, Veysey and Longland – were sound and well qualified. Even though he was papal legate, Wolsey did not take over the king's right to nominate men for high church office. In 1518 Wolsey's proposed candidate for the see of St Asaph in Wales – William Bolton – was rejected by the king in favour of Henry Standish, who had defended royal power over the Church in 1515. In 1528, it was the same story as the king blocked the appointment of Thomas Winter to the see of Durham. Winter was Wolsey's illegitimate son.

The legate as reformer. Wolsey deserves some credit as a reforming legate. He attempted to inspect and regulate the Church for which he was responsible. In 1519 he called a meeting of the bishops. This meeting concerned itself with the familiar topic of how to improve the clergy. In the same year, the leaders of the regular clergy (monks, friars and nuns) were assembled by Wolsey to be given a similar lecture. As legate, Wolsey could, and did, organise official **visitations** to some of the greater and more prestigious houses, probably to set an example to the rest.

It has been argued that Wolsey's main interest in being legate was the financial rewards of the office. Peter Gwyn, who has written the most extensive biography of Wolsey, has estimated that it might have increased his income by about eight per cent. Given that he was already so wealthy, it was not a serious boost to his income.

The legate as humanist. As legate, Wolsey displayed other humanist traits. He was not in favour of an English Bible – a view shared by many English humanists in the 1520s. They associated a **vernacular** Bible with Lollard heresy in England and Lutheran heresy in Germany. In 1522, Luther had translated the New Testament into German. Inspired by this, **William Tyndale** had produced an English New Testament in 1526. The reaction of Wolsey and the king to the illegal appearance of this work in England had been to organise a raid on the London Steelyard, which was seen as a hotbed of Lutheran heretics.

KEY TERMS

Visitations were inspections of churches or religious houses by a legate or bishop or their representative.

Vernacular means that something is written not in Latin or Greek, but in the spoken language of the people of that country.

KEY PERSON

William Tyndale (1492?–1536) was an English reformer and heretic. He fled abroad and translated the Bible into English. He was executed in 1536.

If an English Bible did not appeal to Wolsey, he did have genuine concerns about improving education. Of course, this also enhanced his reputation, but his school in Ipswich and college in Oxford (Cardinal College) were widely welcomed in humanist circles. Wolsey ensured that Cardinal College was supplied with classical texts. The funding for these ventures came partly from the dissolution of some small or failing religious houses. Thus Wolsey fulfilled another humanist demand: he converted Church wealth to educational ends. He also funded public lectureships at Oxford, which were taken up by reputable humanists, and he even encouraged clergy to preach sermons in English. In many ways then, Wolsey should be seen as operating within the mainstream of English humanism rather than in opposition to it.

The legate and Lutheranism. In 1521, Wolsey turned his attention to the Lutheran problem. He held a conference of Oxford and Cambridge theologians to speak out against heresy. He presided over a public bonfire of Luther's books at St Paul's Cross, where Bishop Fisher preached against Luther's errors. This happened again in 1526. Most excitingly, Wolsey persuaded the king to write against the German heresy. The book duly appeared as *Assertio Septem Sacramentorum* (In Defence of the Seven Sacraments). Overall the king and Wolsey along with much of the realm were in full agreement with the Pope's stand against heresy. Antipapalism hardly existed.

KEY TERM

The **Seven Sacraments** were special religious ceremonies that Catholics could receive during their lifetime. They were Baptism, Confirmation, Marriage, Extreme Unction (for those who were dying) the Eucharist (the Mass), Penance and Holy Orders (Ordination). Luther claimed that only the Baptism and the Eucharist were important.

ERASTIANISM

Marsiglio of Padua

Antipapalism was very weak in the 1520s partly because the Pope had little direct impact on the Church in England. The king was really in charge. The idea that the king not the Pope should be in charge of the Church was known as Erastianism. The Italian theorist Marsiglio of Padua had put forward such ideas some 200 years earlier in his notorious treatise *Defensor Pacis* (The Defender of Peace). He claimed that the prince or king – in other words, the secular ruler – should have ultimate control over the Church, not the Pope in Rome.

For his pains, Marsiglio had been excommunicated by Pope John XXII, but his ideas could not be banished. By Henry VIII's reign, the theory was that the king protected the Church, which was free of lay interference and which was governed spiritually by the Pope. The king's Coronation Oath promised as much.

The English Church

The position of the king. In reality, the king's position was much stronger than this. The Pope was unlikely to interfere spiritually with the English Church as Catholic doctrine and practice did not need to be changed. Politically, the Pope accepted that the king controlled most aspects of the English Church and its government, including the crucial matter of appointments to the highest ecclesiastical positions. In effect, the Church, via its senior churchmen, was already a department of state; it was already an Erastian Church.

Privileges of the courts. The Church still had its own law courts, run according to canon law, together with other special privileges. However, these special rights were being eroded. Under Henry VII and Henry VIII, Parliament attacked benefit of clergy. This privilege allowed men accused of crimes, who claimed to be in holy orders, to be tried in a Church court where penalties were lighter. Parliament was also used to attack rights of sanctuary. Criminals could claim rights of sanctuary – freedom from arrest – while they resided inside a church. Disputes in Parliament about the Church's privileged legal position led to the Standish case of 1515.

The Standish case 1515. In this episode, Friar Standish, backed by Parliament, attacked benefit of clergy and was consequently attacked by the bishops. In the end, the king was called in to give his verdict on the dispute, which opened up a serious debate about the power of the Church and the power of the State. The king effected a compromise, but as he did so, he reminded his audience that English kings were subject to no earthly superior: 'We are King of England and kings of England, in time past, have never had any superior but God alone.' The implication of this was that the king was in charge of the

Church in England not the other way round. In 1514 the Pope issued a decree declaring that no layman had authority over a churchman. This was a dead letter in England and could be safely ignored.

HERESY

Quite separate from the various strands of anticlericalism was heresy. Heretics were men and women who challenged fundamental ideas or doctrines of the Roman Catholic Church. Most of those who were anticlerical – men like Erasmus, Colet and More – would never become heretics. These men felt free to criticise the personnel of the Church, but they would never challenge fundamental doctrine. In their eyes, such a challenge would lead to the destruction of the Church and the destruction of society.

The Lollards

There was an underground heretical group in England at the time of Wolsey. They were called the Lollards. The man who had inspired this heretical group – the heresiarch – was John Wycliffe, who had died in 1384. He claimed that the Bible was the only sure basis of belief, being the Word of God, and that it should be available to laymen as well as churchmen. Hence he was strongly in favour of an English Bible. Wycliffe also denounced the papal headship of the Church, claiming that the king should take charge of Church affairs. Furthermore, he rejected the central Catholic doctrine of **transubstantiation**.

By 1500, the Lollards were a small-scale, underground sect. They had very little support and very little hope of denting the power and prestige of the Catholic Church. They were confined largely to areas close to London, the biggest group being in the Chiltern Hills in Buckinghamshire. Bishop Longland of Lincoln, whose diocese covered this area, heard some 350 cases against alleged Lollards. Five were burnt for heresy between 1511 and 1512. They had no national organisation and no agreed faith. They were a fringe group.

Lutheranism in England

It is often claimed that Lollardy was the seedbed for the spread of Lutheran ideas into England in the 1520s, but this is unlikely. Lutheranism was a German heresy and was not immediately attractive to English heretics. In addition, many Lollards believed they had the truth already and did not need Lutheran help. Besides, association with Lutherans and other reformers might bring them to the attention of the authorities. Most Lollards wanted a quiet life.

There was a group of Cambridge scholars and churchmen who took an interest in Lutheran ideas – the so-called White Horse group. Barnes, Bilney, Latimer, Coverdale, Ridley, Frith and Cranmer were the most famous. Most would later be burnt at the stake for their beliefs. While it is clear that Lutheran ideas and Lutheran books had reached England, the support for such ideas was minimal. A few poor scholars were not going to reform the Church.

Most significantly, none of the nobility became Lutheran. The French Wars of Religion in the second half of the century – a terrible series of wars between Catholics and Protestants – happened because the monarchs were weak and significant parts of the nobility converted to Protestantism. This was not the case in England. The nobility, tamed since the Wars of the Roses, remained loyal to the Crown and loyal to the Church.

Meanwhile, there were plenty of men who supported the Church's campaign against heresy – most notably Sir Thomas More. He denounced Lutheranism in a book written in 1526. He also wrote *A Dialogue Concerning Heresies*, which was largely an attack on Tyndale. In 1529 he produced his *Supplication of Souls* – an answer to Simon Fish's *Supplication of the Beggars*.

SUPPORT FOR THE CATHOLIC CHURCH

More's writings remind us that the Catholic Church had plenty of defenders during this period. For many, it was a question of conservatism. They worshipped God and served Him in the same way as their fathers had done. They felt safe and secure within the longstanding traditions, rituals and ceremonies of the Catholic Church. The Church protected them from evil in this world and gave them hope of salvation in the next. For the broad mass of the people, ideas of reform and change were dangerous and destructive.

Church building

The period before 1530 saw no let-up in the building and extension of churches. Important and not-so-important men still poured money into church buildings, church vestments and church ornaments, as they always had. The new steeple on the church in Louth took fifteen years to complete and cost the staggering sum of £305. This was an example of the beautification of churches. In the 1520s, then, the rhythms and routines of the Church carried on seemingly unchallenged.

Catholic literature

Before 1530, the printing presses in England produced more conservative literature than Protestant or anticlerical tracts. Richard Whitford's *A Work for Householders* was a handbook of practical family religion. First published in 1530, it became something of a bestseller. Likewise, William Bond's *The Pilgrimage of Perfection* of 1526 and *The Directory of Conscience* of 1527 proved popular. *The Primer*, a medieval collection of Latin and English devotional works for use at home or in church, sold 37 editions between 1501 and 1520 and a further 41 editions between 1521 and 1530.

The evidence of wills

Further evidence of a flourishing Catholicism comes from the evidence of wills. J. J. Scarisbrick has studied 2500 wills from the period 1500–50, of which all but a handful included something to be given to religious causes. Meanwhile, chantries, fraternities and religious guilds all seem to have been enjoying reasonable health. This meant that many families had invested heavily in traditional Catholicism. It might be argued that this represented habit, rather than heart-felt support for the Church, but at

Evesham Abbey. The magnificent bell tower was built between 1524 and 1532.

least it shows that the Church was not widely seen as seriously corrupt and unpopular.

Visitations

Although the Church was far from perfect, it was making an effort to put its house in order. In 1530 the new and energetic Bishop of London, John Stokesley, conducted a personal examination of the curates in his see. Cardinal

Morton made a visitation of Suffolk in 1499, investigating 489 parishes. He found only eight allegations of sexual laxity among the priests there. In 1511–12 Archbishop Warham made a visitation of 260 Kentish parishes. Church buildings and church services were investigated. Only four priests were found to be ignorant. Between 1514 and 1521 in the huge diocese of Lincoln, some 1000 parishes were investigated.

The limitations and very incomplete nature of the available contemporary evidence mean that we cannot know the full implications and impact of such visitations, but the fact that they were going on at all is surely a sign that the Church did attempt to reform itself. There were disputes about tithes, the principal tax paid by laymen to the Church. But such disputes were not very common and where they did arise the principle of tithing was not called into question. Thus the Church in England was not under attack from a disgruntled laity on the eve of the Reformation. Most of those critical of the Church were churchmen.

The Catholic Church in England remained largely unchallenged in the decades before the break with Rome.

SUMMARY QUESTIONS

1 Describe the main criticisms of the English Church before the Reformation.

2 To what extent did Wolsey embody 'the failings of the pre-Reformation Church'?

CHAPTER 5

1525–33: The king's 'Great Matter' – a study in failure

INTRODUCTION

There was serious opposition to the Catholic Church in parts of continental Europe, leading to the formation of Protestant Churches in parts of Germany, Switzerland and Scandinavia. But, as we have seen, the Church in England was not widely unpopular or under serious attack in the 1520s. The main reason for the Reformation of the Church in England in the 1530s was not the Reformations taking place elsewhere in Europe, but a breakdown in relations between Henry VIII and the Pope. This occurred because the Pope refused to declare that Henry VIII had never been properly married to Catherine of Aragon. This dispute between king and Pope is usually referred to as the king's 'Great Matter'.

HISTORICAL INTERPRETATION

The importance of the divorce between Henry VIII and Catherine of Aragon as a cause of the Henrician Reformation has been much debated. All historians would agree that it is an important factor, but they disagree about its centrality.

A. G. Dickens. In his book *The English Reformation*, Dickens argued that the divorce was not crucial to the Reformation. He believed that reforming ideas, spreading from the Continent in the 1520s, were gaining favour in England, especially in urban areas in the south and east of the country. Such ideas became popular because the Church in England was clearly corrupt and the object of widespread anticlericalism. Wolsey's pomp and power helped to intensify these feelings in the 1520s because of the unpopularity of his rule. Demands for reform of the

Church then gained acceptance among politically important people, both lay and clerical, so that some kind of English Reformation was bound to occur. The king's divorce thus explained only the timing of that Reformation and not the reasons why it happened. In essence, Dickens's Reformation was popular – the people wanted it and the king, for his own reasons, gave way.

G. R. Elton. In *England under the Tudors* and *Reform and Reformation*, Elton emphasised the Reformation as an act of state, caused and influenced by the king and his servants. Here the divorce crisis is the main catalyst for change. A king who had shunned reforming ideas in the 1520s now used the reformers' ideas to take full control of the Church for himself.

Revisionist historians. More recently, 'revisionist' historians led by Christopher Haigh in *English Reformations* and J. J. Scarisbrick in *Henry VIII* and *The Reformation and the English People* have also challenged the idea that reforming ideas were widespread or popular in the 1520s. They see the Church as still well respected and Wolsey as a prudent chief minister. For them, then, the divorce is absolutely central in explaining why religious changes came about in the 1530s. This is underscored by the way that the king later reversed the Reformation when he became worried about its divisive influence and when the divorce and Royal Supremacy were firmly established. In the end, they believe that the king cynically made use of reformers and reforming ideas because he wanted his divorce.

KEY POINTS

- By 1527, Henry VIII had no son to succeed him, and his wife, Catherine of Aragon, was now too old to have any more children. Without a son, Henry believed that there would be a succession crisis on his death.
- Henry believed, very firmly, that he had no son because his marriage to Catherine was illegal in the sight of God, as she was his brother's wife. He wished to marry Anne Boleyn instead.

- Henry's case for an annulment of the marriage was very weak and the Pope would not agree to the idea.
- Cardinal Wolsey, the papal legate, was unable to solve the marriage problem and fell from power in 1529.
- Henry finally decided to declare the marriage illegal in 1533 and in the process broke with Rome, claiming that all matters of dispute (including the annulment of marriages) arising in England could be settled in England without interference from Rome.
- Henry therefore needed the support of the English bishops in order to end his marriage and he took measures to ensure that the reluctant clerics agreed to royal control of the Church.

WHY DID THE KING WANT TO END HIS MARRIAGE TO CATHERINE OF ARAGON?

Introduction
During the late 1520s, Henry VIII became convinced that he was not a married man. Despite serious opposition from inside and outside the realm, and despite the serious weaknesses of his case, his conviction became unshakeable and was to have profound consequences for Church and State in England. It would lead, eventually, to the destruction of the Catholic Church, and its replacement by a Protestant Church of England supervised not by the Pope but by the monarch, bearing the title Supreme Head. The crisis over the king's marriage was unique and unexpected, and was the most important cause of the English Reformation.

The succession problem
Henry VIII had been concerned about his marriage for a number of years, as his union with Catherine of Aragon had failed to produce a male heir. There had indeed been a number of sons, but all had died shortly before or after birth. For Henry this was a serious problem. It meant that there might be a succession crisis when he died. He had a daughter Mary, who was nine years old in 1525, but there was no precedent for a female succession. In the twelfth century, Henry I made his barons and leading churchmen swear two oaths to recognise his daughter Matilda as his

AIARINA ARAGON
ANG: REGIN

A portrait of Catherine of Aragon, by an unknown artist.

heir. However, when he died in 1135, Stephen seized the Crown, and Henry's barons and churchmen meekly accepted him as king.

As it turned out, Henry's daughter Mary did become queen in 1553 and ruled successfully until her death – to be succeeded by Henry VIII's other daughter Elizabeth, who repelled the Spaniards and ruled for forty-five years. Nonetheless, in the late 1520s the omens for a female succession were not promising and Henry feared that there might be civil war in England if he died without a son.

Why did Henry think that his marriage to Catherine was illegal?

As loyal Catholics, Henry VIII and Catherine of Aragon interpreted the death of their sons as divine intervention – God had decided to remove them. As a king appointed and anointed by God, Henry VIII naturally worried about this for many years, not at first in terms of the practical politics of the succession, but in terms of trying to understand the reason for God's anger. Henry's worries about God's intervention seemed to be confirmed by the fact that he did have a son, Henry Fitzroy, who was born to his mistress Bessie Blount in 1519 and created Duke of Richmond in 1525. If he could have a son with her but not with his wife, then it was clear to the king that God was punishing him.

The Bible and the divorce

A biblical text provided the answer to Henry's question about why God had stopped him from having a son. In the Book of Leviticus, in the Old Testament, two verses proclaimed that it was unlawful for a man to marry his brother's wife: 'Thou shalt not uncover the nakedness of thy brother's wife: it is thy brother's nakedness . . . If a man shall take his brother's wife, it is an impiety: he hath uncovered his brother's nakedness; they shall be childless.'

As it happened, Henry had broken this law. He was Catherine of Aragon's second husband and her first husband had been his elder brother, Prince Arthur. Perhaps suddenly or perhaps over a period of months, Henry VIII grasped the full impact of this text in Leviticus. In marrying Catherine, he had broken God's law and God had punished him. If Catherine had failed to have any children at all, the case might have been different. But sons who died shortly before or after birth, given but then cruelly taken away, were surely a sign of divine displeasure. God wanted to make Henry and Catherine suffer. Moreover, Leviticus also made it plain that ignorance of God's law was no excuse.

WHY WAS THE POPE UNLIKELY TO AGREE WITH HENRY OVER THE DIVORCE?

Introduction

In the normal course of events, Henry could have expected the Pope to grant him a divorce or, more correctly, an annulment of his marriage. If his marriage to his brother's wife was sinful in the eyes of God, the Pope would have to declare it null and void. This would mean that he was in fact a bachelor, having never been properly married to Catherine in the first place. Therefore, he could contract a legal marriage with another woman and produce sons to succeed him.

Unfortunately, there were enormous problems with Henry's case for annulment, which meant that no Pope was ever likely to agree to such a request. Despite this obvious fact, Henry VIII clung to the futile hope that papal approval would be forthcoming. Despite constant setbacks, Henry remained convinced that his case was just. Compromise was not possible. In this matter, Henry's conscience, like that of the German monk Martin Luther, was captive to the Word of God.

The Book of Deuteronomy

Nonetheless, the weaknesses of Henry's Leviticus argument were many. In the first place, opponents of the divorce found another biblical text that contradicted the verses in Leviticus. In Deuteronomy there were verses which stressed that it was a man's duty, indeed his moral obligation, to marry his brother's wife, provided that the brother had died, so that he could have the children who had been denied his brother: 'When brethren dwell together and one of them dieth without children, the wife of the deceased shall not marry to another but his brother shall take her and raise up seed for his brother.'

This was very bad for Henry's case. The obvious way to make sense of both texts, Leviticus and Deuteronomy, was to recognise that Leviticus, unlike Deuteronomy, referred to a living brother. Clearly it would be most offensive to God for a man to run off with his sister-in-law while his brother was still alive, but Henry had married Catherine some seven years after his brother's death. This meant that he had obeyed divine law, not broken it.

The Papal Dispensation

There was a further very significant weakness in Henry's case, and one that would have disastrous consequences for the Catholic Church. When he married Catherine in 1509, Henry VIII had been given special permission (a dispensation) by Pope Julius II to allow him to marry his brother's wife. The reasons behind the marriage were political. England wished to retain its alliance with Spain, especially as Henry VIII already had the intention of renewing the Hundred Years War by invading France. Nonetheless the Catholic Church disapproved of marriages between people who were closely related by blood and so a dispensation had to be obtained, and this was duly done.

When Henry officially decided, in 1527, that his marriage was against God's law, this meant that he was questioning the validity and power of the Pope's dispensation. So the king had to argue that the Pope did not have the power to issue such dispensations, when they ran counter to God's law. Pope Clement VII was a reasonable, mild man and in some ways sympathetic to Henry VIII's problem over the succession, but he could never agree that the Papacy had exceeded its powers in granting the dispensation.

It was also unfortunate that the 1520s had seen the beginnings of a Reformation in some parts of Europe, especially in Germany. Reformers there denied that the Pope was head of the Church. In these circumstances, the

List of Popes		
1503–13	**Julius II** (Giuliano della Rovere)	Granted Henry's dispensation
1513–21	**Leo X** (Giovanni de Medici)	Denounced Luther
1522–3	**Adrian VI** (Adrian Dedel)	Charles V's tutor
1523–34	**Clement VII** (Giulio de Medici)	Had to deal with Henry's request for annulment
1534–49	**Paul III** (Alessandro Farnese)	Started the fight back against the Protestants

Papacy was even less likely to undermine its powers publicly or even do a deal privately with Henry, which would strengthen the reformers' arguments about papal corruption.

Catherine of Aragon's opposition

As if this were not enough, there were further problems, of a more practical nature, with Henry's claims about his marriage. First and foremost, there was his wife. If he had been married to an English princess, as his father had been, a solution might have been more easily found. But Henry's wife was a Spanish princess and aunt of the most powerful man in western Europe, the Emperor Charles V. Neither of them was likely to give way without a serious and protracted struggle. Catherine's overt opposition to Henry's plans was the most significant reason for the failure to achieve a divorce – she said no and she kept saying no.

Furthermore, Catherine was genuinely popular in England and clearly seen as the innocent victim of Henry's desire for another woman. She and her supporters argued forcibly that she came to Henry a virgin and that the Leviticus argument could not apply to an unconsummated first marriage. She and Arthur had never been truly married, but she and Henry had. She would never admit that her marriage was illegal. Henry's argument would have left her as a royal mistress for the past eighteen years and their daughter Mary as illegitimate.

Catherine's determined opposition can also be explained by the difficult circumstances she had endured before the marriage took place. In the period between the death of Arthur and her marriage to Henry, Catherine had been humiliated and left without sufficient provision while her father, King Ferdinand of Aragon, and her father-in-law, Henry VII, argued about her dowry and whose job it was to support her. Although officially betrothed to Prince Henry, for many years she despaired of marrying him, so when Henry VIII did propose to her, shortly after his accession, she accepted with alacrity.

A portrait of the Emperor Charles V, painted by Titian.

In addition, the marriage, as royal marriages go, had been extremely happy. Catherine became convinced that it was only evil men around the king who had now filled his head with dangerous ideas. For the most part, she saw Cardinal Wolsey as a convenient scapegoat.

Anne Boleyn's contribution

Catherine's determination to resist Henry's wishes was further fuelled by Henry's growing attachment to Anne Boleyn. The daughter of Thomas Boleyn (soon to be ennobled as Earl of Wiltshire), Anne had spent some time at the French court. Her youth, education and ready wit caught Henry's attention, and her presence at court made Catherine all the more determined to resist Henry's wishes.

A drawing of Anne Boleyn by Frans Pourbus the Younger.

In many ways, Anne was not a very good choice as royal mistress. She refused to sleep with Henry, probably until 1532, because she wanted to be sure of becoming queen – only when this was assured did she consent and fall pregnant. In fact, she was only Marquis of Pembroke when the future Elizabeth I was conceived, probably in early December 1532. Her coyness may have encouraged Henry to pursue the relationship: no one had denied him before and he treated it as an exercise in courtly love. He even wrote her letters (an activity he hated), but he may not have been unhappy with a long engagement as he knew that Anne would be less acceptable as queen if she had been a longstanding royal mistress. Imagine the reaction if Henry had chosen to marry the woman who had already borne him a son – Bessie Blount! More importantly, Henry knew that any child born to Anne must be seen as legitimate, therefore, he wanted to achieve the annulment before Anne became pregnant.

Henry's choice of prospective wife was a major blow to his case for an annulment in another way. It was well known that Anne's sister Mary had been Henry's mistress and there were rumours of a child. This meant, of course, that in the Church's eyes Henry was as closely related to Anne as he had been to Catherine. If his argument from Leviticus was right then he could not marry Anne.

WHY DID IT TAKE HENRY VIII SO LONG TO ACHIEVE HIS DIVORCE?

Reasons for stalemate 1527–9
The king and the succession problem. Henry's campaign to achieve a divorce and secure the succession began in earnest in 1527. He was not to marry Anne Boleyn until 1533. If the real issue was the succession, it is extraordinary that Henry allowed the process to take so long. He needed a legitimate son very urgently indeed. By 1527 he was already thirty-six and a son of his would need to be sixteen or seventeen to be sure of a smooth succession – Henry himself had been seventeen at the time of his father's death.

As Henry well knew, some forty years before in 1483, Richard Duke of Gloucester had taken the throne from his nephew, Edward V, and almost certainly had him and his brother killed in the Tower of London. Two royal sons had been wiped out then, so there need not be safety in numbers. Those boys were twelve and ten at the time of their deaths – their young age and inexperience were crucial in sealing their fate.

The need for a legitimate heir. On the other hand, the events of 1483 showed Henry the need to move cautiously with his annulment. He would have known that Richard of Gloucester claimed the throne on the basis that his nephews were illegitimate, as his brother Edward IV had broken a precontract of marriage when he secretly married Elizabeth Woodville. While few people at the time, or since, actually believed Richard's claims, the stain of illegitimacy was a serious bar to kingship. In the twelfth century, it had prevented Henry I from choosing his eldest illegitimate son as heir, even though he was an able soldier and respected politician. Now it meant that Henry VIII had to prove beyond doubt, to a doubting world, that his marriage to Catherine really was invalid. Only then could he ensure that the son of a future marriage would not be seen as illegitimate.

In addition, the violence and usurpations of the throne during the Wars of the Roses were still within living memory by 1527 and there were still Yorkists who might claim the throne in the future. In 1538 the Henrician regime became convinced that the white rose was blooming again. Henry Courtenay, Marquis of Exeter, and Henry Pole, Lord Montague, were both executed on very flimsy evidence of treason. Their main crime was that they were directly related to Edward IV (see the family tree on page 157).

So while the succession issue demanded a speedy new marriage, the legitimacy issue meant that such a new marriage would take a long time to achieve because it depended on papal approval of the annulment of the Aragon marriage. In the end, Henry proceeded to marry Anne without papal approval and then spent considerable time and effort attempting to convince the world that she was his true wife.

Wolsey's alternative case for divorce. In 1527, Henry VIII was confident of a quick result. In Cardinal Wolsey, he had his own papal legate, one of the highest-ranking churchmen in western Europe, who could surely acquire papal approval for Henry's divorce. However, Wolsey soon appreciated the weaknesses of Henry's case and tried to persuade him to take a less confrontational line. He claimed that the original dispensation granted to Henry and Catherine was invalid because it had assumed that Catherine and Arthur had had sexual relations, when in fact they had not. This would mean that the king's marriage was null and void on a technicality, which would not upset the Pope as much as Henry's argument.

Wolsey's case had the further merit of agreeing with Catherine of Aragon's later testimony that she came to Henry still a virgin. Henry's argument, however, demanded that his brother's marriage had been consummated. Once again he was wrong. Henry never seriously considered Wolsey's argument, which may not have led to a papally approved annulment anyway, but once again it showed that the king was skating on very thin ice.

The impact of the sack of Rome 1527. At the same time, Henry's cause was apparently dealt another paralysing blow when, in 1527, mutinous troops serving the Emperor Charles V sacked the city of Rome. As Protestants rejoiced at this clear sign of divine displeasure towards the Catholic Church, a thunderbolt hurled at the **Antichrist** in Rome, Henry VIII could not afford to be so sanguine. The sacking of Rome meant that now Clement VII was officially, as well as unofficially, captive to the Emperor. Clement did not want to upset Henry VIII and risk further schisms (defections) from the Catholic Church, but now he had no option but to dance to the Emperor's tune.

Charles may not have known or even met his aunt, but Hapsburg pride and Catholic sentiment ensured that he would not allow his family to be disgraced by a shameful annulment. Wolsey thought he saw a brilliant way to solve

> ### KEY TERM
>
> The **Antichrist** appears in the Book of Revelation and refers to the Devil. Radical Protestants taught that the Pope was not even the Bishop of Rome, but the Devil. This helps to explain why religious differences turned so nasty.

the problem of the Pope's dependence on the Emperor. While the Pope was a captive, Wolsey proposed that he should become acting Pope. Armed with such powers, he could quickly grant his master the annulment he craved and Clement, if and when he escaped from Imperial power later on, would be powerless to reverse the decision. Sadly, this particular master plan had to be abandoned when the French cardinals, among others, refused their approval.

Papal compromises. Meanwhile, the Pope played for time and offered other solutions. Clement was prepared to permit bigamy and adultery by legitimising any children born to the king and Anne Boleyn. He even offered to sanction an incestuous marriage between Henry's son, Fitzroy, and his daughter, the Princess Mary. The crucial matter for the Pope was not to make a decision about Henry's case. He could not afford to upset either king or Emperor. If he stalled for long enough, Catherine might die or Henry might change his mind.

Either way, the Pope could not grant the divorce on Henry's terms – and the surprise is that it took Henry VIII so long to realise this. To a king, of course, his will always seems right and few people, even ministers as powerful as Wolsey, could argue with this particular king. Henry remained convinced that he was right and that it was just taking time for the Pope to come round. Henry's unswerving conscience may explain why he never considered the easy way out of his difficulties – the murder of the queen.

English weakness at Rome. Henry's cause was further hampered by the fact that, unlike some other countries, England had no established party among the cardinals attendant on the Pope, and its diplomatic power in Rome was feeble as there were no permanent representatives of English interests there. Instead Henry and Wolsey relied on individual, temporary missions led by men like William Knight, Stephen Gardiner and Edward Foxe, who had only a limited understanding of the complex workings of papal politics.

Additionally, the Papacy could not understand why Henry did not allow Wolsey to settle the matter in England and call on the Papacy later if the second marriage were called into question. Unfortunately, this was not a risk the king was prepared to take. Instead of taking the easier option, Henry held out for the impossible and so created enormous difficulties and dangers for himself and his realm.

The king's hopes revive 1528. In 1528, Henry's hopes – always fairly elastic – revived. The Pope escaped from the clutches of the Emperor, and the king hoped that his recent humiliation at the hands of Imperial troops might encourage him to turn against the Emperor. Annulment of the marriage of the Emperor's aunt might be just the tonic the Pope was looking for to assert his newly won independence. When Clement seemed hesitant and unwilling, Henry proposed to send an Anglo-French bodyguard of 2000 heavily armed troops to help protect His Holiness in these troubled times. In fact, he hoped to use these troops to intimidate the Pope into granting the annulment he craved. The Pope declined the troops and they were never sent, but the episode demonstrates the ingenious nature of some of the king's schemes.

Campeggio and the divorce. Later in 1528, Henry's hopes of a speedy solution revived again as he welcomed a papal legate, Lorenzo Campeggio, to England. As absentee Bishop of Salisbury, he was thought to favour the king's cause and his arrival was to signal the calling of an ecclesiastical court where he and Wolsey would preside and decide on the state of the king's marriage. Before the court met, Henry pressed his arguments on Campeggio with great skill and dexterity.

As so often, the king was now wildly optimistic, confident that since the Pope had agreed to a court in England, he would agree to that court's findings. Meanwhile, Wolsey impressed Campeggio with the seriousness of the current situation. He made clear to his colleague that the divorce was vital politically to assure the succession to the throne, and that failure at this stage would lead to Wolsey's demise and the withdrawal of England's allegiance to Rome. Sadly Campeggio knew, even now, that he could not oblige because the Pope had given him secret instructions not to make a final decision.

Campeggio's plan. Campeggio tried to overcome this rather serious difficulty by putting forward an alternative plan to resolve the problem. In a series of interviews with Catherine, he proposed that she should enter a nunnery, thus divorcing her husband. Jeanne de Valois of France had done no less for her husband King Louis XII and now, in the name of a Roman Church in difficulties, he urged her to follow this example. As can be seen in Source 2, Campeggio, writing to Rome in October 1528, pointed out the advantages of his scheme.

Source 2

We then discussed a proposal for persuading the queen to enter some religious house. With this the king was extremely pleased and, indeed, there are strong reasons for it. The king is determined to allow her whatever she demands, and especially to settle the succession on her daughter in the event of his having no male heirs by another marriage. It was concluded that I and Wolsey should speak to the queen about this on the day following.

The queen stated that she had heard that we were to persuade her to enter some religious house. I did not deny it and constrained myself to persuade her that it rested with her, by doing this, to satisfy God, her own conscience, the glory and fame of her name, and to preserve her honours and temporal goods and the succession of her daughter.

I begged her to consider the scandals and enmities which would ensue if she refused. On the other hand, all these inconveniences could be avoided. She would preserve her dower, the guardianship of her daughter, her rank as princess, and, in short, all that she liked to demand of the king; and she would offend neither God nor her own conscience.

Adapted from a letter written by Campeggio in 1528.

From Source 2 we can see that Catherine's entry into a nunnery would have certain advantages. Such a move would not question the validity of the dispensation or the marriage and would leave Mary as a legitimate child. In addition, it would avoid the problems ahead if, as Campeggio suspected, Henry was in deadly earnest about the divorce. Though she could not know it, Catherine held the fate of the Catholic Church in England in her hand. If she had entered a nunnery, there would have been no major dispute between king and Pope and possibly no English Reformation. However, Catherine refused. Campeggio takes up the story again in Source 3, written nine days after Source 2.

Source 3

After I had exhorted her at great length to remove all these difficulties, and to content herself with making a profession of chastity, setting before her all the reasons which could be urged on that head, she assured me she would never do so: that she intended to live and die in the estate of matrimony, into which God had called her, and that she would always be of that opinion, and would not change it. She repeated this many times so determinedly and deliberately that I am convinced she will act accordingly. She says that neither the whole kingdom on the one hand, nor any great punishment on the other, even though she might be torn limb from limb, should compel her to alter this opinion. I assure you from all her conversation and discourse, I have always judged her to be a prudent lady. But, as she can avoid such great perils and difficulties, her obstinacy in not accepting this sound counsel does not much please me.

Adapted from a letter written by Campeggio in 1528.

The king's speech at Bridewell 1528. Henry VIII became increasingly alarmed at his wife's stubbornness. He was intelligent enough to realise that she was genuinely popular, as innocent parties often are, and that too many people saw the divorce as a crude attempt to trade in an ageing wife for a younger model. One Sunday, at Bridewell Palace in London, the king spoke to assembled notables, clearly hoping to counter the hostility of popular opinion. Henry had the audacity to claim that if Catherine was adjudged to be his lawful wife then 'nothing shall be more pleasant or acceptable to me, for I assure you that she is a woman of utmost gentleness, humility and buxomness – she is without comparison. So that if I were to marry again, I would choose her above all women.'

The Blackfriars Court 1529. In June 1529, the special ecclesiastical court to decide the state of the king's matrimony met at Blackfriars in London. Wolsey and Campeggio presided and most of the nobility and bishops were there, together with the unhappy couple. The court inevitably failed as Campeggio had orders not to decide the case in England and because, as might be expected, Catherine refused to recognise the court. She made an emotional appeal to her husband. She begged him not to cast her aside, affirmed the validity of their marriage, appealed her case to Rome and walked out. In her absence, her defence was conducted fiercely by the Bishop of Rochester, John Fisher. He claimed that the marriage was valid in every way and proclaimed his readiness to die for the sanctity of matrimony in general and Catherine's marriage in particular.

Meanwhile the Pope, alerted to Catherine's appeal, acted speedily for once and issued a decree revoking the court in England and proclaiming that the case would now be decided in Rome. The failure of Blackfriars helped to spell the end for Wolsey, and there was more bad news for him when, after years of fighting, Charles V made peace with Francis I at Cambrai. This left England diplomatically isolated, unable to play France off against the Emperor, and aware that the renewed friendship between Pope and Emperor blocked all hope of a divorce settlement being reached in Rome.

The fall of Wolsey 1529
The growth of hostility to Wolsey. Wolsey had achieved many things since becoming Chancellor in 1515, but Henry had dealt him such a weak hand in the divorce that

he was bound to fail. Touchingly, Catherine of Aragon always blamed Wolsey, not her husband, for the divorce crisis. She angrily believed that Wolsey wanted to humiliate her because the Emperor had not helped him **to become Pope**. Catherine's hostility towards him did not matter much to his position, but now the king was angry with him as well and that mattered very much indeed.

Sensing Henry's hostility towards his chief minister, the Dukes of Norfolk and Suffolk, among many others, gathered to push him over the brink. Parliament was called in 1529 and several anticlerical Acts were passed as a warning to the Church in general, and to Wolsey in particular. The Comptroller of Henry's Household, Sir Henry Guildford, introduced criticism of Wolsey, as can be seen in Source 4. When criticism came from such a man, it was clear that the king agreed with his views.

A drawing of Sir Henry Guildford by Hans Holbein.

Source 4
When the commons were assembled in the Lower House, they began to discuss their grievances and how the spirituality had oppressed them.
First for the excessive fines which the clergy took for the probate of wills, insomuch as Sir Henry Guildford, knight of the garter and controller of the king's household, declared in open parliament that he and others, being the executors for Sir William Compton, knight, paid for the probate of his will, to the Cardinal and the Archbishop of Canterbury a thousand marks sterling. After this declaration they were shown many extortions, done by the clergy for probate of wills, that it were too much to rehearse.

Adapted from *Hall's Chronicle* by Edward Hall, 1548.

The man reporting these events at the start of the so-called **Reformation Parliament** (1529–36) was Edward Hall. His views on the Church were influenced by the fact that he was a reformer. Later, even Sir Thomas More joined the chorus of disapproval against Wolsey. He delivered a fierce attack on his former patron, likening him to a castrated ram.

Wolsey's hopes revive in York. Wolsey was expelled from court. He spent some time at the Carthusian House at Richmond. There, his gentleman usher and biographer, George Cavendish, tells us that the great Cardinal spent much time 'with the ancient fathers of that house in his cell, who persuaded him from the vainglory of this world and gave him shirts of hair to wear, the which he often wore afterwards'. From there Wolsey was sent to York, the seat of his archbishopric, which he had never before visited. There he continued to nurture hopes of being restored to favour. He held a splendid ceremony of enthronement to show that he was not quite finished. Edward Hall gives a hostile account.

Source 5

And to be had in the more reputation among the people, he determined to be installed and enthroned at York with all the pomp that might be, and caused a throne to be erected in the Cathedral church in such height and fashion as was never seen.

Adapted from *Hall's Chronicle*
by Edward Hall, 1548.

Death of Wolsey. Though Henry, as so often, seemed to be indecisive, in the end Wolsey's enemies had their way. Blame for the failure of the divorce proceedings was laid at his door and he paid the price. He was on his way to face charges of treason in London when he died at Leicester Abbey in 1530. Whether Henry would really have executed him, we shall never know. He was needed in London to face a show trial that would put further pressure on the Church, but public execution of this old and broken man might have been counterproductive. Henry VIII did not possess the religious zeal of those Puritans who would later put to death an old and enfeebled Archbishop of Canterbury, William Laud, in 1645. In addition, Henry had not yet acquired the habit of executing those who failed him.

Wolsey's reputation. History has often judged Wolsey harshly because his rule was followed by a Protestant Reformation. In the eyes of Protestants, he represented all that was wrong with the Catholic Church. He was a wealthy, arrogant and supremely powerful cleric who personified the corruption of the Roman Catholic Church. He was guilty of pluralism and of fathering several children. With the Reformation, as with so many great events, historians have been too quick to adopt the line *post hoc ergo propter hoc* (after this, therefore because of this). In this case, critics of Wolsey have argued that, since the Reformation in England started immediately after Wolsey's fall, his crimes and corruption must have caused it. This view was started by one of Wolsey's fiercest contemporary critics, Edward Hall, in his *Chronicle*:

Source 6

The Cardinal, as you may perceive from this story, was of great stomach, for he counted himself equal with princes and by crafty suggestion got into his hands innumerable treasure . . . In open presence, he would lie and say untruth . . . He was vicious of his body and gave the clergy evil example . . . The authority of the Cardinal set the clergy in such pride that they disdained all men and so, when he was fallen, they followed after as you shall hear.

Adapted from *Hall's Chronicle*
by Edward Hall, 1548.

This view is rather unconvincing. After Wolsey the English Church experienced a Reformation not because Wolsey was especially corrupt, but because of Henry VIII's quarrel with the Pope.

Why did the stalemate over the divorce continue after the fall of Wolsey?

Introduction. The fall of Wolsey and the calling of the so-called Reformation Parliament in November 1529 solved nothing in terms of the divorce crisis. From then until 1533, the issue of the annulment was deadlocked. Far from seizing the initiative and browbeating the English Church into proclaiming judgement in his favour, Henry continued to cling to the old and forlorn hope of seeking a papal solution to his marital problems.

During this period, the materials and ideas behind the eventual **Royal Supremacy** did appear and were available to the king and his ministers, but there was no concerted campaign to break with Rome. Instead, we find a feeble and stuttering attempt to put pressure on the Pope to give in to Henry's demands. It is a clear measure of Henry's innate conservatism and indecisiveness in the face of a serious dilemma that, in 1529, after three years of stalemate, he continued for a further three years, in the vain hope that the Pope would somehow change his mind.

The period 1529–32 has sometimes been seen as 'years without a policy', coming as it does between the fall of one chief minister, Wolsey, and the rise of the next, **Thomas Cromwell**. Although this phrase does reflect a lack of direction and confidence, these were not years without a policy, but rather years with the same old bankrupt policy.

Lack of a chief minister. The reasons for this continuing stalemate are not hard to discover. Henry put the humanist and lawyer Thomas More in Wolsey's place as Chancellor. He was well known to the king, having helped him to write a pamphlet denouncing Luther and all his works – the *Assertio Septem Sacramentorum*. An excellent choice for the office of Chancellor in terms of his legal training and international reputation, More was a poor choice in terms of his known opposition to the divorce.

With Wolsey gone, the king had lost a great and dependable churchman, who was crucial to him both as papal legate and as a loyal servant, a man who could speak for the English Church. Without him, the king was face to face with a group of bishops who were mainly hostile to the divorce idea and suspicious of attempts by the Crown to curb their powers and limited independence. Warham, as Archbishop of Canterbury, although old and infirm, was unlikely to help Henry's cause and would do all he could to stall him. Without Wolsey, there was no longer a chief minister to direct and implement policy.

Three contending groups or factions. Instead, Henry operated with three groups of counsellors and advisers, who had rather different ideas about what to do. The

A portrait of Sir Thomas More, painted by Hans Holbein in 1527.

groups were not fixed or organised, but they help to show us the different views presented to the king:

- The first group were conservatives who might be seen as the queen's group. They strove to defend the Catholic Church and the queen, and to fight against heresy. The leaders included Bishops Fisher, Tunstall, West, Clerk and Standish, along with More, the Earl of Shrewsbury and the busy Imperial ambassador, Eustace Chapuys. Although they were to lose in the end, at this time they still had influence in the Council and in Parliament.
- The second group of advisers, made up of reformers, gradually developed around Anne Boleyn and her brother, together with the three Thomases – Cromwell, Cranmer and Audley. This group was not as powerful then as it would be later. Cranmer and Cromwell were not at the forefront of royal policy until late in 1532.
- The third and probably most influential group after Wolsey's fall were aristocrats with whom Henry hunted and felt at ease – the Dukes of Norfolk and Suffolk (Henry's brother-in-law), and the Earls of Wiltshire and Sussex. These men had been united in helping to get rid of the low-born Wolsey, but after his demise they had few ideas about how to proceed.

Faced with these competing and conflicting groups, Henry wallowed and stalemate continued.

Limited impact of the Reformation Parliament. Likewise Parliament did not look like being able to break the deadlock. The first session lasted only six weeks. Three Acts were passed reforming some small areas of clerical abuse and another cancelling the king's debts. Parliament was then **prorogued** and did not reassemble for over a year. This was hardly a concerted campaign to put pressure on the Pope by putting pressure on the English Church.

It was not until September of 1531 that Henry was presented with a great collection of historical sources (the *Collectanea satis copiosa*) which claimed to show that Henry, as king, already possessed a spiritual supremacy over the Church. He was head of Church and State, and thus could grant his own annulment. This was a splendid, if rather involved, piece of royal propaganda, but instead of proceeding immediately to declare that this supremacy existed and to enact it in Parliament, Henry continued to dither, fearful of the consequences.

In January 1531 a little more pressure was applied to the English Church. Fifteen clergymen were accused of *praemunire* (serving the Pope before the king), since they had aided and abetted Wolsey's legateship. The fifteen were all members of the Aragonese circle. The king then widened the attack to the clergy as a whole, who were meeting in Convocation. Parliament had by now been called again, and the main objective was to collect a huge fine from the clergy (which was duly done), since royal funds were running extremely low. However, the king then demanded that the clergy submit to him as 'sole protector and Supreme Head of the English Church and clergy'.

At last it seemed that Henry was moving towards royal control of the Church. In fact, it was not so. Opposition from the clergy, especially Bishop Fisher, was intense and Henry was fobbed off with a compromise when the words 'so far as the law of Christ allows' were added to the king's title. This neutralised his novel claim to supremacy. Once

---

KEY TERM

Prorogue. The king could dissolve parliaments: that is, send them away and have a new election before the next parliament assembled. On the other hand, he could prorogue parliament – send it away, but reassemble the same parliament at a later date. In the sixteenth century, parliaments were occasional not permanent.

Sessions of the Reformation Parliament

3 November–17 December 1529

16 January–31 March 1531

15 January–14 May 1532

4 February–7 April 1533

15 January–30 March 1534

3 November–18 December 1534

4 February–14 April 1536

---

again, far from pressing on with his supremacy, which might have solved the divorce problem, Henry backed down.

Rising hopes of the Aragonese faction. At the end of the 1531 session of Parliament, the king made More deliver a speech to Parliament explaining the case for annulment. Apart from the pleasure the king might have derived from humiliating his Chancellor, the speech achieved little. More refused to resign over this affront, possibly because he and his friends, encouraged by the king's failure to adopt radical measures to achieve the annulment, still hoped for success. One of the leading ladies, Catherine or Anne, might die, or Henry might yet change his mind about his marriage. If he could be persuaded that Mary would make a suitable heir to the throne, perhaps the whole nasty business would be dropped. There was no certainty that a decisive and long-lasting break with Rome was imminent.

The hopes of the Aragonese circle were buttressed by the fact that Parliament would not now be called again for another nine months, during which time royal policy continued to languish. The pace of change quickened, however, in the spring of 1532. The king pushed through Parliament an Act in Conditional Restraint of **Annates**. Vigorous opposition meant that the Act only threatened to cut off these payments to Rome in the future. Thus the Act would have no immediate impact on the situation.

The Submission of the Clergy 1532. More seriously, the king then browbeat the clergy in Convocation into making a formal submission to him. This Submission of the Clergy humiliated the leading churchmen and attacked the independence of the Church in England. Convocation could assemble in future only with the king's permission; no new canons (Church laws) could be passed without royal approval and a special commission would review existing canons. Any canons thought to be hostile to royal rights would be annulled. Henry thus increased his power over the Church, and his Chancellor, Thomas More, resigned in protest, giving a lead to others who had serious reservations about this turn of events. The Submission was

KEY TERM

Annates were payments made to Rome. They were equivalent to the first year's revenue of some of the more important Church offices, including bishoprics.

not enacted in parliamentary statute, so its impact on the situation remained limited.

Cranmer made Archbishop of Canterbury 1532. In itself, of course, the Submission did not bring the annulment any closer; Henry would need a more compliant Archbishop of Canterbury for that. His chance came with the long-awaited death of Warham, in August 1532. In his place Henry promoted **Thomas Cranmer**, who was a Cambridge scholar, chaplain to Anne Boleyn's father and one of the king's pet reformers who had helped to draw up the *Collectanea*. Once again there was little apparent urgency over this move, as it would be another six months before Cranmer was officially enthroned. Once again, Henry was hoping against hope that the Pope would finally relent. Clement VII, for his part, gave his approval for Cranmer's elevation, even though he was a reformer and had not held a bishopric. He hoped that this move would help to mollify the king.

Henry VIII's conservatism. Another reason for the long delay in the establishment of the Royal Supremacy was the king's hostility to religious change. In establishing his supremacy after 1533, Henry VIII would take advantage of anticlerical and Erastian ideas then current in England, but it is clear that before 1533 the king refused to employ such radical ideas. In 1529, for example, Simon Fish had produced the following scathing but hardly convincing attack on the alleged corruption of the clergy in his *A Supplication of the Beggars*.

Source 7
The bishops, abbots, priors, deacons, archdeacons, suffragans, priests, monks, canons, friars, pardoners and summoners are not the shepherds but ravenous wolves going around in shepherds' clothing devouring the flock. And who is able to number this idle, ravenous sort who have begged with so much determination that they have gotten into their hands more than a third part of all your realm . . . And what do all these greedy sort of sturdy, idle, holy thieves do with these yearly exactions that they take from the

A portrait of Thomas Cranmer by Gerlack Flicke.

people? Truly nothing but exempt themselves from their obedience to your Grace.

Adapted from Simon Fish, *A Supplication of the Beggars*, 1529.

Here, then, was a direct appeal to the king to attack clerical corruption. But the king, before 1533, was unmoved.

It was a similar story with canon law. Christopher St German was one of many common lawyers who attacked the Church's canon and papal laws. He believed that the Church's legislative independence should be swept away and that all people should be under English common law. His *Doctor and Student* was a powerful and important treatise putting forward these views. Henry, if he ever read it, seemed unimpressed.

Henry's hostility to heresy. If Henry was unimpressed by Fish and St German, he was actively hostile to William Tyndale. Tyndale was an early English Lutheran. He believed in the centrality of the Bible in Christian theology and believed it was more important than Catholic tradition. He met Luther and undertook a translation of the Bible into English. He finished it in Worms, in Germany, and it was smuggled into England in 1526. His *Obedience of a Christian Man* was a direct appeal to the king as the only man who could end the Catholic Church's corruption and usurped control over the Church in England. It is believed that Anne Boleyn was responsible for bringing a copy of this book to Henry's attention, and he read it with approval. Nevertheless, Henry was not to be pushed too quickly. He had a natural dislike of reformers of all types, as potential troublemakers. In 1531 the king's hostility to reformers was shown in the following letter from Cromwell to his agent in Antwerp, Stephen Vaughan.

Source 8

I have received your letters with also that part of Tyndale's book which you directed to the King's Highness. After I had received these things, I went into the Court and there presented the same to the king. At my next visit there, it pleased the king to send for me, declaring unto me not only the contents of your letters but also the matter contained in Tyndale's book. However, his Highness nothing liked the said book as it was filled with seditious slanders, lies and fantastical opinions, showing therein neither learning nor truth. Talking further with his Grace, it was clear that he thought that you held Tyndale in too much affection. In your letters you commend his manners, modesty, simplicity and knowledge of worldly things rather than his works, which the king thinks are full of lies and abominable slanders designed only to infect and intoxicate the people. Your favouring of the said Tyndale, who assuredly shows himself in my opinion rather to be full of venomous rancour and malice than with any good learning, virtue, knowledge or discretion, has put the King's Highness in suspicion of you . . . He is very pleased to have his realm destitute of such a person as Tyndale, for his Highness right prudently considers that if he were present, he would do as much as he could to infect and corrupt the whole realm.

As touching Frith, whom you also mentioned in your letters, the King's Highness . . . does much regret and lament that he should set forth and apply his learning and doctrine in spreading and sowing such evil seeds of damnable and detestable heresies.

Adapted from a letter written by Thomas Cromwell in 1531.

It is clear from this source that the king did not approve of heresy. Tyndale and Frith were heretics whose ideas might undermine the proper working of society. Cromwell is clearly keen to warn Vaughan off, but there is perhaps a note of disappointment in his letter. He had set off to court in high hopes that Tyndale's ideas might appeal to Henry – the king, however, had not taken the bait!

So Tyndale the heretic could only operate from the supposed safety of self-imposed exile. In the end, even this failed to save him. Before being burnt at the stake in Antwerp, in 1534, he is alleged to have cried, 'Lord, open the King of England's eyes.' Clearly, he had little faith as yet in the king's reforming zeal.

And he was right. Henry VIII feared heresy; it was troublesome and, even worse, foreign. He, Cranmer and Cromwell would use the ideas of reformers of all types to help to create and legitimise the annulment, the Royal Supremacy and the break with Rome, but they only used these ideas because the Pope had failed to grant the divorce. Even then, the king remained hesitant in practice and conservative in principle. Without Henry VIII, there would have been no Reformation. Some would argue that, even with him, there was no Reformation.

Anne Boleyn's pregnancy 1533. The event that actually led directly to the break with Rome and the birth of the Church of England was Anne Boleyn's pregnancy. Anne, unlike the Pope, finally changed her mind. As soon as the pregnancy was known, the king convinced himself that it was the long-awaited son. Even now he did not abandon hope of a papal climb-down. As late as March 1533, Henry was telling Eustace Chapuys, the Imperial ambassador, that he hoped the Pope would 'do his pleasure in this affair'.

Two months earlier, as soon as he had found out about the pregnancy, the king had instructed Cranmer to marry him to Anne Boleyn. Not until May 1533 did the same Archbishop formally annul the Aragonese marriage and declare the Boleyn marriage legitimate. After such a long wait and after so many dramatic twists and turns, it was something of an anti-climax. However, Henry would now move with some speed to make a reality of the break with Rome and the Royal Supremacy over the Church. The Church in England would become the Church of England.

SUMMARY QUESTIONS

1 Outline the problems faced by Henry VIII in attempting to end his marriage to Catherine of Aragon.

2 To what extent can the period 1529–32 be seen as 'years without a policy'?

SOURCE QUESTIONS

1 According to Campeggio in Source 2, what were the advantages for Catherine of the 'nunnery solution'?

(3 marks)

2 What are the strengths and weaknesses of Sources 4, 5 and 6 as evidence of Wolsey's pride and unpopularity?

(5 marks)

3 What does Source 8 reveal about Henry VIII's attitude to heresy in 1531? *(4 marks)*

4 To what extent can Source 8 be seen as reliable evidence of Cromwell's attitude to heresy in 1531? *(7 marks)*

CHAPTER 6

1533–8: How important and wide ranging were Henry VIII's reforms of the Church?

KEY POINTS

- The king used Parliament to establish his supremacy over the Church:

  1533 **Act in Restraint of Appeals.** This prevented Catherine of Aragon from appealing to Rome against the annulment of her marriage.

  1534 **The Succession Act.** This made Princess Mary illegitimate and made people take an oath agreeing with the annulment and the supremacy. More and Fisher refused to take the oath.
  Act of Supremacy. This made official the Royal Supremacy over the Church.
  Treason Act. This widened the definition of treason so that denial of the king's supremacy was now treason.

- The king used his Supremacy to enrich himself at the Church's expense, most notably by dissolving all English monasteries in the period 1536–9.
- At the same time, religious reforms were introduced which seemed to be moving England in a Protestant direction:

  1536–40 Dissolution of the monasteries – 500 religious houses destroyed.

  1536 The Ten Articles

  1536 & 38 Cromwell's religious injunctions

  1537 The Bishop's Book

  1538– Introduction of English Bibles into parish churches.

HISTORICAL INTERPRETATION

There is a longstanding debate about the nature and impact of the reforms of the Church introduced in the

1530s. Historians like A. G. Dickens and G. R. Elton saw this as the decisive decade in the establishment of English Protestantism. The king, aided by reformers like Cranmer and Cromwell, broke with Rome and set about the destruction of corruption and superstition in the Church.

The revisionists, led by Christopher Haigh, have countered this by pointing to the unpopularity of reforming ideas, the limited nature of the reforms introduced by the king and the turn back to Catholic doctrines in the last years of the reign. More recently, Andrew Pettegree has suggested a middle line, pointing out that Protestantism did build up a powerful following in the 1530s and 1540s, which meant that it could not be destroyed thereafter.

HOW DID HENRY VIII USE PARLIAMENT TO ESTABLISH HIS SUPREMACY?

Introduction

In the early 1530s, Henry VIII took the momentous step of declaring that **the king and not the Pope exercised supreme power over the Church in England**, both politically and spiritually. He did this primarily to legalise not only the annulment of his so-called marriage to Catherine of Aragon, but also to legalise the celebration of his real marriage to Anne Boleyn. The timing of this move was determined by Anne's pregnancy. It was vital that no one, then or in the future, could question the legitimacy of his longed-for heir. Thus the Church of England was born out of Henry VIII's marital difficulties, and its first Supreme Head was a monarch of doubtful morals.

Erastian kingship

The idea that the king should be in charge of the Church in his own country had a long history. **Marsiglio of Padua**'s famous tract *Defensor Pacis*, which included such ideas, was published some 200 years before Henry's problems. In the 1530s an English translation of this work was sponsored and published by Thomas Cromwell. In the 1520s in Germany, Martin Luther had stressed the powers of the princes and their duty to protect and reform the Church. So Henry was already working in an Erastian climate.

KEY ISSUE

The king not the Pope exercised supreme power over the Church in England. This was the key idea in the Henrician Reformation through which England achieved the break with Rome. It sounded revolutionary and dramatic, whereas in practical terms it added little to the king's powers. It did, however, make Henry a priest, which was new.

KEY PERSON

Marsiglio of Padua (1275–1342) was an Italian political theorist. He published *Defensor Pacis* in 1324 and fled from Italy in 1326. He was excommunicated by Pope John XXIII.

Furthermore, we know that Henry himself had been concerned about the relationship between State and Church at the time of the so-called Standish case in 1515 (see page 52). He wondered then whether his clergy, with their oath of loyalty to Rome, were perhaps only half his subjects. As early as 1516, the king had been heard to claim that 'Kings of England have never had any superior but God alone.' An official Royal Supremacy over the Church would increase his powers, give him access to new sources of wealth and revenue and sort out his matrimonial difficulties all in one go. Once again, one wonders why the King did not make himself Supreme Head sooner.

Parliament and the Supremacy

In order to make everyone aware of the Supremacy, Henry turned to Parliament and made use of the skills of the reformer Thomas Cromwell. But the crucial feature of the Acts of Parliament passed at this time to give concrete form to the Henrician Supremacy was that they were declaratory. Parliament did not give the king new powers; it affirmed the new order as though it were the old order. The official line was that Henry VIII was Supreme Head of the Church because he always had been. This was an exciting legal fiction that helped to pull the rug out from under the feet of potential opposition. In a conservative age, how could people oppose something that was not new?

The Act in Restraint of Appeals 1533

The first significant Act in establishing the king's Supremacy was the Act in Restraint of Appeals passed in March 1533. Thomas Cranmer, a known reformer, recently elevated to the Archbishopric of Canterbury, had already married Anne to Henry, but had not yet declared that Henry was not married to Catherine. This Act helped him out, as it declared that all legal cases – spiritual or temporal – which arose in England could be settled in England. Therefore no one, least of all disgruntled Spanish princesses, could take their case on appeal outside the realm, and certainly not to the Pope in Rome.

Even better for Henry was the fact that the king was the supreme authority in all legal cases in England. Therefore, it was quite within his powers to grant his own annulment or divorce or whatever he wanted. The justification offered for this boundless power was that, when you thought about it, England was not just a kingdom but was in fact an empire. So the king was not the king at all but the Emperor.

It was a pity that no one had addressed Henry or any of his predecessors by such a title, but the theory was that emperors could not possibly have any earthly superiors. And this despite the fact that Charles V, who clearly was an emperor, did not claim to exercise spiritual powers. Nonetheless the Act claimed that Henry did hold such powers and went on to declare, not too convincingly, that these powers had always belonged to the English Crown. Here then was the basis for divine right monarchy and nothing had changed. The magnificent phrases of the preamble to the Act encapsulate Henry and Cromwell's assertion of royal power.

Source 9

Where by divers sundry old authentic histories and chronicles it is manifestly declared and expressed that this realm of England is an empire, and so has been accepted in the world, governed by one supreme head and king having the dignity and royal estate of the imperial crown of the same, unto whom a body politic, comprising all sorts and degrees of people divided in terms and by names of spirituality and temporality, are bound and owe to bear next to God a natural and humble obedience. He is furnished by the goodness and sufferance of Almighty God with plenary, whole and entire power . . . to render justice and make final determination . . . in all causes occurring within this realm . . . without the interference of any foreign prince.

Adapted from the Act in Restraint of Appeals 1533.

Cranmer annuls the marriage

In fact, the Act possessed a serious loophole, in that it prevented *future* appeals to Rome, whereas Catherine had lodged her appeal to the Holy See in 1529. Ignoring this difficulty, Cranmer then declared that the king's marriage to Catherine was null and void in the curiously undistinguished setting of the Priory of St Peter in Dunstable. This site was chosen as it was close to where Catherine was residing at Ampthill. If the king hoped that Catherine, impressed by the new Act of Parliament, would now throw in the towel, he was sadly mistaken. Catherine refused to appear and Cranmer might have done better to have held his court in full public view in London. Another small problem with the new Act was the question of how one of the king's subjects, the Archbishop, could cite the king when he was supposedly not subject to any earthly power.

The Succession Act 1534

The importance of Henry's marital problems in activating the reforming laws of the 1530s is indicated once again by the next important Act passed through a compliant Parliament. In the session of Parliament between January and March 1534, the first (as it turned out) Succession Act was passed. This declared that the only heirs of Henry VIII were his children by Anne Boleyn. Cranmer's sentence condemning the so-called Aragonese marriage was given official backing and Parliament was told that Cranmer's judgement must be right as it was backed by the universities of Bologna, Padua, Paris, Orleans, Toulouse, Angers and divers others.

Catherine was merely the widow of Prince Arthur and should be styled 'Princess Dowager', which meant that Princess Mary was illegitimate. Penalties for denying any of this were necessarily harsh and the Act was to be proclaimed 'in all the shires within this realm'. Just to ensure that everyone agreed with its provisions, a further clause declared that all subjects were to take an oath to the Act.

Source 10
And for the more sure establishment of the succession of your most royal Majesty . . . be it further enacted that all the nobles of your realm spiritual and temporal and all your other subjects shall make a

corporal oath that they shall truly, firmly and constantly maintain . . . the contents of this present Act.

Adapted from the Act of Succession 1534.

Further strength was added to this and other Acts by the fact that they were framed as petitions to the king from his loyal Parliament, rather than merely being royal commands.

The Act of Supremacy 1534

Also in 1534 an Act for the Submission of the Clergy gave legal force to the submission made by the clergy in 1532 and made them fully the king's subjects. Later in the year, during the parliamentary session held in November/December 1534, the Supremacy Act was passed. In a sense, the Act in Restraint of Appeals had already declared that the king was Supreme Head of the Church. The new Act repeated this message in case anyone was in doubt. The repetitious nature of the legislation of this period is a tribute not to the king's reforming zeal – in many ways he remained a conservative in religious matters – but to the government's continuing anxiety and determination. The king's authority over the Church was spelt out again in an Act of 1536 'extinguishing the authority of the **Bishop of Rome**'.

The Treason Act 1534

Now that everyone was clear about the Supremacy, the king and Cromwell needed to ensure that everyone agreed with them. As already noted, the Act of Succession carried with it a demand that important people should swear an oath to the Act. Most, of course, did. Then, just to ensure continuing obedience, Cromwell, now Principal Secretary to the king, produced a new Treason Act in 1534, just after the Supremacy Act, which changed the nature of treason.

In the past, this most terrible of crimes, carrying a mandatory death sentence and loss of lands and goods, involved *actions* by the accused that were intended to deprive the king of his life or powers. Now, the new

The **Bishop of Rome** was now the Pope's official title. Later on there would be moves to destroy all references to him as Pope in devotional books. Fiercer Protestants denounced the Pope as the Antichrist.

Treason Act declared that treason could be *spoken*. Anyone claiming that Henry was not Head of the Church was now guilty of treason and could be executed. In fact, very few were found guilty under this new Act, but it certainly helped to keep people loyal and marked another important extension of royal power.

HOW DID HENRY VIII EXPLOIT HIS SUPREMACY FOR FINANCIAL GAIN?

Financial advantages of the Supremacy

With his title secure and severe punishments awaiting the unwary, Henry could now turn to the financial exploitation of his new (or, rather, old) powers. By early 1534, the king had passed an Act granting himself Annates – payments of the first year's revenue of certain greater benefices (such as bishoprics) – which in the past had gone to Rome. By the end of the same year, he had extended this financial pay-off by granting himself First Fruits – the first year's revenue on all ecclesiastical benefices and, in addition, an annual Tenth from the Church – a tax of ten per cent of the annual value of all ecclesiastical benefices. So began the financial exploitation and spoliation of the Church.

Cromwell becomes Vicegerent in Spirituals

In January 1535, Cromwell was appointed Vicegerent in Spirituals – a new title meaning that he could act as the king's deputy in church affairs. He had promised to make Henry 'the richest prince in Christendom' and, being a keen reformer, he saw that the monasteries would make a useful financial target. As Luther and other reformers had decided that Purgatory did not exist, the benefits of the monastic life were nullified and, in some parts of Europe, monasteries were already being dissolved. The problem in England was that there had been no national impetus towards reform of this type and only limited anticlericalism. Therefore, to announce the sudden dissolution of all the monasteries might have been very risky and damaging to the regime.

EARL OF ESSEX.

A portrait of Thomas
Cromwell, after Hans
Holbein.

Cromwell's plan for dissolution

Cromwell's political brilliance now took a hand once more.
He dreamed up a cunning plan to destroy the monasteries
without appearing to do so. During 1535, he sent out two
sets of commissioners to investigate the Church. The Head
of the Church wanted to know the value of the Church he
controlled. One set of commissioners, working rather
rapidly, set out to supply a complete record of the
Church's accumulated wealth and income. These men
visited parish churches and cathedrals (the secular Church)
as well as monasteries and nunneries (the regular Church).
At the same time, other commissioners set out to
investigate the well-being of the monasteries, to check up
on corruption and spiritual degeneracy. The Head of the

Church thought it would be only right and proper that he should pose as a reformer. Anyone asking awkward questions was told that the king's aim was to reform not destroy.

The reports on the monasteries

The reports came in to Cromwell, who then declared to the king that many of the monasteries fell far short of the high standards that should be expected. As well as a number of religious houses that were impoverished or decayed, there were many examples of bad behaviour by monks, nuns and abbots. Most unusually, it was found that only the small monasteries were corrupt – especially those with fewer than twelve inmates or an annual value of less than £200 per year. On the other hand, large monasteries were given a clean bill of health. Religion was flourishing there and the rules were being obeyed.

Men like Layton and Leigh, who reported on many monasteries, were hostile to them as institutions. They knew what evidence Cromwell wanted and duly obliged. One monastic Visitor, John ap Rice, writing in 1536, complained about Leigh in a letter to Cromwell.
'At Bruton he behaved very insolently. At Bradstock and elsewhere he made no less ruffling with the heads than he did at Bruton. Wherever he comes he handles the fathers very roughly.' The speed with which the commissioners operated indicated that this was not a genuine attempt to investigate the monasteries properly. Nonetheless, it was hard for contemporaries to claim that the king was mistaken, and easy for the Vicegerent in Spirituals (Cromwell) to find evidence of corruption, however slight or long ago.

Tregonwell's Report. The following report by Tregonwell – one of the more balanced commissioners – shows how even his report could be used selectively to misrepresent the state of the smaller monasteries. He wrote it at the time of his visits in 1535.

Source 11
I went to Godstow where I found all things in good order, both in the monastery and the convent, except

that one sister, 13 or 14 years ago, when in another house, had broken her chastity. For her correction and punishment, the Bishop of Lincoln sent her to Godstow, where she has now lived in virtue ever since.

From there I went to Eynsham where I found a raw sort of religious persons. All kinds of sin had been committed by them, for which offences they have now been punished by their **Ordinary** in his visitation. As far as I can tell, the abbot is chaste of his living and right well supervises the repairs of his house. He is negligent in the overseeing of the brethren but claims that this is because of his daily illness, which infirmity did appear, by his face, to be true.

Adapted from Tregonwell's Report, 1535.

So some sins had been committed, but punishments had been meted out. The abbot at Eynsham was a little negligent, but then he was not well.

The Act for the Dissolution of the Smaller Monasteries 1536

In the spring of 1536, Parliament was presented with an extraordinary government **bill** declaring that the smaller monasteries should be closed down immediately because of their sins. It should have been evident to all that it was inherently unlikely that small monasteries were corrupt while larger ones were shining beacons of virtue. Yet faced with this bill, it was hard to voice opposition. Cromwell had the evidence he needed, much of it clearly exaggerated by himself and his commissioners.

Source 12

Manifest sin, vicious, carnal and abominable living, is daily used and committed amongst the little and small abbeys, priories and other such religious houses of monks, canons and nuns, where the congregation of such religious persons is under the number of 12 persons. The governors of such religious houses consume and waste the ornaments of their churches and their goods and chattels to the high displeasure of

> ## KEY TERM
> The **Ordinary** was an official, usually the local bishop, who had the task of inspecting and regulating religious houses.

> ## KEY TERM
> **Bill.** This is the name given to an Act of Parliament or Statute before it was approved by the Commons, the Lords and the King.

Almighty God, slander of good religion, and to the great infamy of the King's Highness and the realm, if redress should not be had. There can be no reformation of this problem unless such small houses are utterly suppressed and the religious persons in them committed to great and honourable monasteries, where they may be compelled to live religiously for reformation of their lives.

Adapted from the Act for the Dissolution of the Smaller Monasteries 1536.

This passage reveals one reason why the dissolution was achieved with relative ease. Cromwell claimed in the Act that the large monasteries were untainted by corruption and that errant monks, from the unhealthy smaller houses, would be moved to the large and worthy institutions. The king thus preserved the façade of a reformer while acting as a destroyer. The official line was that the king so loved monasticism that he was determined to root out corruption in order to enhance it. To adopt a gardening metaphor, he was pruning out the dead wood in order to improve the health of the plant.

In fact, he was closing down the small monasteries not because they were corrupt, nor because he had turned against the ideal of monasticism, but because he coveted their wealth. This was hidden from Parliament by Cromwell's marvellous propaganda about corruption. Faced with this, Parliament could do little. Some members who were reformers themselves might well have been enthusiastic and many others might have pondered the gains that they could make from such a dissolution. The Act was passed without serious opposition.

The process of dissolution

Armed with the power to dissolve the smaller houses, Cromwell's agents began to dissolve the larger houses as well. Once the process of dissolution began, the distinction between small and large monasteries was conveniently forgotten. Commissioners were sent to large houses and demanded their surrender. Of course, it was soon widely rumoured that a general and forced dissolution of the monasteries was taking place, but Cromwell was equal to the problem. In a letter to one abbot, written in 1538, he brilliantly maintains the lie that surrenders were happening voluntarily.

Source 13

I doubt not that you have recently received the king's letters which told you that as long as you acted as good and faithful subjects, his Grace would not in any way interrupt you in your state and kind of living. His pleasure is that you should apprehend anyone declaring anything to the contrary. The king knows that in such cases there are always some malicious and cankered hearts which, upon a voluntary surrender, would persuade and blow abroad a general and violent suppression. Some governors and companies of a few religious houses have lately made free and voluntary surrenders into his Grace's hands but the king has commanded me to tell you, for your quietness and repose, that, unless there had been overtures made by the said houses, his Grace would never have received the same. You may be sure that you shall not be disturbed by his Majesty but that his Grace will be your shield and protector.

Adapted from a letter written by
Thomas Cromwell in 1538.

The scale of the lies is breathtaking and it is no wonder that many monks and indeed laymen were uncertain about the king's intentions. Many religious houses were fobbed off with the idea that they were in fact being reformed, not dissolved, by the Supreme Head, and companies of confused monks no doubt believed the lie. Other houses were made to pay stiff fines and told that, in this way, they could save their houses. The Abbott of Rewley believed the cruel lie, as is made clear in this touching letter that he wrote to Cromwell in 1536.

Source 14

I submit myself full and wholly to your mastership, as all my refuge, help and succour is in you, glad of my voluntary mind to be bound in obligation of one hundred pounds to be paid to your mastership, so our house may be saved.

Adapted from a letter written by the Abbot of Rewley in 1536.

In fact, monks and abbots were faced with a stark choice between surrender and punishment. The abbots at Colchester, Reading and Glastonbury chose martyrdom rather than surrender, but they were in a minority. The king and Cromwell could not be resisted and they offered pensions to those who acquiesced in the destruction of their houses.

The plundering of the monasteries and the Second Dissolution Act 1539

It was the most breathtaking plunder of the English Church that had ever been seen and it was accomplished by methods that bordered on terrorism. Some 500 religious houses were dissolved. A huge array of wondrous medieval artwork was destroyed or carried off to be melted down for profit. Valuable lead was stripped from roofs, and buildings were plundered of their stone and left as empty shells, which still today provide haunting testimony to the greed and vandalism of Henry and Cromwell.

So by 1539, when the Act for the dissolution of the larger monasteries (or abbeys) was introduced into Parliament, the members were faced with a *fait accompli* (an accomplished fact). The Act claimed that the abbeys, appalled by their sins, had voluntarily surrendered to the king. Once again Cromwell had outmanoeuvred Parliament. Now the members could not oppose the Act because most of the abbeys had already been dissolved and few landowners or merchants wanted to miss out on a share of the spoils.

The sudden influx of goods and property to the Crown was so great that Cromwell was forced to set up a special financial court – the **Court of Augmentations** – to deal with it all. Perhaps appropriately, the first Chancellor of

The Court of Augmentations. The title means that the court dealt with increases (or augmentations) in the king's lands and property. The court was really used for accounting purposes – the revenue and goods went into the king's coffers.

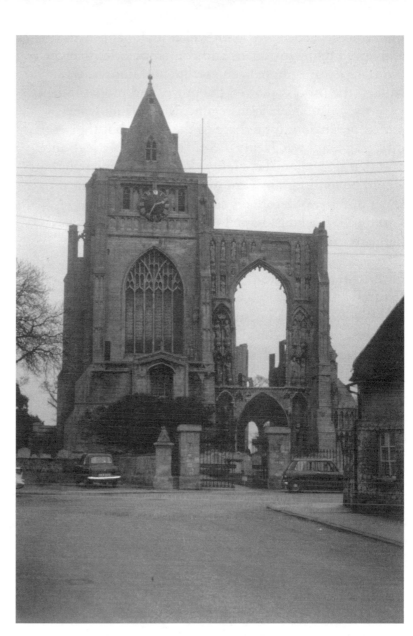

Crowland Abbey, Lincolnshire. The great nave of the Abbey Church (on the right) is ruined. The north aisle was converted into a parish church.

KEY PERSON

Sir Richard Rich was one of Cromwell's servants. He lied in court in 1535 in order to convict Sir Thomas More of treason and was rewarded with the office of Attorney-General for Wales. He later became Lord Chancellor and died in his bed.

this court was **Richard Rich**, Cromwell's servant and toady, who had, by this time, perjured himself and murdered Thomas More. The fact that the same man ended up as Chancellor of England, the most important lawyer in England, points to the terrible political and moral climate of the times.

Overview of dissolution

So it was that the king and Cromwell, with the acquiescence of the political nation, destroyed monasticism. The speed with which it all happened convinced many historians and contemporaries that the monasteries must have been corrupt and unnecessary. In fact, the process showed the power and propaganda expertise of the Henrician regime. Many landowners joined in, anxious for a share of the spoils, but the directing hand was Henry's. Sir Thomas More had once said that if the lion (i.e. Henry) knew his own strength, it would be hard for any man to curb him. Encouraged by a small number of reformers such as Cranmer and Cromwell, the king showed that More's prophecy was perfectly correct.

Financial implications of the plundering of the Church

Henry's plunder and destruction of the Church did not end there. Cromwell had claimed that he would use the Supremacy in general and the dissolution of the monasteries in particular to make Henry the richest king in Christendom. As well as pulling down abbeys, the king now gained regular taxes from all clergy and his new bishoprics scheme would allow him to plunder land belonging to the secular Church in the name of reform. **Six new bishoprics** were set up and allocated lands from the existing sees, but in the transfer of these lands from one see to another, quite a lot was diverted to the Crown.

However, the opportunity created by the great transfer of land and property to the Crown, to clear debts and increase royal income for the foreseeable future, was lost. As Henry needed to pay off debts, to construct coastal defences against the possibility of foreign invasion and to bribe the leading magnates into submission, the monastic lands, instead of being retained, were hastily sold off. Instead of endowing the Crown with long-term income, they were sold for short-term gain.

In the 1540s, the king decided to relive his youth by embarking on war with France and with Scotland once more. By the end of the reign, just eleven years after the first dissolution, Crown finances were in a worse state than they had been before the onset of the Henrician Reformation. Archbishop Cranmer had even believed

Six new bishoprics. Henry set up new bishoprics centred on monastic buildings and lands at Oxford, Peterborough, Gloucester, Chester, Bristol and Westminster. The last was abandoned in 1550 during the reign of Henry's son, Edward VI.

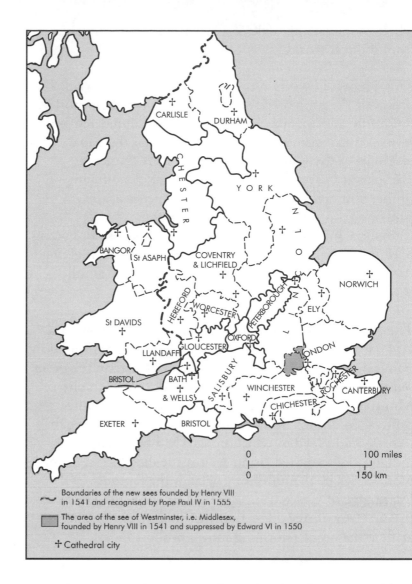

English and Welsh dioceses after the Reformation.

Boundaries of the new sees founded by Henry VIII
in 1541 and recognised by Pope Paul IV in 1555

The area of the see of Westminster, i.e. Middlesex,
founded by Henry VIII in 1541 and suppressed by Edward VI in 1550

✝ Cathedral city

Henry's promise that money from the dissolution would
be spent on education and the poor.

Limited theological impact of the dissolution

The dissolution of the monasteries was justified on the
basis of their alleged, but largely invented, corruption and
scandalous living, not on the grounds that such institutions
should not exist. Many Protestant theologians, however,
were teaching that Purgatory, the halfway house for the
dead between Heaven and Hell, did not in fact exist. Thus
they believed that monasteries and **chantries**, which existed
partly to say prayers for the dead in Purgatory, should not
exist either. In addition, many Protestants rejected the

KEY TERM

Chantries were endowments
in churches supporting
prayers and Masses on behalf
of the dead. They were so
called because prayers were
chanted or sung by the priest.

whole monastic rationale of a life spent apparently cut off from the real world.

King Henry, however was not a Protestant theologian. He dissolved the monasteries because he wanted their money. Politically and financially, he enjoyed his supremacy and seemed unconcerned at the renunciation of the papal headship of the Church. Religiously, he remained a Catholic at heart. He had written a book denouncing Luther and defending the Seven Sacraments of the Catholic Church, he enjoyed the ceremonies of the Catholic Church, such as Creeping to the Cross and going on Pilgrimage, and he showed little real interest in giving the Church of England a distinctive and non-Catholic theology.

The religious changes brought in before 1539 show us a king moving with caution and hesitation, often inspired by political or diplomatic considerations rather than religious ones. After the Anabaptist excesses in the German city of **Munster** in 1535, King Henry, along with most other princes, could not rid himself of the idea that too much reform might lead to rebellion. In 1536 he suffered the indignity of a massed rising against the dissolution of the monasteries in the north of England, the famous Pilgrimage of Grace (see page 149). It is against Henry's residual fear of new ideas that we should measure and analyse the other reforming moves of the 1530s.

HOW IMPORTANT AND FAR REACHING WERE THE OTHER RELIGIOUS REFORMS OF THE PERIOD 1536–9?

The Ten Articles 1536
These Articles appeared largely at the request of Cranmer and some of the more reforming bishops, who thought there should be a statement of religious orthodoxy in the post-papal English Church. The king was interested in the prospect of some kind of agreement with the German league of Protestant princes (the **Schmalkaldic League**), whereby he could defy the Emperor Charles V and pose as the European champion of reform. However, the religious

Munster in northern Germany was taken over by Protestant extremists or Anabaptists. Led by a tailor, Jan of Leyden, they introduced communism and polygamy, declaring that Munster was the New Jerusalem referred to in the Book of Revelation. Books apart from the Bible were burnt and unbelievers were killed.

The **Schmalkaldic League** (1531) was a small group of German Protestant princes set up to defend themselves against the Catholic Emperor Charles V.

price demanded by the German princes proved too high for the conservative king.

Although the Ten Articles were based, in style, on the German Wittenberg Articles, on key issues they refused to adopt a distinctly Protestant or Lutheran line. In the ceremony of the Mass, for example, the Ten Articles declared that Christ's body and blood were actually present 'substantially'. This could be seen as Catholic or Lutheran. On the means of achieving salvation (or justification), the Articles proclaimed that 'sinners attain this justification by contrition and faith joined with charity'. If charity was taken to mean **good works**, then this was a very Catholic formulation. Three of the seven sacraments of the Catholic Church (the Eucharist, Baptism and Penance) were discussed and all were seen as necessary for salvation. The other four sacraments were not mentioned, but neither were they condemned as unnecessary.

KEY TERM

Good works. The Catholic Church taught that salvation was achieved by good works as well as faith. Luther and other Protestants taught that faith alone was necessary and good works were of no value as a means of salvation.

In addition, the Ten Articles were passed only through Convocation. Unlike the later Six Articles, which were approved by Parliament, they did not have the force of law. Instead, they have all the hallmarks of religious compromise and of being a rushed interim statement in which difficult issues were largely avoided. As with many other religious pronouncements of the period, they were distinctly English but largely indistinct. The English talent for ambiguity may have been encouraged by Henry's pride. He did not wish to be seen as subservient to the wishes of a few German princes. He was a king and his own man.

The Bishops' Book 1537

Officially called the *Institution of a Christian Man* (the implications of this for women are not made clear!), this volume on theological matters hoped to clarify some of the issues left unresolved by the Ten Articles. The book was the subject of considerable debate between conservative and reforming bishops, especially between Stokesly of London and Foxe of Hereford. The four lost sacraments were found again, but were seen as less important than the other three.

The main problem with this book is that it lacked royal approval. The king declared that he did not have time to do more than glance at the volume, which seems highly unlikely for a king who enjoyed theological debate more than most. Lacking royal approval, the volume was soon known as 'The Bishops' Book'. When Henry did find time to review the book, he sent Cranmer 250 changes to the text. The main thrust of these changes was to ensure that 'good works' and not just faith played a part in salvation.

Cromwell's Injunctions 1536

Whatever the intricacies of theology involved in the Ten Articles and Bishops' Book, they had little impact on the way in which people worshipped. One wonders, indeed, how many people beyond the bishops and keen reforming clergy would have read them! By contrast, Thomas Cromwell's two sets of Injunctions, issued in 1536 and 1538, did more to dismantle ancient aspects of Catholic ceremonial.

The 1536 set placed emphasis on reform via education. The clergy were ordered by Cromwell to teach the Pater Noster (Our Father), the Articles of Faith and the Ten Commandments to congregations and to young people. Wealthy clergy were to support scholars at schools and universities, while parents were urged to educate their children. There was nothing uncatholic about any of this, of course, but the Injunctions went on to declare that the clergy were to publicise – and presumably show their approval of – the Supremacy and the Ten Articles.

Two further items would have a more profound impact on the population at large. One repeated the reduction in the number of **Holy Days** (or holidays) that had been approved by Convocation a little earlier. The other was a command that rectors should provide Bibles in English and Latin for people to read in church. The Catholic Church and many Catholic reformers, such as Sir Thomas More, were not against vernacular bibles in principle, but they thought that those allowed to read the scriptures should be restricted to clergy and intellectuals, to prevent disputes on matters of theology. For now, this article was largely ignored.

KEY TERM

Holy Days were annual saints' days when no work would be done and they were often accompanied by exciting local religious ceremonies. Protestants thought that they were superstitious and encouraged idleness, so they sought to end them.

Cromwell's Injunctions 1538

In September 1538, when circumstances favoured the reformers once again, when the suppression of the larger monasteries was taking place and Henry was once again courting the German Lutheran princes, Cromwell was allowed to issue a second set of Injunctions. Most were extensions of the 1536. Now images that were the object of pilgrimage were to be taken down. Candles before images were forbidden and sermons were to be preached against the veneration of images and relics. This fitted in nicely with the attacks being made on the monasteries. In February 1538 the Rood of Grace from Boxley Abbey was destroyed at St Paul's Cross in London, and in July images of the Virgin from Walsingham and Ipswich were burnt.

An English Bible

In addition to attacks on superstitious practices, the 1538 Injunctions made a more determined effort to introduce an English Bible into every parish in the land. Cromwell had commissioned Miles Coverdale to produce a Great Bible. However, the printing in Paris (not London) was delayed and when the bibles did finally appear, the reformers' influence over the king was beginning to crumble. Nonetheless, the English Bible that was introduced marks a major development in the history of the English Church.

The frontispiece of the Bible appealed to Henry's self-esteem. It shows the Supreme Head flanked by Cranmer and Cromwell, distributing the Word of God to the faithful. It enhanced Henry's sense of his imperial powers as second only to God, and it was used as powerful propaganda to boost the Supremacy itself. The Old Testament, after all, contained many references to godly kings. Here was Henry, in similar guise, doing great and godly things for his people.

Restrictions on access to the Bible

Access to the Bible, however, was restricted. Individuals who wished to possess their own bible had to have a licence. Later on, the king realised that the English Bible might prove divisive. He complained about men debating about the Word of God in alehouses. In 1543 Parliament brought in an Act for the Advancement of True Religion.

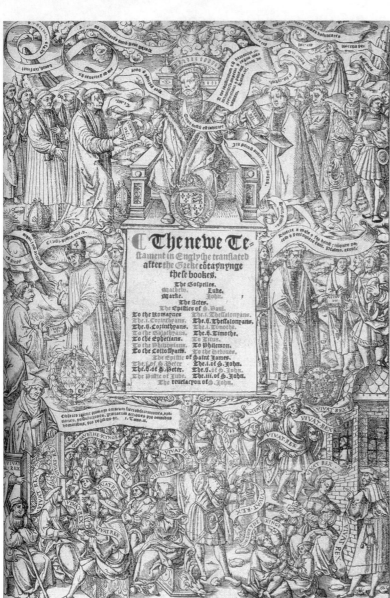

The title page of the Great Bible, published in 1539.

It condemned 'crafty, false and untrue' translations of the Bible and limited Bible reading to the politically powerful. Noblemen and gentlemen might read the Bible to their families at home. Substantial merchants might read it by themselves, while the common people – even supposing they could read – were not to read the scriptures at all.

This law again suggests that the Henrician Reformation was not widely or radically reforming in nature. The king had made himself Head of the Church, dissolved the monasteries, cracked down on superstition and brought in an English Bible. In matters of faith and theology, however, he had not brought in heretical or Lutheran ideas. From 1539 onwards, Henry made it plain that religious reform was over and that the Reformation was on hold. There would be no more Protestant reform until after the king's death in 1547.

SUMMARY QUESTIONS

1 Describe the role of Parliament in carrying out the Henrician Reformation.

2 Explain the main reasons for the changes in religion during the 1530s.

SOURCE QUESTIONS

1 What evidence is there in Source 11 to indicate that the monasteries were in good order?　*(5 marks)*

2 How far does Source 12 challenge the view of the monasteries given in Source 11?　*(7 marks)*

3 Using all the Sources 11–14 and your own knowledge, consider the view that the dissolution of the monasteries was successfully carried out by means of deception and propaganda.　*(20 marks)*

CHAPTER 7

1547–58: The reigns of Edward and Mary

FRAMEWORK OF EVENTS 1547–58

1547   Execution of Earl of Surrey (January)
Death of Henry VIII and accession of Edward VI (January)
Edward Seymour becomes Lord Protector (January)
Seymour becomes Duke of Somerset (February) and obtains the right to nominate Councillors (March)
Somerset defeats the Scots at Battle of Pinkie (September)
Parliament meets (November–December) New Treason Act. Act for dissolving the Chantries
Publication of Book of Homilies

1548   Enclosure Commission appointed to enforce existing laws (June) Sporadic riots in Southern England
French army in Scotland (June)
Mary, Queen of Scots goes to France (July)
Proclamations order the removal of images from churches and disuse of superstitious ceremonies

1549   Parliament (November 48–March 49) passes Act of Uniformity imposing First Edwardian Prayer Book. Tax on sheep and cloth. Act permitting priests to marry.
More Enclosure Commissions. Rioting in Southern England (spring)
Western Rebellion and Kett's Rebellion (summer)
War with France – French besiege Boulogne (August)
Bonner, Bishop of London deprived for opposition to Prayer Book (September)
Fall of Somerset (October) Warwick v. Wriothesley
Bad harvest

1550   Warwick takes charge as Lord President of the Council (February).

HEINEMANN ADVANCED HISTORY

Peace with France and Scotland – Treaty of
Boulogne (March)
Princess Mary refuses to use New Prayer Book
Bad harvest

1551 Gardiner deprived of his bishopric (February)
Warwick made Duke of Northumberland (October)
Somerset tried for treason (December)
Third bad harvest in a row

1552 Execution of Somerset (January)
Parliament meets (January–April) Second
Edwardian Prayer Book
Royal Commission reports on Crown's financial
problems (December)

1553 42 Articles of Religion (June)
Death of Edward VI (July)
'Reign' of Lady Jane Grey (6–19 July)
Accession of Mary (July)
Execution of Northumberland (August)
Parliament meets (October–December) Repeal of
Edwardian religious laws

1554 Marriage Treaty with Spain (January)
Wyatt's Rebellion in Kent (January)
Lady Jane Grey executed (February)
Parliament meets (April–May)
Mary marries Philip (July)
Pole arrives as Papal Legate (November)

1555 Parliament (November 54–January 55) restores
Papal Supremacy (January). Heresy laws revived
First Protestant martyr executed (February)
Hooper burned in Gloucester (February)
Philip leaves England (August)
Latimer and Ridley burned in Oxford (October)
Death of Bishop Gardiner (November)
Cranmer deprived: Pole made Archbishop of
Canterbury (December) Holds Legatine Synod in
London
Very bad harvest

1556 Philip becomes King of Spain (January)
Burning of Cranmer (March)
Worst harvest of the century; beginning of a series
of epidemics

1557 Philip returns to England (spring)

War with France (June) French defeated at Battle of
St. Quentin
Pole deprived of legatine powers by Pope Paul IV
(April) and investigated for heresy in Rome (June)
1558 Loss of Calais (January)
Parliament meets (January–March)
Deaths of Mary and Pole (November)

THE RULE OF SOMERSET 1547–9

Seymour takes charge

In January 1547, with Archbishop Cranmer at his bedside,
Henry VIII died. His long and tortuous campaign to leave
the realm in the hands of an adult male heir had ended in
failure. Despite the divorce campaign, break with Rome
and of course, six wives, Henry's heir, Edward, son of his
favourite wife, Jane Seymour, was a boy of nine. Though
no one was to know it at the time, Edward would not live
to be an adult. He died in 1553 and was succeeded by his
elder sister, Princess Mary. It is one of the greater ironies of
English history, that, if Henry VIII had been less keen on
the Book of Leviticus and had accepted the idea of a
female succession, then he would have been succeeded
smoothly enough by an adult woman of thirty years and
the country might have been spared the great upheavals of
the Henrician Reformation, as well as the conflicts that
now lay ahead. Mary, it turned out, was entirely capable of
governing the realm well. Given the terrible sufferings
inflicted on her by her father over the previous twenty
years, it is surprising that she was so well balanced.

Henry's failure to provide an adult heir was potentially
very serious. In 1547, the Crown was seriously in debt and
England was diplomatically and religiously isolated. France
and Scotland were still smarting from invasion by Henry
VIII, while Charles V seemed to have turned the
Protestant tide in Europe by defeating the German
Protestant princes at the Battle of Muhlberg (1547).
Internally there seemed little chance of political or religious
stability. Henry's last years had been marked by faction
fighting at Court over the country's religious future.
Conservatives wished to minimise the influence of known

reformers like Cranmer and Seymour, while the reformers chafed under a religious settlement based on the **Act of Six Articles** of 1539 which was essentially Catholic. Just days before Henry's death, the conservatives suffered a double blow when the Duke of Norfolk was imprisoned and his son, the Earl of Surrey, was executed.

Without the steadying influence of the old king there was every chance that there would be serious conflict. The Catholic powers of Spain and France might invade in the name of Princess Mary or the country might be gripped by civil war – or both might happen simultaneously. Well might **Bishop Latimer** take as his text while preaching before King Edward in 1549, the passage from Ecclesiastes which cries out, 'Woe to thee, O land, where the king is a child'. Henry VIII's legacy was one of uncertainty.

Within hours of his death, there occurred a very English and bloodless *coup d'état*. **William Paget** kept the news of the king's death secret for a couple of days which allowed **Edward Seymour**, the new king's uncle, to take charge of the boy and the realm. Henry VIII's will had decreed that a Regency Council of sixteen named Councillors should rule in Edward's name until he came of age. However, with the conservatives temporarily in disgrace (Norfolk avoided execution only because of the king's death), Seymour managed to persuade his fellow Councillors, mainly by means of bribes and titles, that a Protector was needed to create a stronger and more united government and that he was the ideal candidate. His pre-eminence in 1547 rested not on his administrative capabilities but on the fact that he was the king's uncle. Luckily for Edward VI, this royal minority proceeded more smoothly than the previous one 64 years earlier when Edward V's uncle, Richard of Gloucester, went on to usurp the throne.

In March 1547, Seymour's attempt to seize power received a boost when **Lord Chancellor Wriothesley**, the leading conservative to survive in power, was removed from his office. In the same month, a special commission pronounced that Seymour was legally Protector of the realm with 'full power and authority' to transact all the business of government without reference to the King's

Council. Having taken supreme power, Seymour awarded himself a dukedom (that of Somerset) and began to rule without consulting the other Councillors.

Somerset's government

Somerset was able to rule by issuing proclamations. During his 30 months as Protector he issued some 75 of them, compared to just 35 issued by his successor Northumberland in a period of nearly 4 years. Since the passing of the Act of Proclamations in 1539, the Crown was able to pass and enforce royal proclamations as though they had the force of law. The theory was that, in dangerous and unsettled times, when **Parliament** still met only infrequently, proclamations could be used to ensure strong and effective government. This Act suited Somerset well, except that it demanded that each proclamation should be signed by twelve Councillors. This arrangement was fine for Henry VIII, whose Councillors did as they were told, but not so good for Somerset, whose high-handed methods soon made him unpopular in that quarter. Happily, Somerset had the Act repealed by Parliament which met for six weeks at the end of 1547. In this way he managed to preserve the tradition of issuing proclamations without the legal necessity of getting other Councillors to agree with him.

In the same Parliament, Somerset passed a new Treason Act. Far from following the harsh tradition of Henry VIII's Treason Act of 1534 which had extended the definition of treason to include words, Somerset's new Act was much more liberal. It swept away the 1534 Act as well as the Act of Six Articles (1539) and all restrictions on the printing and study of the Scriptures. As Somerset was committed to the reforming group at Court, this Act was an important step in paving the way for more Protestant reforms in the future. However, Somerset's move was irresponsible in that it created expectations of change without having a new religious settlement to hand. Meanwhile there was a flood of Protestant propaganda on the one hand and growing Catholic unease on the other, as the religious future of the country was once again thrown into doubt. Somerset got the worst of both worlds! This was not quite how Somerset had planned it. The Act was probably designed as a

HEINEMANN ADVANCED HISTORY

KEY PERSON

Lord Chancellor Wriothesley. Thomas Wriothesley, later Earl of Southampton, was a leading conservative force in the 1540s. He succeeded Thomas Audley as Lord Chancellor of England in 1544 but lost his office when Somerset took power in 1547. His fortunes revived briefly in 1549 when he helped to oust Somerset and became Earl of Southampton but he then tried to remove Northumberland. As a result he lost power and helped to drive Northumberland more firmly into the reforming camp.

KEY TERM

Parliament. One of the interesting developments of the Reformation period was the increasing frequency with which Parliament met. Under Edward and Mary (1547–58) it met every year except 1556 and 1557.

KEY TERM

The **chantries** were essentially 'chapels' endowed by individuals or institutions to say masses for the dead to help reduce their time in Purgatory. As Protestantism denied the existence of Purgatory, they were seen as unnecessary.

popularity boost for a man whose hold on power was rather tenuous. It was meant to win favour with Parliament and the political nation at large by discarding very publicly the repressive measures of the previous regime. Henry VIII, who had swept away Empson and Dudley in similar style in 1509, would have approved.

Somerset's grip on power was aided by the fact that the young king never seems to have interfered in his Protector's exercise of power. King Edward seems to have been a committed Protestant and would no doubt have approved of the general direction of Somerset's reforming policies. Though apparently intelligent and well-educated, Edward was probably not consulted in detail by his uncle and so remained Somerset's most useful political ally. Somerset ruled in his name but not under his authority.

SOMERSET'S POLICIES

War against the Scots

The keystone to Somerset's policies was not so much religion as war. He had made his name in the early 1540s as a commander in the wars against France and Scotland. Now in 1547, like Henry VIII before him, he strove to consolidate his hold on power with victory in war. He hoped that a glorious and successful campaign against the old enemy would unite a troubled realm and calm fears about his *coup d'état*. For Henry VIII the main enemy had always been France, with Scotland as something of a side show. For Somerset the priorities were reversed. He had burnt Edinburgh in 1544 and now he aimed to complete the conquest of Scotland by converting her to Protestantism and marrying her infant Queen Mary to young King Edward. The scheme was certainly ambitious and proved to be a complete failure. By attacking Scotland, Somerset, predictably enough, provoked war with France. By spending huge amounts of money on campaigning, garrison troops and cart loads of English Bibles, he further increased royal debts. This in turn increased taxes and inflation and worsened the plight of the poor. Increased royal debt meant that more Church wealth had to be plundered. With monastic wealth all used up, the target this time was the **chantries**. They had to be dissolved in order to pay for a pointless war and for the political support which Somerset craved. This was another clear example of religious policy being determined by fiscal needs. Money and lands which had been donated for spiritual purposes were now stolen and used for secular ends.

Religious policy

It is hard to know whether the religious changes under Somerset deserve the title of 'policy'. Somerset generally proceeded cautiously but without any real sense of direction. The first step was the Dissolution of the Chantries. The removal of these institutions, based more in towns and therefore more visible than their monastic counterparts, was another step along Protestantism's destructive path. Earmarked for closure under Henry VIII they were sacrificed to the demands of a fatally flawed foreign policy.

More genuinely reforming was the *Book of Homilies* published by Cranmer in 1547, designed to help those priests who were not used to preaching sermons. This publication highlighted a central problem in the efforts of the Reformers to make England into a Protestant nation – the lack of a Protestant preaching ministry. The existing clergy had been told to introduce an English Bible into their parishes, but beyond this most remained essentially Catholic, administering the sacraments in accordance with the Catholic Act of Six Articles. It would take at least a generation to produce ministers who were committed Protestants and even then they would often have to tailor their Protestant enthusiasm to the more conservative demands of their parishioners.

In 1548 proclamations demanded the removal of images from churches and the ending of many ceremonies now deemed superstitious, such as the use of **ashes** and holy water. The next year saw one of the landmarks in the English Reformation, the first *English Prayer Book*. Devised by Cranmer, this book essentially translated the Latin ceremonies and words into English and put forward a moderate interpretation of the Eucharist. It was sufficiently ambiguous to allow for the real presence of Christ and

KEY TERM

Ashes were sprinkled on people's heads in a special ceremony on Ash Wednesday, the first day of Lent.

many Catholics, including Bishop Gardiner (by this time in the Tower!) gave it their approval.

While it was far from radical in terms of its theology, the new *Prayer Book* did emphasise the growing importance of parliament in the process of religious change. Under Henry VIII, all the great reforming statutes had been passed through Parliament, but their introduction and authority stemmed essentially from the king. He was Supreme Head of the Church and that power was granted to him not by Parliament but by God. Under Edward, Parliament's authority was more pronounced. The new *Book of Common Prayer* was enforced by an Act of Uniformity passed by parliament. With the king still a minor – only twelve years old in 1549 – and with the authority of the Protector still a novelty in legal terms, control of religious affairs had passed to Parliament. Another Act of 1549 officially allowed clergy to marry and in some dioceses up to one-third of the clergy did so. This still left the majority unmarried.

From his deathbed, Henry VIII points at his successor Edward VI. The first three men to the right of Edward are Somerset, Northumberland and Cranmer.

Social policy and rebellions

Somerset has often been called the **Good Duke** as he seemed to promise a better deal for the common man. Like Wolsey before him, he attempted to curb enclosures which were continuing to drive men off the land. Advised by **John Hales**, Somerset set up Enclosure Commissions in 1548 and 1549 which toured the country in search of illegal enclosures. However well-meaning the policy, it was a failure. Attempts to introduce new laws against enclosure and in favour of dairy farming were rejected by Parliament, where landowners once again saw the moves as undermining their rights. On the other hand, the excitement over enclosures and the promise of better times, stirred up agrarian unrest as those at the receiving end of new enclosures saw their expectations dashed.

Apart from enclosures, the main cause of the problems was inflation. R. B. Outhwaite has calculated that prices of foodstuffs in the 1540s had more than doubled compared to seventy years earlier and were some 30 per cent higher than in the 1530s. Meanwhile, the purchasing power of agricultural labourers and building craftsmen – the amount they could buy with the same money – was only 85 per cent that of the previous decade. One of the main causes of this inflation was the debasement of the coinage carried out in the 1540s to fund warfare and the rebuilding of coastal defences. Somerset was advised to restore the currency by **Sir Thomas Smith**, his Secretary of State but his words fell on deaf ears.

Meanwhile, the economic problems and Somerset's policies combined to spark off **rebellion in the summer of 1549**. In the south-west the rebels objected mainly to the new *Prayer Book*, while in East Anglia, enclosure was the main grievance. The rebellions were eventually put down by force but they helped to spell the end of Somerset. With his religious, social and foreign policies in ruins (the French laid siege to Boulogne in August 1549) and with the growing resentment of the Councillors at his failure to consult them, it was only a question of time. Another serious bout of faction fighting in the autumn of 1549 brought the end of the Protector, again by means of a bloodless *coup d'état*. The charges drawn up against him by the Privy Council tell the tale with some clarity and perhaps a little exaggeration.

Source 15
The lords and others of the King's Majesty's Privy Council, considering the great rebellion of the people in sundry parts of the realm and the great slaughter and effusion of blood that lately hath been, and considering the great insolency and disobedience that yet remaineth amongst the King's Majesty's subjects, whereunto if speedy remedy be not provided, both his Majesty's most royal person and the whole state might be brought into hazard and peril, and remembering also that this and sundry other great disorders had proceeded from the ill government of the Lord Protector, who being spoken unto both in open council and otherwise privately, hath not only refused to give ear to their advice but also hath followed his own fantasies, from which all the said disorders hath grown and arisen . . .

Adapted from the official charges brought against Somerset in 1549.

THE RULE OF NORTHUMBERLAND 1549–53

Somerset overthrown
Somerset's fall was engineered by William Paget, Thomas Wriothesley and **John Dudley**, the Earl of Warwick. The latter made a name for himself by crushing the rebels in East Anglia and now saw his chance to topple Somerset. The Protector's fall was then followed by a fresh outbreak of faction fighting and it was Dudley who emerged as the new power in the land. He waited nearly two years before awarding himself a dukedom (that of Northumberland) and he proved to be a little less grasping and greedy than Somerset, who had used his period in office to accumulate large estates in the West Country. Unlike Somerset, Northumberland did not seek to become Protector but ruled through the Council as Lord President of that body. Somerset was sent to the Tower and, although released in

KEY PERSON

John Dudley, Earl of Warwick (1502–53). Son of the Dudley who was executed by Henry VIII in 1510, he became Earl of Warwick as a reward for supporting Somerset's coup in 1547. In 1549 he overthrew Somerset and made himself Duke of Northumberland in 1551. He was executed for high treason when his attempt to prevent the accession of Queen Mary in 1553 ended in failure.

1550, he never regained serious influence and was eventually executed in January 1552.

Foreign policy

Northumberland ended the war with France and Scotland but it was by means of a humiliating English climb-down, underscoring the failure of Somerset's aggressive policy. The city of Boulogne was handed back to the French, while Scotland not only remained free of English dominance but was now more firmly allied with France than ever. Young **Mary, Queen of Scots**, far from marrying King Edward, had been sent off to France to marry Henry II's son Francis – later Francis II.

Religious policy

Like Somerset, Northumberland now decided to court popularity by moving the religion of the realm in a more Protestant direction. Somerset's *Prayer Book* had left the **radicals** dissatisfied as it failed to clearly distance English theology from Rome. In 1550 **Bishop Hooper of Gloucester** had objected to the use of traditional Episcopal vestments in his consecration to his see and, as a result, his consecration was delayed. Meanwhile **Bishop Ridley of London** carried out a campaign to move altars away from the east end of churches and into the nave where they were to be used as Communion tables. This move was designed to stress that Christ was not actually present under the forms of bread and wine in the Eucharist ceremony.

In the same year, 1550, the radicals' progress was confirmed with the introduction of the new Ordinal – the service for the ordination of new priests. The centrepiece of Northumberland's and Cranmer's religious reforms, however, was another new *Prayer Book* which was introduced in 1552. This was more clearly Protestant in tone than its predecessor. The Mass was abolished and replaced by a Communion service and the wording of that service stressed that the ceremony was a memorial service. Communicants took the bread in remembrance of Christ's suffering and death. At the same time colourful Catholic vestments were largely replaced by Protestant black and white. In 1553, Cranmer also issued 42 Articles of Religion, which were clearly influenced by the ideas of the Frenchman and leading continental reformer, **John Calvin**, who had brought in his own reforming ideas in the free city of Geneva. In particular his contentious idea of **predestination**, now became part of the English Church's theology.

The end of Northumberland

The new religious reforms, however, all hinged on the survival of King Edward and, by 1553, there were serious concerns about his health. Sadly, Henry VIII's longed-for son was struck down by a mortal illness at the age of only fifteen. Traditionally it has been argued that it was Northumberland who, faced with this crisis, attempted to alter Henry VIII's third Succession Act of 1543 and place the Protestant **Lady Jane Grey** on the throne rather than King Edward's half-sister, the Catholic Princess Mary. Early in 1553 Lady Jane was married to Guildford Dudley, Northumberland's son which seemed to confirm that the Lord President was scheming to put his daughter-in-law on the throne with his grandson as the next king. However, this view seems to be unduly simplified and unfair on Northumberland. It was King Edward who was the real driving force behind the scheme and it was not clear, when Lady Jane Grey married Dudley, that the King would die within a few months. When it did become clear that the end was near, it was Edward himself who summoned the Council and demanded that they accept his will, in which he declared that the Crown should go to Lady Jane and her heirs. Unfortunately his will had no force in law. Minors could not make wills at that time and even a legal royal will could not overturn statute law. The Succession Act of 1543 was still very much in force and this declared unambiguously that Mary should be Edward's heir. The puzzle is that Edward should not have tried to make Elizabeth the next queen. At least she was included in the Succession Act and was a Protestant of sorts. Mary's claim might be set aside by Parliament because of her religious persuasion. Probably Edward saw Lady Jane as a more sincere Protestant and, as a married lady, one who might produce a future Protestant king in the near future.

Failure of Lady Jane

Whatever the merits of Edward's choice of heir, he, like his father before him, could not command events after his death. Although the habit of the political nation had always been to acquiesce in change, and although many observers expected Jane to rule because she was a Protestant, Princess Mary successfully defied the new settlement and brought off the first successful seizure of power since her grandfather's in 1485. First she evaded capture by Northumberland and retreated from London to the safety of Norfolk. There she proclaimed herself queen and many gentry rallied to her call. When Northumberland set out from London with troops to deal with her, the rest of the Council, led by the Earls of Arundel and Pembroke, abandoned the plot and declared for Mary in London amid scenes of rejoicing. Northumberland's army began to desert and he soon surrendered. Mary took power by another bloodless coup. The political leaders of the nation had voted for legality rather than religious expediency. In many parts, her accession was greeted with rejoicing. In some parishes, altars and images were set up once again and Latin service books reappeared in an outburst of local enthusiasm which predated the official changes back to Catholicism. This enthusiasm may have been linked to opposition to the new *Prayer Book* introduced at the end of Edward's reign and must reflect on the limited impact of Protestant doctrine during Edward's reign. This extract from the Yorkshire clergyman, Robert Parkyn, seems to capture the mood.

Source 16

And so the said Queen Mary was proclaimed at York on the 21st day of July and at Pontefract, Doncaster, Rotherham and many other market towns on the 22nd of July . . . she to be right inheritor and Queen of England and Ireland, whereat the whole commonalty in all places in the north parts greatly rejoiced, making great fires, drinking wine and ale, praising God. But all such as were of heretical opinions, with bishops and priests having wives,

did nothing rejoice, but began to be ashamed
of themselves, for the common people would point
at them with fingers in places where they saw
them . . .

Adapted from the *Narrative of Robert Parkyn.*

Mary's religious reforms

With Mary's peaceful accession, England experienced yet
more religious reforms but this time they were Catholic,
not Protestant, reforms. As the daughter of Catherine of
Aragon, Mary saw her accession, quite naturally, as
divinely ordained (as indeed did many of her Protestant
opponents!) After so many years of suffering both for
herself and for her fellow Catholics, God had given her the
chance to bring back the old Faith. She had refused to
abandon the Latin Mass or conform in any way to the
Edwardian changes, and now her fortitude and faithfulness
were rewarded.

**Lady Jane Grey,
attributed to Master
John, c1545.**

Rarely can a monarch have come to power with as clear a
set of aims as did Queen Mary. Within two years, she had
not only brought back Catholic doctrine and ceremony,
abolishing the *Prayer Book*, but she had also destroyed the
Royal Supremacy and brought back the Papal Headship
over the Church. The insular and schismatic Church of
England became, once again, the Church in England, part
of the wider Roman Catholic Church. Although the
changes were dramatic, Mary did proceed with caution.
In her first parliament, between October and December of
1553, an Act was passed, with some opposition, which
repealed all of the religious laws passed during Edward's
reign. Thus, at first, the English Church returned to the
last years of Henry VIII's reign, with the Act of Six Articles
and the Royal Supremacy. It was not until January 1555
that Parliament repealed all the Acts passed against the
Papacy since the beginning of the Reformation Parliament
in 1529. This move seems to have been unopposed, since
it was made clear that the nobility and gentry could keep
hold of their ex-monastic lands!

Persecution of Protestants

With the destruction of these laws, the medieval heresy laws were automatically revived and these were used from 1555 onwards to track down and execute those Protestants who refused to give up their faith. Several hundred were burnt at the stake in the next three years and this marks the most serious and most un-English bout of religious persecution in English history. Critics were quick to blame Mary and the Imperial ambassador, Simon Renard, for this ruthless policy, but in truth the policy was implemented by a few of the bishops, most notably **Bishop Bonner** of London. Nonetheless, one must remember the religious divisions which Mary had inherited and the views of the Catholic bishops about the Protestant problem. Most believed that England had been led into Protestantism by a small group of evil men, who had misled the nation. For many centuries the Catholic Church had taught that obstinate heretics, those who refused to recant, should be burnt at the stake in order to save the Church from heresy. Unfortunately for Mary and the bishops, Protestant heresy had not only been active in England for some twenty years but, periodically, it had received royal approval. So, by 1555, there was bound to be a core of Protestant opinion, mainly in London and the south-east, which would prove hard to undermine. Nonetheless the persecution might have proved a success in the long term, since there were very few Protestant martyrs from the ruling classes. Only four bishops were executed and none of the victims were of noble or gentry status. Zealous Protestants from those classes conformed or fled abroad to await better days rather than face persecution at home.

Cardinal Pole returns

Cardinal Reginald Pole, who had been a Catholic exile during the troubled days of schism and heresy, now returned to England as Papal Legate, to reunite the English Church with Rome. Later he replaced Cranmer as Archbishop of Canterbury. He had always been a moderate Catholic reformer supporting the ideas of Cardinal Contarini, who took the view that the way to destroy heresy was not to wage war on the heretics but rather not to deserve their criticism. If the Catholic Church waged war on corruption and returned to proper spiritual values

KEY PERSON

Edmund Bonner was a diplomat and Henrician Catholic who accepted the Royal Supremacy. He was Bishop of London from 1540 until 1549, when he was deprived of his office. He was restored to his see by Mary and was committed to the destruction of Protestant heresy. He was imprisoned in 1559 when Elizabeth became queen, and died in 1569.

KEY PERSON

Cardinal Reginald Pole (1500–58) was a Yorkist through his mother the Countess of Shrewsbury who was executed by Henry VIII in 1541. He opposed Henry VIII's divorce and went into exile. He lived in Italy from 1532 and was made a Cardinal by Pope Paul III. There was hope that he would return to England to head the Pilgrimage of Grace in 1536 and talk of a marriage between him and Princess Mary to ensure a Catholic succession. He returned to England as Papal Legate in 1554 and reunited England with Rome. He was made Archbishop of Canterbury and died within hours of Queen Mary in 1558.

Protestants brought from Colchester (Essex) to London for interrogation by Bishop Bonner in 1556. On the advice of Cardinal Pole they were released after re-affirming their belief in Christ's real presence in the Eucharist.

then Protestant heresy would lose its rationale. So, as Archbishop, he took initiatives to improve the quality of the clergy, by introducing seminaries in every diocese and holding a legatine synod to investigate the state of the Church. These were sensible moves towards long-term success and the Catholic revival of the reign was underpinned by increasing numbers of young men coming forward for ordination and by an able and purposeful bench of bishops. All but one of them resigned rather than accept the Protestant Settlement of Queen Elizabeth.

All in all the Marian reforms were not as savage and uncompromising as seen elsewhere on the Continent. There was no English Inquisition, no English Jesuits and no confiscation of ex-monastic lands. The vast majority of the English nation, with its traditional support for legitimate authority in Church and State, showed no signs of serious opposition to moderate Marian Catholicism.

The Spanish marriage

Mary sought to bolster the return of Catholicism by her marriage to Philip II of Spain. She announced this to her Council early on in the reign and, despite reservations from some, a marriage treaty was signed and the marriage took place in July 1554, just a year after her accession. This marriage brought back England's natural alliance with

Spain (who controlled the Low Countries) and of course, might have produced the Catholic heir which Mary desperately needed, as her current heir according to the 1543 Act of Succession was the Protestant Princess Elizabeth.

The marriage to Philip led to opposition. Sir Thomas Wyatt led a rebellion early in 1554 against the planned marriage but was quite quickly defeated. In fact the rebels had over-reacted to the marriage as they thought that it would lead to Spanish control of England. By the marriage treaty, Mary remained sovereign and although she made war on France in alliance with Spain, this was no more than previous rulers had done. Calais, the final outpost on the Continent was taken by the French in 1558 but it was no great loss. Trade was not adversely affected and the government saved money by not having to finance the costly Calais garrison.

The end of the reign

Despite serious misgivings by some, the first female ruler in English history had been a success. Mary had clear aims and objectives in religion but she ruled with the help and advice of her Council. There was faction fighting within the Council but this, in reality, was no worse than what had gone before and at least did not lead to any executions. Mary may not have been too concerned about the details of administration but the reforms in government under Henry VIII had helped to create a stronger central government which could function effectively without the guiding hand of an adult male ruler. Although government functioned effectively in this period, the success of Mary, Pole and the Catholic bishops in restoring Roman Catholicism was to be short-lived. Less than six years after her accession, Mary died without a child to succeed her, so that the throne passed to Anne Boleyn's Protestant daughter. Once more God seemed to have intervened in the affairs of men (and women) and He now turned His favour once again on the Protestants. It is to Mary's credit that, unlike Edward VI, she did not attempt to pervert the succession to suit her religious convictions.

SUMMARY QUESTIONS

1 What were the main changes in religion during the reign of Edward VI?

2 'During Mary's reign, the successes clearly outweighed the failures.' To what extent do you agree with this viewpoint?

HEINEMANN ADVANCED HISTORY

AS ASSESSMENT: POLITICS AND RELIGION 1485–1558

Sources exercise in the style of AQA

You will need to have read Chapter 1 before doing this exercise.

1 Study the sources below and answer the questions.

Source A

The King, our sovereign lord, remembers how by unlawful maintenances and the giving of liveries, signs and tokens, and retainers by indenture, promises, oaths, writing or otherwise; embraceries* of his subjects . . . by the taking of money by juries, by great riots and unlawful assemblies; good rule in this land is almost defeated . . . The laws of the land have little effect, to the increase of murders, robberies, perjuries and the insecurity of all men and to the losses of their lands and goods to the great displeasure of almighty God.

From the Star Chamber Act 1487.

(*embraceries = corrupting of juries)

Source B

A decree made to confirm an order taken by the Mayor and commons of Plymouth for the expulsion of Nicholas Lowe and Alice his wife, out of Plymouth for their misdemeanours and evil living in the keeping of brothels, night watching beyond reasonable hours, maintaining and keeping dicers, carders, gamblers and other misgoverned and evilly disposed persons. And Sir John Croke, knight and his sons and servants, by the same decree, ordered not to maintain or uphold the said persons in the said case against the Mayor and commons. And for having done so up to the present, they are ordered to keep the peace upon pain of a fine of £200.

A case before the Council in Star Chamber, 6 May 1494.

Source C

He cherished justice above all things; as a result he vigorously punished violence, manslaughter and every other kind of wickedness whatsoever. Consequently, he was greatly regretted on that account by all of his subjects who had been able to conduct their lives in peace, far removed from the assaults and evil doings of scoundrels.

From a description of Henry VII by Polydore Vergil, 1513.

Questions

> 1 Study Source A. Using your own knowledge, explain the meaning of the phrase, 'the giving of liveries'. *(3 marks)*

How you should answer. This is a comprehension via own knowledge question. Remember that this question carries only 3 marks, so the answer should not be too extensive – a short paragraph should be enough. You will need to explain what was involved in the 'giving of liveries' and add in further own knowledge (e.g. about the Star Chamber Act of 1487) in order to reach full marks. For this type of question, mark schemes usually award 1 mark for basic or general explanation; 2 marks for developed explanation; 3 marks for developed explanation with additional piece of relevant own knowledge.

> 2 Study Source C. What are the strengths and weaknesses of this source as evidence of Henry VII's ability to enforce law and order during his reign? *(7 marks)*

How you should answer. This is a question about evaluating a source. Sometimes questions ask about the reliability or value of the source – in this case, it is strengths and weaknesses. There are two points to bear in mind as you answer this. First, you should make specific comments on both the strengths and weaknesses of the source. Second, the question directs you to focus on the king's 'ability to enforce law and order'. In other words, you should not talk about strengths and weaknesses of the source in general.

On the strengths side, Polydore Vergil did reside in England during Henry VII's reign and so was in a position to judge the effectiveness of Henry's policies. On the other hand, Vergil was an outsider, an Italian, and he is writing soon after Henry's reign. Perhaps he is looking back rather nostalgically; he certainly does not give any specific examples of Henry's ability to enforce law and order.

> 3 Study Sources A, B and C and use your own knowledge. 'Henry VII was successful in restoring strong government in England between 1485 and 1509.' Explain why you agree or disagree with this opinion. *(15 marks)*

How you should answer. This is a typical mini-essay question that demands integration of source use and own knowledge in order to answer a specific question about the reign as a whole. This will be the longest answer because of the marks on offer and because you will need to make direct use of all three sources and include relevant own knowledge. Therefore it will be necessary to write a short plan before you start on your answer. A plan is also important since, to reach the top level, you need to put forward a judgement at the start of your answer that will be sustained throughout the essay.

Using the sources, you can see Henry VII's determination both nationally and locally to uphold law and order. From own knowledge, you can discuss measures to curb over-mighty nobles, use of bonds and recognizances, the Council Learned in the Law and the king's ability to increase his income. At the top level, you will need to produce a well-sustained account that cross-references the sources and own knowledge, drawing conclusions about the success or otherwise of Henry VII in restoring strong government. Remember that the best answers will probably not agree or disagree completely with the quotation, but will offer a balanced answer. However, the answer should not be too well balanced as this will adversely affect the clarity of your answer.

Style. This is how a good answer might start.

Henry VII did much to restore strong government after the upheavals of the Wars of the Roses, though the scale of his achievement has often been exaggerated. Source A shows up the king's determination to restore strong government by acting against unlawful maintenance and retaining of armed men by members of the nobility. Such crimes had helped to sustain the civil conflict during the Wars of the Roses. Source B shows up the importance of the Star Chamber Act, passed early in the reign, by giving two specific examples of action taken at a local level by the King's Council seven years later. The suspended fine mentioned at the end of Source B, 'upon pain of a fine of £200', is a good example of the king's more systematic enforcement of bonds and recognizances during his reign.

After looking at a wider range of measures taken by Henry to restore strong government, you might conclude by giving a more balanced evaluation of Henry's success, to sustain the judgement made in the first sentence.

Although the king was clearly determined to restore strong government, he was not wholly successful. In Source C, Vergil, who was on intimate terms with the king, may exaggerate Henry's success, especially as he is writing soon after Henry's death. While Sources A and B show Henry's determination to restore law and order, they do not tell us how effective the policy was. While the disruptive power of the nobility was curbed, the reign saw serious disruption from two pretenders to the throne, a tax riot in Thirsk that led to the murder of Northumberland and a tax rebellion in Cornwall where the rebels marched all the way to London unchallenged.

Sources exercise in the style of Edexcel
You will need to have read Chapter 1 before doing this exercise.

1 Study the sources below and answer the questions.

Source A
A true friendship and alliance shall be observed henceforth between Ferdinand and Isabella, their heirs and subjects, on the one part, and Henry, his heirs and successors, on the other part. They promise to assist one another in defending their present and future dominions against any enemy whatsoever.

Both countries agree to help one another to defend their lands against any enemy. The people of each country are allowed to live in one another's countries and to trade there.

Neither country shall give any help to rebels from the other country, or allow them to remain in their lands.

> From the Treaty of Medina del Campo
> between England and Spain, March 1489.

Source B
We have read your letter and think that you have acted correctly concerning the marriage treaty. We know that King Henry has asked the Pope to allow the marriage even though the parties are young. Everything has been done as it should be. When you speak to the king about the marriage, you should insist that there must be an alliance and we look to you to improve the terms of the treaty. The duties on goods brought into England from Spain should be lowered. If the king will not agree, then we will raise duties on English goods here.

> Extracts from letters written by King Ferdinand and Queen Isabella to
> the Spanish Ambassador in England, de Puebla, 10–15 January 1497.

Source C
Henry VII's major concern was to secure his throne and his succession against a series of claimants – in particular Lambert Simnel (1486–7) and Perkin Warbeck (1491–9), each of whom received support from foreign powers. In other words, dynastic threats dominated Henry's dealings with foreign rulers . . . There is no doubt, too, that Henry was obsessed by the problem of internal security

throughout his reign, because his original claim to the throne was so weak. He relied on a network of agents and informers.

From Roger Lockyer and Dan O'Sullivan,
Tudor Britain 1485–1603, 1997.

Questions

1 What does Source B reveal about the aims of Ferdinand and Isabella in their dealings with Henry VII? *(3 marks)*

How you should answer this question. This is a comprehension question that does not require own knowledge, beyond that needed to understand what the source is saying. The source shows that the Spanish wished to see the marriage (between Catherine of Aragon and Prince Arthur) take place as a means of strengthening the alliance between the two countries. In addition, the source reveals that the Spanish wished to use the marriage as a means of improving the terms of trade for Spanish goods being sent to England.

2 Using your own knowledge, explain how Lambert Simnel and Perkin Warbeck caused problems for Henry VII. *(5 marks)*

How you should answer this question. This is a straight own knowledge question and you should not use the sources in your answer. In other words, you will gain no credit just for saying that they were claimants or that they received foreign aid, since you are told this in Source C. For full marks, you will need to give details about each of these men in terms of how they caused problems for the king. In addition, you must be careful not to move on to a related but slightly different question of your own, such as 'How great a threat did they pose?' or 'Which was the greater danger to the regime?'

3 Study Sources A and C. To what extent does Source A support the views expressed in Source C about the aims of Henry VII's foreign policy? *(7 marks)*

How you should answer this question. This question asks you to compare sources. You must focus on the aims of foreign policy in each source and look for agreement and disagreement in order to answer the 'to what extent' part of the question. Having looked again at the two sources with the question in mind, you should be able to start your answer with a clear and relevant idea followed by quotations from both sources. Then try to find an 'aim' in Source 1 that is not in Source 3, in order to show that the agreement between the sources is not complete.

Style. This is how you might answer this question.

Source A does support Source C in terms of the aims of Henry VII's foreign policy. Source C claims that this policy was dominated by 'dynastic threats' and Source A backs this up with its references to the two rulers helping each other defend their lands 'against any enemy'. Source A also makes it clear that Spain will not help 'rebels from the other country' or let them stay 'in their lands'.

However, Source A also refers to the need to improve trade between the two countries, showing that eliminating dynastic threats was not the sole aim of Henry VII's foreign policy. Source C does not mention improvements in the terms of trade as an aim of Henry VII's foreign policy.

Essay question in the style of OCR

You will need to have read Chapters 3, 4 and 5 before answering this question.

1 Wolsey was Henry VIII's chief minister from 1515 to 1529. He faced problems in:
   i)   foreign affairs
   ii) government
   iii) religion
   iv) obtaining papal approval for the king's 'divorce' from Catherine of Aragon.
   (a) Explain the problems faced by Wolsey in any two of these areas.

   (30 marks)

   (b) Compare the importance of at least three of these problems as causes of Wolsey's fall from power in 1529.   *(60 marks)*

How you should answer question (a). First, you need to pick out the two areas that you know most about in terms of the problems arising from them. You will need to set out a brief plan on each of your chosen areas, highlighting what you see as the main problems. This should ensure that your answer is well organised and reasonably thorough. Deal with each chosen area separately and try to write a similar amount on each. In particular, be aware of the danger of writing too much on one area, such as the divorce problem. If you choose this area, make sure you focus on the problem of obtaining papal approval, not on all the problems associated with the divorce.

Mark schemes will usually say that, to reach the highest mark band, candidates will need to 'explain rather than describe' and will 'set their answers in the context of Wolsey's administration'. Top-band answers will be thorough, wide ranging and well balanced. Remember that what is being evaluated by the examiner is the quality not the quantity of your response. The OCR descriptor for 24–30 marks in an essay of this kind states:

'The response explains key issues in the question convincingly and relevantly. The answer is successful in showing a high level of understanding. The answer focuses on explanation rather than description or narrative. The quality of the historical knowledge supporting the explanation is sound and is communicated in a clear and effective manner. The answer is well organised. The writing shows accuracy in grammar, punctuation and spelling.'

How you should answer question (b). This is a three-way comparison question and so it will need a clear and effective plan to ensure success. The easiest and probably most convincing line to take here is to argue that the failure to obtain papal approval for the divorce was the most important reason for Wolsey's fall and this failure allowed criticism of Wolsey on other fronts to influence the king. Having established one factor as the most important, you might then consider the relative importance of your other two factors in bringing about Wolsey's fall. If you think that one of them is more significant than the other, you should state this at the beginning of your section on the more important factor.

The top-band descriptor for this 60-mark essay is very similar to that for the 30-mark essay, so candidates need to produce an essay that is wide ranging and with a sustained judgement running through it. As always, it is very useful to state your overall answer to the question in the first sentence or two of your essay. This will give the answer a clear focus at the outset, which will then, hopefully, be maintained throughout the essay.

Essay question in the style of Edexcel
You will need to have read Chapters 3, 4 and 5 before answering this question.

EITHER

1 a Describe the domestic policies of Cardinal Wolsey in Church and State in the period 1515–29.   *(15 marks)*
  b How much opposition did these policies arouse?   *(15 marks)*

OR

2 a Show how Wolsey's position and power brought him unpopularity.
   (15 marks)

  b Why, despite this unpopularity, was he able to continue as chief minister to Henry VIII for fourteen years?   *(15 marks)*

How you should answer these questions. Detailed comments on these questions are not necessary as most of the relevant points have been made already. Just ensure that you look carefully at each question to assess what it is asking you to do. Questions 1a and 2a are more descriptive, while Questions 1b and 2b require more explanation and analysis. Always look carefully at the mark allocation. In these cases, the two answers should be about the same length.

Sources exercise in the style of Edexcel

You will need to have read Chapter 6 before doing this exercise.

1 Study Source A and answer the questions.

Source A
The prior is not elected by the convent as he should be: but simply at the order of the lord abbot. The same prior is frequently drunk. Many of the monks devote themselves more to hunting than is proper and they play tables with dice; they play dice instead of attending Matins. In choir they do not sing but gossip. The lord abbot settles the officers of the convent at his own pleasure although the majority of the monks disagree. The sacrist has in his chamber, secretly, a certain maiden and he has also lived incontinently with others. The hosteller has no bread, beer or beds for receiving guests.

From visitation reports by the Bishop of Lincoln
on the abbeys of Romsey and Peterborough, June 1518.

1 Study Source A. What does this source reveal about the shortcomings of the monks in these abbeys? *(5 marks)*

How you should answer this question. This is a straight 'use the source' question. Use brief and relevant quotations to answer the question and, where appropriate, give your explanation of those quotations. Mark scheme descriptors for higher levels of response might well talk about the need for 'developed statements in which references to the source are explained rather than simply cited or identified'. The more shortcomings you find, the better your answer. Note that you are not being asked to talk about the reliability of the source in this question.

2 Why did Henry VIII decide to dissolve the monasteries in the 1530s? *(7 marks)*

How you should answer this question. This is, essentially, an own knowledge or recall of knowledge question, although the source also acts as stimulus in giving you the official reason for the dissolution: namely, the corruption of the monasteries. For a top-level response you need to give a range of reasons, official and unofficial, and make explicit comments about the relative importance, in your view, of these causes.

3 What can be said for, and against, the view that the dissolution of the monasteries was 'merely an act of plunder'? *(18 marks)*

How you should answer this question. This is a typical wide-ranging question requiring own knowledge and a sustained line of argument in both parts of the answer. You will need to plan out your main ideas in favour of the statement (probably the longer part of the answer), but also address the other side of the question, against the statement, even if you think it misguided. For example, you might look at why reformers did not believe in the need for the monastic way of life, the many tales of corruption (as in Source A) and the motivation of those who bought monastic lands and goods.

Mark scheme descriptors for the highest level of response will talk about the need to provide 'sustained argument which examines the idea of plunder in an authoritative and detailed way and which covers most aspects of the question, argues both ways and covers a range of appropriate areas. The candidate will need to show an ability to analyse historical phenomena of some complexity and to convey that analysis in logical and well-structured ways.' Needless to say, such answers will probably be produced only if you plan your answer carefully before you start.

A2 SECTION: ENGLISH REFORMATIONS 1533–58

INTRODUCTION

These sections of the book focus on reactions to the Henrician Reformation of the 1530s and explain how and why there were further changes in English religious practice in the 1540s and 1550s. They go on to consider whether or not there was a mid-Tudor crisis.

Historical interpretations

The English Reformation, in terms of its causes, impact and popularity, has been the subject of a great deal of debate amongst historians, particularly over the last 40 years. Geoffrey Elton in *The Tudor Revolution in Government* (1953) and *England under the Tudors* (1955) placed the English Reformation firmly in the realm of high politics. He believed that the pre-Reformation Church was corrupt and unpopular in the 1520s and that these defects were personified by Cardinal Wolsey. Wolsey's failure to achieve the Divorce from Catherine of Aragon gave the reformers led by Cromwell and Cranmer their opportunity to bring in Protestant reforms which set the English Reformation in motion. At the same time Elton was concerned to highlight the reforms in government brought about by Thomas Cromwell in the 1530s. For Elton this decade saw a 'revolution in government' stimulated by the break with Rome and the establishment of the Royal Supremacy. England became a more centralised and unified realm. Government became more bureaucratic and the authority of the king and parliament was enhanced. The success of Protestantism was furthered in Edward's reign and the restoration of Catholicism under Mary was seen as a backward and sterile move which was bound to fail. Overall Elton established the Reformation as an 'Act of State'.

A. G. Dickens in *The English Reformation* (1964) was less concerned with high politics and government than Elton. His work on Protestantism and Lollardy in Yorkshire led him to focus on the spread of Protestant ideas amongst more ordinary men and women. For him the English Reformation occurred not because Henry VIII had a major disagreement with the Pope but because English intellectuals were taking on continental reforming ideas and demanding changes to the Church. Once again the corruption of the pre-Reformation Church was stressed and examples of anti-clericalism were highlighted. While acknowledging that

Henry VIII did play a significant part in the changes in religion, Dickens saw the Reformation as a popular movement rather than an 'Act of State'.

Revisionism

Against this background can be set the views of the so-called revisionist historians led by J. J. Scarisbrick and Christopher Haigh. Scarisbrick in his biography of Henry VIII (1968) stressed the importance of the Divorce Crisis and the part played by the king in bringing about change. In 1984 he produced *The Reformation and the English People* which began to look more sympathetically at the resistance to the religious changes under Henry VIII and Edward VI. Elton and Dickens had presented the English Reformation as a very powerful and almost 'inevitable' set of changes which swept the land; now Scarisbrick pointed out that the changes had not been universally welcomed.

Christopher Haigh has written more than anyone else in the revisionist vein. In *The English Reformation Revised* (1987) he did much to attack the idea that there was a powerful and growing feeling of anti-clericalism against the English Church in the decades before the Reformation. In *English Reformations* (1993) he sought to demonstrate that the Reformation was far from being the powerful and well directed force portrayed by Dickens and Elton. He examined a great deal of evidence from English shires which seemed to show that the progress of Protestantism at the local level was patchy and varied, with many people clinging to the old ways. At the same time he argued that there were serious changes in the government's religious policy during the 1530s and 40s. After toying with Protestant ideas in the 1530s, Henry VIII re-adopted Catholic theology in the 1540s. The Protectors under Edward VI were motivated by political considerations and made little headway in a land which was still fundamentally Catholic. This in turn meant that Mary's reign could be seen as a triumph. David Loades in his *The Reign of Mary Tudor* (1979) did much to promulgate a more favourable view of the Marian regime which was backed up by Robert Tittler in his *The Reign of Mary I* (1983).

Other revisionists such as Robert Whiting in *The Blind Devotion of the People* (1989) have used local studies – in his case in Devon and Cornwall – to show that Protestant ideas were more acceptable in some areas than in others and that such ideas were often modified by local experience and custom.

Opposition to the Henrician Reformation

If it is the case that the Henrician Reformation was not widely popular and reflected only the views of the king and a small group of influential reformers, we need to explore the opposition to the changes and explain why such opposition failed, in the short term, to reverse the Reformation.

In the 1530s there was serious disquiet about the changes introduced and one large-scale rebellion, the Pilgrimage of Grace in 1536. This rebellion was the most spectacular of the Tudor period and was clearly opposed to the king's reforming policies. Henry VIII and Cromwell dealt ruthlessly with all opposition, both real and suspected. The power of the Crown was too great and the power of the nobility too diminished for there to be a successful uprising against the Reformation.

Nonetheless, in the 1540s, the king's policies showed a clear change in direction. Henry VIII now introduced further changes to the Church which indicated that, although he had broken with the Pope, he did not wish the English Church to adopt Protestant ideas or doctrines. The reforming minister Thomas Cromwell was executed for being too Protestant and new religious articles were introduced that were entirely Catholic in nature. By the time of the king's death in 1547, the Church of England might be described as essentially 'Catholic without the Pope'.

One of the reasons for these changes was fear of foreign invasion. In the late 1530s, the king was concerned that the rulers of Spain and France might invade England. This threat was later defused when Henry VIII returned to his traditional stance of friendship with the Emperor, Charles V, and hostility towards Francis I of France.

The last years of the king's reign also saw renewed faction fighting at court. This was intensified by the king's successive marriages to Anne of Cleves, Catherine Howard and Catherine Parr. By and large the conservative faction, whose views mirrored those of the king, prevailed. However, just before Henry's death in 1547, the conservative faction fell out of favour. This allowed the reformers, led by Edward Seymour, to take charge in the next reign.

Edward then Mary 1547–58

With Henry VIII's death the Church was subject, rather unexpectedly, to further changes that pushed it in a more Protestant direction. The new king, Edward VI, favoured the reformers and his reign saw the sweeping away of Henry VIII's religious laws. Two English Prayer Books were introduced and the chantries and many religious guilds were dissolved. No sooner had this happened than Edward died and was succeeded by his half-sister Princess Mary, who was a staunch Catholic. She totally reversed the Protestant Reformation introduced by Edward. Catholic ceremonies were brought back, Cardinal Pole became Archbishop of Canterbury, England was allied to the greatest Catholic power in Europe, Spain, and the papal headship of the Church was restored.

Both sets of changes in this period showed up the power of the monarchy to influence religious change. Edward VI and his two 'Protectors',

Somerset and Northumberland, were all Protestants. Mary, the daughter of Catherine of Aragon, was a Catholic. Elizabeth, who succeeded Mary, was the daughter of Anne Boleyn and the child of the Henrician Reformation. She would ensure that, in the longer term, the Church of England would be Protestant and Mary's Catholic triumph short-lived.

Henry VII had restored the power of the monarchy after the Wars of the Roses and started the process of curbing the power of the nobility. Henry VIII had further elevated Crown power by taking control of the Church and exploiting its spiritual and financial resources. Edward and Mary showed that the power of the monarchy was sufficiently great to survive the rule of a child and the rule of a woman. In this sense, there was no mid-Tudor crisis during the reigns of Edward and Mary. The extraordinary and contradictory changes and serious problems of the period demonstrate in fact the enduring and enhanced power of the Crown since the reign of Henry VII and the concomitant acquiesence and passivity of the English aristocracy.

As for the people of England, it is clear that they did not seriously influence the religious change of the period. Rather, they followed the lead given to them by their political masters, with varying degrees of enthusiasm. Popular rebellions were serious but regional affairs did little to influence government policy.

SECTION 1

1533–8: How serious was the opposition to the reforms of the Church?

OVERVIEW OF FACTION AND OPPOSITION

The changes triggered by the king's annulment of his marriage to Catherine of Aragon, by his marriage to Anne Boleyn and by the establishment of his Supremacy all had profound consequences in the 1530s. Most importantly, these changes led to opposition of various types. Some appeared as mass opposition, like the Pilgrimage of Grace in 1536, some as the opposition of individuals like Bishop John Fisher and Sir Thomas More. Elsewhere, there was real conspiracy, as in the strange episode of the Holy Maid of Kent, and imaginary conspiracy, as in the so-called Exeter Conspiracy of 1538. In addition, there was some trouble from native Protestants who thought Henry VIII unduly slow-moving and conservative, and a lot of trouble from foreign powers like the Emperor and the Pope who disliked schism and heresy. These powers threatened to lead a Catholic crusade, which would invade England in the name of Princess Mary and depose her father.

Opposition, real and imagined, made the government more watchful and vigilant as well as keen to make people outwardly and openly conform to the new changes. Central government was strengthened at the expense of local government, as it tried to enforce the important changes in Church and State. At the centre, the changes caused the emergence of faction fighting on a scale, and with a deadly intensity, rarely seen before or after. This faction fighting was instigated mainly by Thomas Cromwell and his circle of associates, but in the end it destroyed its creator. In 1540, Thomas Cromwell, recently ennobled as the Earl of Essex, was arrested in the Council Chamber, disgraced and beheaded.

Historical interpretations

The extent and importance of opposition to the religious changes in the 1530s has been of crucial importance in the debate amongst historians about the reasons for and impact of the Reformation. More traditional historians like Dickens and Elton saw Catholic opposition to the changes as limited and essentially doomed. Revisionists such as Christopher Haigh, J. J. Scarisbrick and Eamon Duffy emphasise the strength and endurance of opposition to the Reformation. They claim that the failure of opposition shows more about the growing power of the Crown, rather than the popularity of religious change.

OPEN OPPOSITION TO SUPREMACY AND MARRIAGE

The Holy Maid of Kent and her circle 1527–34

One of the earliest opposition groups was that surrounding the so-called Holy Maid of Kent – **Elizabeth Barton**. Employed as a plain serving girl, she had begun to have religious visions and claimed that God had cured her of an unpleasant disease. She was duly fêted as a visionary, received a number of important and credulous visitors and was sent off to a local nunnery – nothing terribly dangerous or unusual so far. However, in 1527, as the king went public with his matrimonial doubts, she emerged from her nunnery, this time uttering terrifying prophesies about what would happen to king and country if Henry proceeded in his attempt to annul his marriage. In particular, she denounced the hapless Anne Boleyn and claimed that the king would die quite quickly if he married her.

Wolsey and Warham were impressed, John Fisher was distinctly encouraged and the king was denounced to his face. Elizabeth's associates, particularly Edward Bocking, a Canterbury monk who became her spiritual and, it seems, political adviser, began to gather a circle of friends and admirers and to draw in other men and women known to be worried about what the Henry was doing. Fisher and More were both drawn into the affair. More typically displayed greater caution than Fisher. Also involved were a number of monks and the Imperial ambassador, Eustace Chapuys. In 1533, Bocking attempted to publish copies of *The Nun's Book*, a collection of the Nun's prophecies, in order to foment further opposition and alarm. The charges drawn up against Bocking by Cromwell, in 1534, tell their own tale.

Source 1

Edward Bocking frequently railed against the king's marriage before the false nun. She, to please him, pretended to have a revelation from God that the king was no longer accepted as king by God because of his marriage. This is proved by the great book written by Doctor Bocking.

Adapted from the official charges against Edward Bocking, 1534.

Cromwell was alerted to the danger and, as usual, he exaggerated the size of the problem. As the affair was based in Kent, the Nun's backers hoped to attract support from across the Channel. Cromwell was right to realise that an attempt to publish propaganda tracts was rather more serious, as opposition goes, than a few amateur plotters with limited influence.

Arrest and execution 1534. Faced with this, Cromwell had the Nun and her friends arrested and staged a grand ceremony where Barton and her

Elizabeth Barton (1506–34). In 1525 she fell ill, perhaps with epilepsy, and began to fall into trances where she would cry out against sin and vice. By the next year she was widely recognised as a Holy Maid. After her visions condemned the king's marriage to Anne Boleyn, she was found guilty of treason and hanged at Tyburn.

Eustace Chapuys
was the Imperial
ambassador in
England, based in
London and
representing the
Emperor Charles V.
He was shocked by
the king's
annulment and
attack on the
Church and was
determined to
encourage
opposition. He
sent back rather
exaggerated reports
of the scale of the
Pilgrimage of
Grace and
encouraged the
Emperor and the
Pope to invade
England on the
basis of the king's
widespread
unpopularity.

supporters would confess their crimes before a gathering of the leaders of the political nation. **Chapuys** reports that the crowd were at first reluctant to condemn her and that the Nun was steadfast in adversity, but he may well have been trying to impress Charles V by exaggerating the scale of the opposition to Henry's reforms.

Elizabeth Barton and her close adherents were hanged at Tyburn in April 1534. In a way it is remarkable that the she and her friends had been able to survive for seven years while making damaging attacks on the State, the nation and the king's policies. It is a testament to the more deadly nature of politics in the early 1530s that she was dispatched when she was. After 1533, those who attacked the king's marriage with Anne Boleyn were guilty of treason. Such people might refuse to recognise Anne Boleyn's children as heirs and, even worse, might support Princess Mary in an effort to topple her father. The king and Cromwell decided that such opposition should be eliminated.

The opposition of Bishop Fisher

The same point can be made in connection with John Fisher. He had vocally and publicly opposed the king's attempts to annul the Aragon marriage right from the start. Displaying tremendous courage and bravery, while many around him dithered in confusion, he delivered sermons and wrote books denouncing the king's aims. For eight years he was unwavering in his approach. In 1533 he had even written secretly to the Emperor, urging him to use force against the king. He was later arrested and convicted of lesser treason over the Nun of Kent affair.

Arrest and execution 1535. In April 1534, however, as the Nun and her close adherents suffered at Tyburn, Fisher refused to take the oath to the Act of Succession. He was sent to the Tower, but still the king held back. Perhaps he retained some respect for the man who had preached the oration at his father's funeral in 1509, or perhaps he feared the consequences of executing a man of international reputation. It may be that the Pope – by now Paul III – hastened Fisher's execution by awarding him a cardinal's hat in 1535. The linking of Fisher's opposition with the real danger of invasion from abroad, in the name of Pope and Emperor, may have been the last straw for Henry. Fisher was beheaded as a traitor in 1535. His head was placed on London Bridge and later thrown in the river.

Fisher's death ensured that attempts to reach a settlement with Rome would be fruitless. Before his death, Paul III had been conciliatory towards Henry, hoping to do a deal to recover English allegiance if he withheld the king's excommunication. Like many others, the Pope thought of the breach with Rome as a temporary political expedient,

which Henry might abandon when circumstances changed. Fisher's death helped to ensure that no such compromise would occur. The breach with Rome would not be healed until Catherine of Aragon's daughter was crowned queen in 1553.

The opposition of Sir Thomas More

Another opponent of the changes, always associated with Fisher, was Sir Thomas More, Chancellor of England. The king had broken his word to More about keeping him out of the Divorce and in 1532 More had resigned his office over the Submission of the Clergy. Having failed to halt or reverse royal policy, More's opposition was passive. Like Fisher he refused to take the oath to the Act of Succession but, unlike Fisher, he refused to say why he would not take it.

Arrest and execution. According to the law, even according to the new Treason Act of 1534 (which came into force in February 1535), More could not be found guilty of treason since he had never 'maliciously' denounced the king's title as Supreme Head of the Church of England. The law as it stood could only imprison him indefinitely for refusing to take the oath. More lingered in prison for over a year, then, on 1 July 1535, he was brought to trial.

As More had been very careful not to deny the king's title of Supreme Head, Cromwell had to proceed by means of **perjured evidence**. Richard Rich, apparently created Attorney General for Wales for his troubles, claimed that he had heard More deny the king's Supremacy in the Tower just a few weeks before, when he and two others had come to take away More's books. It is to their credit that Southwell and Palmer, the two men with Rich, claimed that they had been so busy with the books that they had failed to hear or take note of what was said by More and Rich. Their silence and Rich's reward confirm that the trial was rigged and there is evidence that, just to be on the safe side, the jury was rigged as well. One juror, a London draper called John Russell, was an informer who had unsuccessfully accused More of corruption in a Chancery case. This **rigged trial** was to foreshadow others and indicates how the government was becoming increasingly paranoid and increasingly ruthless.

More's reputation. More had not denied the king's title or offered any overt opposition to the regime. When interrogated by Cromwell in the Tower, he said, 'I am the king's true faithful subject and pray for his Highness and all the realm. I do none harm, I say none harm, I think none harm, but wish everybody good. And if this be not enough to keep a man alive, in good faith, I long not to live.' His wish was to be granted soon afterwards. At his execution he claimed that he died 'the king's good servant, but God's first'. More's death has assured him of a posthumous

KEY CONCEPTS

Perjured evidence is where someone lies under oath in court, usually to get an innocent person condemned for a crime they did not commit.

A **rigged trial** is a trial in court where the outcome has been decided before the case starts. In this case, it would have been counterproductive for Cromwell if More had been found innocent. Disregard for justice and the law was a hallmark of Cromwell's methods in government.

reputation as a saintly and brave man who stood up against changing times and embraced death rather than deny his principles. Two film versions of Robert Bolt's play *A Man for All Seasons* have further enhanced More's reputation as a courageous statesman.

It is perhaps easy to exaggerate More's saintliness and to forget that, behind the witty and urbane humanist, there was a savage and narrow-minded critic of heresy and heretics. In addition, there is something more commanding in Fisher's open and outspoken opposition than in More's **passive resistance**. Nonetheless, More remains one of the notable characters of the period and the manner of his death meant that few others would risk open opposition to the king.

The opposition of the Carthusian monks

Among those few others who did risk the king's anger were a group of **Carthusian monks**, including the prior, from the London Charter house, together with the priors of the Charter houses at Axholme in Lincolnshire and Beauvale in Nottinghamshire. They too would suffer at the hands of Cromwell's brutalised regime. Unlike More, the three priors had denied the Royal Supremacy over the Church, saying that no layman – not even the king – could be head of the Church.

Execution of the priors. The three priors, Houghton, Lawrence and Webster, together with Richard Reynolds and John Hale were executed at Tyburn. Having refused a last-minute offer of pardon if they would change their minds, they were subject to the full horrors of the law. Each was hanged, cut down while still alive and disembowelled. To add to the agony, they were butchered in turn, so that they had to watch the sufferings of their fellows.

A crowd of thousands gathered to watch the cruelty and it is unlikely that the government won much popular approval for its actions. On the other hand, as Voltaire would remark later about similar barbarity from an English government, such violence against harmless men would 'encourage the others'. If peaceable monks were treated this way, it would encourage others to avoid any appearance of opposition to the regime.

More monks executed. However, even with their prior executed, the remaining Carthusian monks in the London Charter house still refused to submit to the royal will. In May 1535, three more monks, Middlemore, Exmere and Newdigate, were locked up in the Tower. There they were tied to posts with iron collars around their necks and 'great fetters' riveted to their legs. They were left for seventeen days, unable to sit and 'never loosed for any natural necessity'. A few days later they were executed at Tyburn. Some monks did submit in the end, but ten more were starved

KEY CONCEPT

Passive resistance. At a time when outright or violent opposition to the government was seen as a sin, many resorted to non-violent protest – a refusal to conform to the government's wishes.

KEY PEOPLE

Carthusian monks. An order of monks noted for their spiritual and solitary lives.

to death, tied to posts in Newgate prison. This was barbarity and cruelty rarely seen before in English history. Henry VIII's reign, which had started with such high hopes of glory and reform, had become home to institutionalised violence and depravity.

The executions of More, Fisher and the Carthusians marked a turning point in government policy towards real or imagined opposition. The regime had demonstrated that even passive or cloistered opposition would not be tolerated. The Henrician regime demanded clear affirmations of loyalty and approval, especially as it soon detected only grudging acceptance of the changes from most of the political nation. Most disliked the changes and were worried for the future; many acquiesced in the sure knowledge that the changes would soon be reversed. In a more credulous age than our own, some believed that God would punish the king and his people for their sins.

Opposition from abroad

One constant worry for Henry VIII was that opposition at home might be fanned and encouraged by opposition from abroad. The Holy Maid of Kent affair and Fisher's opposition had involved appeals to the Emperor, Catherine of Aragon's nephew. There was hope, even in 1535, that France and the Holy Roman Empire, both Catholic powers, might come together, under the auspices of the Pope, to launch a grand Catholic crusade against England.

The king's treatment of Catherine of Aragon. Catherine of Aragon had been at pains not to encourage such plans of invasion from abroad. Though she would not enter a nunnery in order to help the king, she refused consistently to encourage plots against her husband. In 1533 she wrote to the Pope, asking him not to promulgate the excommunication of her husband. 'I do not ask his Holiness to declare war. I would rather die than provoke a war.'

Nonetheless, after his marriage to Anne Boleyn, Henry continued to see his first wife as a threat. He demanded that she acknowledge publicly that she was Princess Dowager (i.e. Prince Arthur's widow) not queen and that her daughter Mary, as offspring of an illicit union, was illegitimate. Catherine naturally refused to do as Henry wished, and she and Mary paid a high price. Henry threatened that Catherine would follow the example of More and Fisher. For the last five years of her life, he prevented her from seeing Mary. It is hard to understand such callous treatment unless we see that Catherine and Mary now represented a real, if unwitting, threat to the regime. Frightened men like Henry VIII easily become cruel and by 1535 there were more reasons for Henry to feel worried.

THE RISE OF FACTION

KEY TERM

Aragonese faction or circle. The name given to those who actively supported Catherine in her struggle with the king and hoped to see a reversal of Henry's reforming policies. After Catherine's death, some of these men hoped to use Princess Mary to overthrow their enemies at court.

KEY PERSON

Princess Mary (1516–58) was the only surviving child of Henry and Catherine of Aragon. She was well educated and Catherine believed that she should be the king's heir. She was in trouble during the Protestant regime of her brother, Edward VI, but became queen in 1553 and brought back Catholicism.

The death of Catherine of Aragon and its consequences

The Royal Supremacy and Henry's marriage to Anne Boleyn had given rise to serious opposition from a wide variety of individuals. It also gave rise to renewed faction fighting at court, which had an intensity and persistence rarely seen before. By the end of 1535, Anne Boleyn had not yet produced a son and there were already rumours that the marriage would not last. At court, therefore, the **Aragonese faction** began to have real hopes that the second marriage would fail and that Catherine might yet be restored.

So it was with considerable relief that Henry heard, in January 1536, that Catherine had died at Kimbolton Castle. The king had sent her there as it had a reputation for bad air and disease. Now that she was dead, he could not hide his joy. He wore yellow for mourning and celebrated her demise with a Mass, a banquet, dancing and jousting. Her death was also good news for Henry because it might pave the way for a new understanding with the Emperor. With his aunt safely dead, surely Charles might return to the safe and sensible foreign policy of an English alliance against France. After all, Henry had never enjoyed pretending to like the French – they were, in his eyes, England's natural enemy. Now the king could again realise his military ambitions against France, and England would be saved from the prospect of invasion. Although Charles seemed accommodating, however, Catherine's death in fact unleashed a greater danger.

The threat from Princess Mary. Mary, aged twenty, was now head of the Aragonese faction. After years of terrible hostility from her father towards her mother, deprived of access to both of them and officially pronounced illegitimate, it was no wonder that she grew embittered and looked around for revenge. The Imperial ambassador, Chapuys, was full of schemes which, without Catherine's restraining influence, might now be carried to fruition. Most of the plans revolved around Mary being spirited out of the country, marrying a Habsburg prince, invading England in the name of the Catholic Church and overthrowing her tyrannical, schismatic and unpopular father. As a result of these schemes, together with increasing signs of internal unrest, which would break out into popular revolt in 1536, the regime grew ever more watchful and suspicious.

The king's doubts about the Boleyn marriage

At the same time, Cromwell had to deal with a new and unexpected problem. Having just witnessed the death of the king's first wife, Cromwell was soon set the task of getting rid of the second. Just when Anne seemed more secure, with the death of her rival, she in fact became more vulnerable. As long as Catherine lived, Henry was bound to support his second wife and her associates, who had, after all, delivered the annulment that he had so desperately wanted. Now that Catherine was dead, this was no longer the case.

The key to the fall of Anne Boleyn was her failure to produce a son. After all the years of negotiation, bluff and bluster to get rid of Catherine, Henry had married another woman who had then failed to produce the longed-for male heir. If her first child, born in September 1533, had been a boy, she would have been invincible, her position safe and secure. With a son on her knee the Tudor dynasty would be secure and God's blessing on the king (and queen) made clear. Sadly, the first child was a girl, named **Elizabeth** after Henry's mother. The birth of a daughter was a serious blow. Henry had convinced himself that it would be a son – a daughter might be a sign of divine displeasure.

The birth of Elizabeth did not end the marriage, but as luck would have it, no son was then forthcoming. It is quite likely, in biological terms, that this had more to do with Henry than with Anne, but the king did not see it that way. Another pregnancy probably ended in a stillbirth in June 1534. Anne was then delivered of a fourteen-week foetus, probably a boy, on the day that Catherine of Aragon was buried in January 1536. This event must seriously have shaken Henry's confidence in his second marriage. The timing of the event might be serious evidence of God's anger. Deep down the king might well have wondered if God thought the marriage illegal because of his affair with Anne's older sister Mary. The **Book of Leviticus**, the touchstone of his case against Catherine, had come back to haunt him.

The fall of Anne Boleyn 1536

Henry's doubts, combined with Anne's fiery temper and unpredictable behaviour, eroded his faith in his wife. Furthermore, Anne was a supporter of reform and the king did not think that women should dabble in theology. At the same time, he had found a new lady-love at court. He had begun flirting with **Jane Seymour** as early as 1534. Her gentle nature and quiet demeanour attracted the king as an antidote to his wife's temper. She reminded him of Catherine of Aragon, but without the stubborn streak.

In April 1536, Henry let it be known that he wished to have the Boleyn marriage annulled. Astonishingly, after less than three years, the marriage that had taken so long to effect and that had divided and endangered the realm, was now to be annulled in its turn. This wife, however, was not a Spanish princess; her relatives were not Habsburg Emperors but the king's servants. She had won few friends on her way to power and had many enemies who would queue up to get rid of her. The heightened

KEY PERSON

Princess Elizabeth (1533–1603) became queen in 1558 when she succeeded her half-sister Mary. Despite Henry's misgivings about being succeeded by a female, women ruled England perfectly well for half a century.

KEY CONCEPT

The **Book of Leviticus**, remember, said that a man must not marry his brother's wife. Sexual relations with your wife's sister might be just as bad!

KEY PEOPLE

Jane Seymour
(1509–37) was the eldest daughter of eight children born to Sir John Seymour of Wolf Hall in Wiltshire. She was one of the ladies-in-waiting to both Catherine of Aragon and Anne Boleyn. She married Henry eleven days after the execution of Anne, but died in 1537 soon after giving birth to the future Edward VI.

Edward Seymour
(1506?–52) was Jane Seymour's brother, whose power and influence at court rose with the king's marriage to his sister. In 1553 he made himself Protector for his nephew, Prince Edward.

Richard of Gloucester was the younger brother of Edward IV. He used a claim of illegitimacy to overthrow his nephews Edward V and Richard Duke of York. He was crowned as Richard III, but was killed at Bosworth just two years later.

tension and cruelty at court would mean that her family and friends would be the victims of the bloodiest purge yet seen at the Tudor court – worse than anything seen, away from the battlefield, even during the Wars of the Roses. The author of this purge was Thomas Cromwell.

Another annulment? The Seymour group, led by Jane's brother **Edward**, together with the remnants of the Aragonese group, hoped to get rid of Anne by means of a quiet annulment, followed by a quiet retirement to the country. They placed their hopes on a pre-contract of marriage between Anne and the Earl of Northumberland's son, which would invalidate her marriage to the king. Such an argument was used, admittedly rather unconvincingly, by **Richard of Gloucester** in 1483 to invalidate his nephews' claim to the throne. In the circumstances of 1536, it might well have worked. After all, Henry's claim to the throne was not in doubt and, unlike her predecessor, Anne would probably go quietly. Her daughter would be made illegitimate, but unlike Princess Mary, she would not be a political threat to the regime or the next wife. Surely, she could be found a safe husband who would keep her out of trouble.

Anne Boleyn is accused. Unfortunately for Anne, Cromwell had other ideas. The low-born Secretary realised that he and other reformers were vulnerable to an attack launched at Anne, since he was so closely associated with her. In fact, he probably miscalculated as the Seymour and Aragonese groups were fairly easy-going. Nonetheless, Cromwell decided that the safest solution to the king's new marital problem was the execution of the queen, on the grounds of adultery. Only Cromwell possessed the cynical determination to destroy his opponents and to transform the Boleyn crisis into a political coup of the first order. The other players in the drama went along with the accusations against Anne with varying degrees of distaste or disbelief, but it was Cromwell who drove them on. In April 1536, he presented bold and false accusations against Anne to the king. She was accused of multiple adultery and, for good measure, incest with her brother George Boleyn. The scale and number of the charges astonished bewildered onlookers like Cranmer, as Source 2 shows.

Source 2

If the reports of the queen be true, they are more to her dishonour not yours. I am clean amazed for I never had better opinion of any woman, but I think your Highness would not have gone so far if she had not been guilty. I wish and pray that she may declare herself innocent. Yet, if she be found guilty, I consider him not a faithful subject who would not wish her to be punished without mercy.

Adapted from a letter written by Cranmer in 1536.

The Archbishop was a simple soul, of course. Anne Boleyn did declare her innocence loud and clear at her trial, but it did her no good. The bravado of Cromwell's charges astonished contemporaries like something out of Stalin's Russia. Many thought that the charges must be true because they were so awful. Adultery and incest, however, would not be enough on their own to lead Anne to the block. Legally, adultery was not in fact treason and so was not a capital crime. So Cromwell had to claim that Anne and her lovers had conspired to kill the king. One of the accusations against Anne was that she had told her lovers that she would marry one of them as soon as the king was dead.

Trial and execution. Henry Norris, William Brereton, Francis Weston, the hapless Mark Smeaton, a musician, as well as Anne and her brother were tried before Cromwell and Norfolk, Anne's uncle, in what was clearly a rigged trial. After the trial of Thomas More, Cromwell was an old hand at such affairs. All except Smeaton, who was tortured, denied the incredible charges. It was to no avail. Cromwell seemed to revel in the task, making use of rumour, gossip and the hot-house atmosphere among the queen's circle.

Anne may well have been flirtatious; probably her conversation was indiscreet and laden with the innuendo of courtly love. After all, she was young and lively, with a middle-aged and bad-tempered husband. But she was surely innocent of such terrible crimes. The charges were a fiction; she and her friends were the victims of judicial murder. On 19 May, Anne was beheaded by a headsman brought over specially from **Calais**, armed with a sword rather than an axe. On the scaffold, Anne claimed rather touchingly that there never was 'a gentler or more merciful prince' than her husband.

Annulment. Two days before Anne Boleyn died, Cranmer, who had annulled the king's first marriage, obligingly annulled the second. Astonishingly, he claimed that Henry's adultery with Anne's sister rendered the marriage invalid from the start. Leviticus had won the day once again. And once again it was Cranmer who cleared the way for a new marriage.

Impact of the Boleyn purge

The purge of the Boleyn faction – Anne, her brother and three gentlemen of the Privy Chamber – was presented by Cromwell as a justifiable attack on opponents of the king. Unlike Fisher and More and the Holy Maid of Kent, this opposition came from within the court, indeed from within the king's bedchamber, and was all the more dangerous for that. Whether Henry really believed the charges is very

KEY PLACE

Calais, the French port just across the Channel from Dover, was England's last outpost on the Continent and last remnant of England's conquest of France during the Hundred Years War. It had a garrison of English troops and was therefore expensive to maintain.

hard to say. The day after he had appointed a commission to inquire into Anne's supposed crimes, Henry was writing to his ambassador in Rome that he still hoped for male heirs, 'by our most dear and most entirely beloved wife, the queen'. Cromwell created the coup and Henry obligingly played the part of the wronged husband. When the storm broke he would claim that Anne had beguiled him into marriage by means of witchcraft. Clearly, the king had now taken a big step away from reality, one that would continue to produce and encourage faction fighting at court.

Marriage to Jane Seymour and the birth of Prince Edward

Anne's death left the way clear for a marriage to Jane Seymour. With indecent haste, Henry announced his betrothal to Jane on the day of Anne's death. Speed, however, was necessary as Henry still had no son. Nine years and two wives after his first doubts about the succession problem, he was no nearer a solution. True, he had gained another daughter, but in the wake of her mother's execution, Elizabeth joined Mary in the ranks of royal bastards. At the same time, Henry Fitzroy, Henry's illegitimate son, was clearly ailing and would die within a month of Anne's execution.

However, God's anger seemed to have subsided, as Jane Seymour produced the son Henry so fervently desired. In September 1537, Prince Edward was born. The irony was that this time it was the mother and not the son who died. Jane probably died of gangrene within a few days of the birth. Sadly for Henry, God was still punishing him. Although the son had been granted, the queen, whom he loved dearly, was taken from him.

POPULAR OPPOSITION TO THE HENRICIAN REFORMATION – THE PILGRIMAGE OF GRACE 1536

Introduction

In the autumn of 1536, Henry VIII was faced with possibly the greatest and best organised popular protest yet seen on English soil. The risings began in Louth, in Lincolnshire, but soon sprang up all over the north of England. The geographical extent of the uprising was impressive, as were the numbers involved – some 30,000 or so armed men eventually assembled on the banks of the River Don near Doncaster. Equally worrying was the organised nature of the risings. This was not a chaotic rabble, but a mass movement under the leadership of a one-eyed lawyer, **Robert Aske**.

KEY PERSON

Robert Aske (d.1537) was born around the beginning of the century. He was a lawyer, based in London, who had been in the service of the Earl of Northumberland. He led the Pilgrimage of Grace and complained about the destruction of the abbeys and about the 'new men' around the king. Despite receiving a pardon from the king, he was hanged in 1537.

The rebels took an **oath** to stick together in their Pilgrimage and to conduct themselves peacefully during the rebellion. Only one man was killed before the rebels dispersed peacefully. The rebels issued **a series of Articles** outlining their complaints and demands. Most disturbing for the Cromwellian regime in London was the ease with which, in some three weeks, the rebels took control of the north – none of the local ruling class wished or dared to oppose them. York, the key to the north, was taken over without a shot being fired and, as the rebels turned south, **Lord Darcy**, sympathetic to the rebels, surrendered Pontefract Castle. The rebels had effortlessly cowed or won over most of the gentry and aristocracy, and had taken over a substantial part of the kingdom.

The king's weakness

The strength of the rebels was only too apparent, but what was worse was that Henry, like earlier monarchs, was ill-armed to resist such an all-embracing uprising. He had no standing army, but instead had to rely on the loyalty of peers like Norfolk and Suffolk raising what troops they could from outside the region. In addition, as the documents below show, the king's commanders found it hard to raise troops, especially as the king was so reluctant to spend money.

Source 3

The £10,000 sent to us will not dispatch the army here and will pay those who go northwards only until Sunday next. We cannot advance further or disorder will ensue. My Lord Steward here needs £20,000. All complain they cannot live on 8 pence a day.

From a letter written by the Duke of Norfolk
in October 1536.

Source 4

And whereas you, Sir Anthony Browne, were directed to repair to Suffolk with 2,000 men and you have in readiness about 560, you shall march forward with those you have. As to the wages of 8 pence a day, you must have special regard for your charges, which will grow excessive unless you take care not to exceed our old rate of wages.

Henry VIII answers the Duke, October 1536.

Adapted from a letter written by Henry VIII
in October 1536.

In the end, the government raised only 8000 assorted soldiers to challenge the 30,000 rebel troops on the other side of the River Don. Not surprisingly, the Duke of Norfolk reported to the king that a battle against the rebels was not an option. Further anxiety was roused in

KEY TERMS

The **oath** was the so-called Oath of Honourable Men, devised by Aske in York, at the Council of the pilgrim captains in October 1536. All the pilgrims took the oath.

A series of Articles. These were the York Articles and the later Pontefract Articles drawn up by the leaders of the rebellion in the two towns.

KEY PERSON

Thomas, Lord Darcy (1467–1537) was an important rebel leader. He owned lands in Yorkshire and Lincolnshire. In 1513 he went with the English invasion force to France. He played a part in the fall of Wolsey but became disillusioned with the new men and the new policies and plotted with Lord Hussey and Chapuys for an invasion of England by the Emperor. He was beheaded in 1537 for his part in the Pilgrimage.

The movement of rebels in the Pilgrimage of Grace.

Map legend:

+   Monasteries involved in the Pilgrimage
••••••••▶   Route of Lincolnshire rebels
———▶   Main routes of Yorkshire rebels
– – –▶   Route of Kirkby Stephen and Cumberland rebels
·····▶   Route of Westmorland rebels

London as the government had to face the idea that the rebellion might be co-ordinated with an Imperial/Papal invasion of England from the Continent. Chapuys, the Imperial ambassador, could hardly conceal his glee when he heard of the rising. He sent a stream of letters to his master exaggerating the scale of the affair and claiming that an invasion of

England, presumably from the Emperor's territories in the Low Countries, would easily overthrow the schismatic Henry, avenge Catherine of Aragon by putting Princess Mary on the throne and bring England back to papal obedience. Yet more pressure was put on the nervous regime when **Cardinal Reginald Pole**, a descendant of the Yorkist kings, appeared in the Calais area. This was not to be his hour, but he would bring England back to full papal obedience nineteen years later.

Rebel weaknesses

Despite the government's obvious weaknesses, the position was far from hopeless. Although many gentry and peers were involved in the rising, none of the titled nobility threw in their lot wholeheartedly with the rebels. The man most likely to make a success of the rising was Henry Percy, sixth Earl of Northumberland. However, he encouraged the rebellion only indirectly. Four of the rebel captains, Aske, Constable,

KEY PERSON

Cardinal Reginald Pole (1500–58) (see the family tree on page 157) was the son of Sir Richard Pole and Margaret, Countess of Salisbury. Educated at Oxford and Padua, he was in Italy from 1521 to 1527 and still on good terms with Henry. He was very much opposed to Henry's divorce from Catherine, and this soured his relations with the king. After 1532 he remained abroad. In 1536 he was made a cardinal and in 1549 he came within a few votes of becoming Pope.

A portrait of Reginald Pole by an unknown artist.

Lascelles and Stapleton, were members of his council. Yet the Earl remained in London throughout and remained aloof from the rising. By contrast, Henry Clifford, Earl of Cumberland, far from being solicited as a potential leader, was often under attack from the rebels. He was a notorious rack renter and found himself besieged in Skipton Castle. He was also hated by the Percies, which meant that there was no chance of a united northern baronage. This was vital if the rebels were to achieve long-term success.

Some of the great men who did join the rebellion were less than whole-hearted. Lord Darcy, for example, would later claim that he had been forced to join the rebels because Pontefract Castle was so badly provisioned that it could not withstand a siege. A further and probably decisive factor in the king's favour was that the rebels were loyalists. The gentry and commons of the north were not attempting to overthrow the king. In time-honoured fashion, the commons were exercising their right to protest at the changes – real and potential, now and in the future – that were taking place. The gentry seemed to agree with their complaints and all presumed that, once aware of their concerns, a caring monarch would move to put things right. Lord Darcy again provides a typical example of this attitude. 'For my part,' he claimed, 'I have been, and ever will be, true to the king our sovereign Lord, for as I ever said, one God, one Faith, one King.'

Failure of the Pilgrimage

Such sentiments failed to mollify his sovereign Lord. Darcy was beheaded on Tower Green for his part in the uprising. Given the loyalty and peaceful nature of the rebels, their only real hope of success was that Henry would be so frightened or (much less likely) so concerned that he would sack his low-born counsellors, reinstate the nobility as his chief advisers and turn the clock back to 1529. Norfolk and Suffolk and other conservatives who hated the reforming measures introduced by Cromwell and Cranmer no doubt hoped that this would indeed be the king's reaction.

Unfortunately for them and for the rebels in the north, Henry was unrepentant. Faced with rebellion, peaceful and respectful though it was, his instinct was to teach them a sharp lesson. As he did not possess the armed forces to crush them directly, he and Cromwell resorted to subterfuge. They appeared to go along with the rebel demands, inviting the leaders to London under a free pardon while also granting a parliament to meet in the north. When the loyal rebels had dispersed in triumph, Henry was able to destroy the leaders with ease and then send in troops to execute as many rebels as they could capture. In the end, Aske and the rebels were betrayed by their loyalty to their king.

Government propaganda against the Pilgrimage

Furthermore, the king and his servants put out some serious propaganda to strengthen the government's hand. How was it possible for the rebels to take an oath together, while honouring their oath to the king? The north of England was bombarded with propaganda on the sinfulness of rebellion. Richard Morison, who had once lived in the household of Reginald Pole, produced a pamphlet entitled *A Remedy for Sedition.* 'When every man will rule, who shall obey?' he wondered, and his point was unanswerable. The king might be surrounded by evil counsellors, but only if the king agreed that they were evil.

In addition, Henry won the propaganda war abroad. Cromwell's letter to the English ambassadors in France, written in December 1536, is a masterly tissue of lies, designed to dampen down any thoughts of an invasion:

Source 5

We have received your letters and perceive that the recent insurrections [i.e. the risings in Lincolnshire and Yorkshire] have been reported in a very exaggerated manner. The rising happened because of false reports spread among the people by certain seditious men who are in danger of the laws. When the people learnt that they had been deceived, they lamented their offences and desired our pardon. Both Lincolnshire and Yorkshire are at our mercy. Within six days we had in readiness against each of these two insurrections, two such armies as would have devoured the rebels and remained capable of giving battle to the greatest prince christened. Thank God my subjects were so ready to fight against the rebels that we were rather forced to keep them back than to spur them on.

Adapted from a letter written by Cromwell on the king's behalf in 1536.

Reasons for the Pilgrimage

Defence of the Church. So, what had it all been about? The most significant and all-embracing reasons for the rebellion were the changes in religion and attacks on the Church, both secular and regular. The Act for Suppressing Smaller Monasteries was passed in March 1536. By the summer, commissioners were at work in the north amid widespread rumours that a total dissolution of the monasteries was intended. A year earlier, commissioners had been sent out to evaluate the wealth of the Church as a whole and had produced the *Valor Ecclesiasticus.* Thus there was a general feeling that the monasteries might not be the only part of the Church on Henry VIII's list. The rumour spread that there was to be an attack on the Church as a whole – secular and regular.

So it was that the rebellion began in defence of a parish church not a monastery. In Louth in Lincolnshire, the people of the town, inspired by the local clergy and a shoemaker known as Captain Cobbler, rose to defend their parish church. The commons were guarding the church's treasure house, fearing that the Bishop of Lincoln's registrar or other commissioners were about to seize the treasure. When the registrar arrived to carry out a visitation of the local clergy, he was seized. Immediately the rebels marched to a nearby nunnery at Legbourne, where royal commissioners were at work. On 4 October in Horncastle, the Bishop of Lincoln's chancellor fared even worse than his colleague – he was lynched and killed by the mob.

Monasteries restored. Elsewhere the pattern of revolt was similar. Risings flared up where monasteries were being dissolved – monks and priests were often foremost in stirring up popular protest. In all, sixteen out of fifty-five suppressed monasteries were restored during the revolt. In York, the nunnery of St Clements was set up again. In Lancashire, Sawley Abbey was restored. One of the local leaders in Cumberland was the vicar of Brough. Aske always claimed that the rising was mainly motivated by religious concerns, and this was true.

York and Pontefract Articles. The rebels wore the badge of the five wounds of Christ, believing they were engaged in a crusade to protect the Church and to reverse the Henrician Reformation. In their Articles, religious grievances had pride of place. The first of the York Articles sent to the mayor by Aske claimed that 'the suppression of so many religious houses' was of 'grete hurt to the common welthe'. Article 4 complained about the activities of Cromwell and Rich, the Chancellor of the Augmentations, and Article 5 attacked reforming bishops, especially Cranmer, Shaxton, Latimer and Longland.

In the later Pontefract Articles, religious grievances again head the list. Article 1 condemned the heresies of Luther, Wycliffe, Tyndale, Barnes and the Anabaptists. Article 2 wanted to see the papal headship of the Church restored 'as before it was accustomed to be', even though it didn't want to restore the payment of first fruits to Rome. Article 3 wished to see Mary restored to the succession, indicating their belief that the Aragonese marriage was valid. Articles 4 and 6 sought to reverse the suppression of the monasteries and in particular of the Observant Friars, while heretic bishops, with Cromwell and Rich as 'maintayners of the false sect of heretiques', were the target of Articles 7 and 8.

Naturally enough, there were many non-religious articles as well. The gentry and peers opposed the Statute of Uses of 1536, which would restrict their ability to bequeath property without paying great fines. The rebels were also motivated by a regional spirit, which deplored the spoliation of the north by a southern government. Many articles claimed that taxes were too high, but this is a standard complaint that could be made anywhere at any time. The most important reason why thousands of people joined the protest in the autumn of 1536 was opposition to the attack on their Church.

The destruction of the rebels 1537

Meanwhile, Henry, having sent the rebels home with empty promises of pardon and a parliament in the north, prepared to strike. The opportunity he craved was given to him by **Sir Francis Bigod**. His abortive rising of January 1537 was used as an excuse to claim that the rebel leaders had broken their word. The Duke of Norfolk returned to the north and declared martial law. Groups of rebels were hanged in Cumberland, while the gentry leaders of the Pilgrimage were rounded up and taken to London. Some 178 people, including Aske and Darcy, were executed for treason.

As luck would have it, Henry's control over the north was strengthened by the death of the Earl of Northumberland in July 1537. He had made Henry VIII his heir and so all his lands reverted to the king. Cromwell then brought in a permanent Council of the North staffed by loyal servants, while Sir Thomas Wharton was made Warden of the West March in 1544. The feudal power of the northern nobility was thus seriously eroded. When the people and the magnates of the north rose again, thirty-three years after the Pilgrimage, once again in the name of the Catholic Church, the end result was the same – failure and humiliation.

IMAGINARY OPPOSITION? THE EXETER CONSPIRACY 1538

The alleged conspiracy. One final episode of opposition deserves to be investigated. In 1538 the government claimed to have uncovered a dangerous conspiracy among conservative noblemen designed to overthrow the king and bring back Catholicism. This was the so-called Exeter Conspiracy, named after Henry Courtenay, the Marquis of Exeter. He was supposed to have conspired with Lord Montague and his brothers Geoffrey and Reginald Pole. The Marquis's wife, Gertrude, had travelled in disguise to see the Maid of Kent several years before and Reginald Pole was a cardinal living in exile in Rome. The dangerous nature of the plot was reinforced by the fact that both families – Courtenays and Poles – were Yorkists with a claim to the throne.

Trial and execution. Geoffrey Pole was made to give evidence and the Marquis and Lord Montague were duly executed. Henry's vindictiveness even reached as far as Montague's elderly mother, the Countess of

KEY PERSON

Sir Francis Bigod
was a Protestant Yorkshire gentleman. Although a critic of monasteries, he realised that Henry had deceived the rebels and sought to stir up the north in 1537 to prevent royal revenge. He failed to take Hull and was captured in Cumberland in February 1537 and executed.

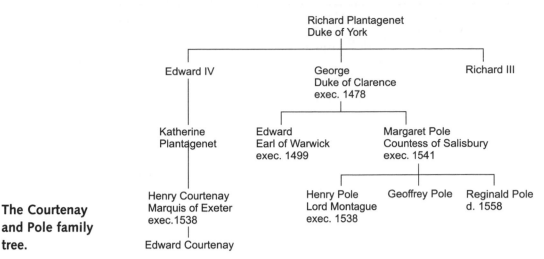

The Courtenay and Pole family tree.

Salisbury, an apparently harmless woman whose crime was that she was the niece of both Edward IV and Richard III. The plot was almost certainly an invention by Cromwell, who used unexceptional testimony from servants to incriminate his noble victims. Source 6 describes the examination of the servant John Collins in 1538.

Source 6

The said Collins says that he heard Lord Montague much praise the learning of Cardinal Pole. He further says that he heard Lord Montague say that knaves rule about the king and he trusted that one day the world would amend and that honest men would rule about the king. He heard Lord Montague say that he trusted to see the abbeys up again and say that Cardinal Pole should marry the Lady Mary and that she should have title to the Crown.

Adapted from the interrogation of John Collins in 1538.

The reason for this cruel strike was probably Cromwell's feelings of insecurity in the autumn of 1538. As with the destruction of the Boleyn group in 1536, Cromwell was at his most dangerous when he felt vulnerable. The discovery of a nasty plot in 1538 would, he hoped, shore up his power base. The king was always more forgiving when someone defused a serious threat to him and his government.

Opposition timeline

1534 Destruction of Elizabeth Barton and her supporters.
1535 Execution of More and Fisher
1536 Dissolution of the Monasteries begins
      Execution of Anne Boleyn and her circle
      Pilgrimage of Grace
1537 Sir Francis Bigod's abortive uprising
1538 Exeter conspiracy

SOURCE QUESTIONS

1 Using your own knowledge, explain what is meant in Source 1 by
  'railed against the king's marriage'.   *(4 marks)*

2 Using Source 1 and your own knowledge, explain why Cromwell
  might have seen the Holy Maid of Kent as a serious challenge to the
  Henrician regime.   *(7 marks)*

3 To what extent does Source 4 back up the evidence of Source 3 about
  the state of the king's forces in 1536?   *(5 marks)*

4 Using Sources 3–5 and your own knowledge, consider the view that
  the Pilgrimage of Grace was 'a serious rebellion carried out by loyal
  subjects'.   *(20 marks)*

SECTION 2

1538–47: In what ways and to what extent was the Reformation reversed?

OVERVIEW

The trial and condemnation of the Protestant John Lambert, in 1538, was a clear sign that the king was becoming disenchanted with the reforming direction that affairs had taken. The next year, an Act of Parliament, the Act of Six Articles, confirmed this disenchantment and in 1540, Thomas Cromwell, the architect of the Reformation was disgraced and executed. The Reformation was put on hold for the rest of the reign. Meanwhile, after three years of being a bachelor, the king was embroiled in three more marriages within the space of three years. He also sought to rediscover his youth by adopting an aggressive foreign policy. He invaded France, capturing Boulogne, and attacked the Scots, defeating them at the battle of Solway Moss.

This was also a period of intense faction fighting between those who wanted more reform and those who wanted less. Ultimately, the king did not allow such conflict to influence the direction of affairs, although it did contribute to all three of his marriages during the period and the sudden ending of two of them. Right up until his death, Henry remained the master, with courtiers and noblemen terrified of his moods and temper. He liked to play tricks on them just to remind them who was boss. However, even Henry VIII could do little to influence events from his grave and, during his son's brief reign, the reformers would have their day.

WHY WAS CROMWELL OVERTHROWN IN 1540?

The trial of John Lambert 1538
This trial began the process of reversal and was an indication that Cromwell's reforming ideas were not as popular with the king as they had once been. It was also clear encouragement to all those who deplored the recent changes to the country's religious beliefs and practices. Perhaps surprisingly, the trial took place at the instigation of Cromwell. Realising that the king was in heresy-hunting mood, the Vicegerent in Spirituals, who had recently murdered Exeter and Montague as alleged papists, now decided that Henry needed a Protestant heretic to persecute. Once again, Cromwell was attempting to preserve his influence and display his loyalty.

Lambert made a convenient victim. He was accused of denying the **real presence** in the Eucharist. The king himself attended the trial, dressed all in white, as a clear indication of his personal commitment against heresy. Cranmer's intervention in the trial proved rather feeble as he seemed to give Lambert the benefit of the doubt. The king, Gardiner and other bishops were in no doubt about Lambert's guilt, as Source 7 clearly shows.

Source 7

Lambert was sent for by the Archbishop [Cranmer], brought into open court and forced to defend his cause. The king commanded Cranmer to refute Lambert's assertion that the body of Christ was not present in the sacrament of the altar. Cranmer began his disputation very modestly saying, 'Doctor Lambert, let this matter be handled between us indifferently. If I convince you by the Scriptures, that your argument is wrong, you will willingly refute the same. If you prove your argument true, I promise that I will embrace the same.' When they had contended, Lambert answered so well that the king seemed to be greatly moved, the Archbishop entangled and the audience amazed. Then the **Bishop of Winchester**, fearing that the argument would be lost, interrupted the Archbishop. Through the pestiferous [evil] counsel of this one Bishop of Winchester, Satan did here perform the condemnation of Lambert.

Adapted from John Foxe's *Book of Martyrs*, 1563.

Execution of Lambert. Foxe's view of the trial was, of course, partisan. However, the king had no doubt about his verdict and pronounced the sentence of guilt. Lambert was burnt alive on 22 November 1538. The condemnation and death of Lambert was more than just the death of one heretic. It showed that the king was firmly against any change in the crucial Catholic doctrine of the Mass. On the day of the execution, Henry issued a proclamation insisting on the real presence and the observance of Church ceremonies. In addition, **clerical marriage** was declared unlawful (not that it had ever been declared lawful). This stipulation caused Cranmer to send his German wife back to Germany!

The threat of invasion

The king's anxiety about the spread of heresy in his realm was fuelled by a dangerous turn in foreign affairs. In 1538, Charles V and Francis I, who had been at war for so long, made peace at Nice. Worse still, they met with the Pope at Aigues-Mortes and declared war on all **schismatics**. Admittedly, there were quite a lot of schismatics in Europe to choose from, but Henry thought he might be near the top of the list.

KEY CONCEPT

The **real presence** was the doctrine that Christ was actually present in the bread and wine at Communion. Catholics believed in this doctrine, while many Protestants did not.

KEY PERSON

The **Bishop of Winchester** was Stephen Gardiner (1487–1555). He supported the king's Supremacy but wanted traditional religious practices and beliefs to be retained. He was the leading churchman in the conservative group in the 1540s and was later imprisoned for his beliefs.

**Clerical
marriage.** The
Catholic Church
declared that
priests, like Christ,
should not marry,
but be married to
the Church
instead. Protestants
generally approved
of clergy marrying
because it was not
forbidden in the
Bible.

Schismatics were
those guilty of
schism or
separation from the
Catholic Church:
in other words,
heretics.

Transubstantiation
was the Catholic
belief that in the
Mass, the bread
and the wine were
entirely
transformed
miraculously into
the body and blood
of Christ.
Challenging this
idea was
fundamental to all
Protestants.

Henry's diplomacy usually centred upon being allied with one or other of
the great powers of Europe. Through most of the 1520s he had been
allied with Charles V and against Francis I. Through most of the 1530s,
when he had fallen out with Charles V, Francis I had been only too
happy to play the part of ally. Now Charles and Francis had joined
together in common cause. The French wanted to fight against the old
enemy and Charles V wanted to avenge Catherine of Aragon.

At the time of the Pilgrimage of Grace in 1536, there had been rumours
of a Catholic crusade to oust Henry VIII; now it seemed that such a
crusade was about to become a reality. Faced with this situation, the king
thought it best to put a stop to reformation. Perhaps Charles and Francis
would not invade if they realised that the English Church was not
controlled by a heretic king. For Henry this policy was reinforced by his
personal worries about the spread of heresy, which had been evident
throughout the 1530s.

The Act of Six Articles 1539

Reasons for its passing. So, in 1539, further evidence appeared that
England was in fact a Catholic country. To the dismay of visiting
Lutheran representatives, hoping to bring about the harmonisation of
Lutheran and English Churches, the king brought in the Act of Six
Articles. He asked the Duke of Norfolk to request the House of Lords to
consider six key theological issues. This was a signal to the conservatives
that their star was now in the ascendant. Although the six items were
posed as questions, the king and the Lords knew the answers that were
wanted. As a result, the Act, which took up very Catholic positions on
the matters in question, was passed without serious opposition in
Parliament and in Convocation.

Impact of the Act. Denial of **transubstantiation** was made punishable by
burning. Denial of clerical celibacy, of Communion in one kind only for
laymen, of vows of chastity, of Masses for the dead and of auricular
confession were all punishable by hanging or life imprisonment. After the
feeble moves towards a Protestant theology, this was clear and
unambiguous: Catholic doctrines were now being enforced by
parliamentary statute, the highest form of law. Not many people were
persecuted under this Act. Some authorities may have been unhappy
with the savage penalties, or it may be that there were not many
committed Protestants in England. In any case, Henry had set the seal on
the beliefs of the Anglican Church, and they remained in force until his
death.

Opposition to the Act. Protestants at home and abroad were outraged,
but there was little that they could do. Cranmer made some token signs
of opposition in Convocation, but quickly caved in. Bishops Shaxton and

Latimer nobly resigned their sees, which left the bench of bishops dominated by conservative men. Gardiner's triumph was completed as he was invited back to the Privy Council. Protestant theologians abroad were aghast, but not really surprised. They had never thought that Henry was one of them. In September 1539, Martin Bucer, a Protestant leader based in Strasbourg, condemned the Act.

Source 8

I lament the decision of Parliament in London on transubstantiation in consequence of which two of the most pious bishops – **Latimer** and **Shaxton** – have been taken [imprisoned]. In November there will be a new parliament in which they will proceed to extremities with these people and many others, for there are many in England who know Christ truly and cannot keep silence. The crafty Bishop of Winchester is behind all this as he has warned the king that if he proceed with the Reformation, it will lead to commotion and the principal Lords of England will be against him.

Adapted from a letter written by Martin Bucer in 1539.

The Cleves marriage

Though the passing of the Act of Six Articles was a clear move to reverse the Reformation, the king was still pursuing negotiations with the Protestant princes of Germany. While the danger of Charles and Francis remained, Cromwell had managed to persuade the king of the advisability of a marriage alliance with the Emperor's German opponents. A number of possible wives were being considered for the king and, two years after the death of Queen Jane, Henry thought that a new wife might help stop the onset of old age. Now nearing fifty years old and increasingly plagued by ailments that restricted his mobility, the king was looking to recapture his youth.

Since his prospective brides around Europe could not come to him, Henry sent **Hans Holbein,** the brilliant painter of so many Tudor statesmen, to vet **Anne of Cleves**. The portrait of Anne was unduly flattering, the king was impressed and he allowed Cromwell to persuade him to proceed with the marriage. The king's enthusiasm led to him going, in disguise, to meet his new bride as soon as she arrived in England in order to 'nourish love'. Unfortunately for her and, as it turned out, for Cromwell, what the king saw did not please him. He dubbed her 'the fat Flanders mare' and it was only with difficulty that he could be persuaded to go through with the marriage ceremony.

KEY PEOPLE

Nicholas Shaxton and **Hugh Latimer** were reforming bishops of Salisbury and Worcester respectively.

Hans Holbein the younger (1497–1543) was a German artist and the most important painter at the court of Henry VIII. He came to England in 1526 with a letter of introduction to Sir Thomas More from their mutual friend, Erasmus. He went to Switzerland in 1528, but returned to England in 1532 and spent the rest of his life there. His wonderful paintings of the king and his courtiers give us a splendid insight into the characters of the leading men and women of the Henrician period.

Cromwell undermined

Heresy. Soon afterwards, however, the diplomatic reasons for the marriage fell apart. Charles and Francis were soon at odds again and the king did not need the Protestant German princes or his new wife. Cromwell, who was blamed for the marriage, was under pressure to end it. Buffeted by this and already undermined by the Six Articles, Cromwell was in more trouble when a special commission reported on the spread of heresy in Calais, which England still owned from the time of the Hundred Years War. This commission hinted that Cromwell was aware of the heresy in Calais, but had been unwilling to enforce the Six Articles.

Robert Barnes. Furthermore, one of Cromwell's religious allies, Robert Barnes, a Lutheran who had been used in the Cleves negotiations, got the Vicegerent into further trouble. He preached in favour of **justification by faith alone** as a response to Bishop Gardiner's recent sermon campaign. Barnes was indiscreet and foolish. He and two other heretics, Jerome and Garrett, were sent to the Tower.

Catherine Howard. Even worse was to follow as the conservative Duke of Norfolk aimed to exploit the king's marital unhappiness by dangling his alluring young niece, **Catherine Howard**, in front of the disgruntled monarch. Henry was quickly captivated by her and this allowed Norfolk to further recover his influence with the king, which had languished on and off since the fall of Norfolk's other niece, Anne Boleyn.

As it turned out, 'niece marrying' would, once again, prove disastrous for Norfolk. However, in the short term, the king's attachment to Catherine Howard allowed Norfolk and Suffolk to intrigue against Cromwell. They had resented Wolsey, only to find their triumph short-lived when Cromwell rose to prominence as the king's secretary. Now, with Gardiner, they were poised to destroy another low-born favourite.

The fall of Cromwell 1540

Cromwell had made many other enemies. The dissolution of the monasteries had evoked genuine outrage and Cromwell and Cranmer were seen as the architects of a dangerous and divisive change in the religious life of the nation. Gardiner and other conservative bishops also saw their chance to be rid of the scheming and bloody favourite, the man who had made faction fighting such a dangerous and lethal game.

However, the king had one final trick to play before throwing Cromwell to the wolves. In April 1540, the king ennobled him as Earl of Essex. Some have argued that this was a trick on Henry's part, to make his downfall more terrible for being unexpected. But it may be that it was only at the last minute, some time in June, that the king agreed to

Cromwell's arrest on grounds of heresy and treason. The end of Cromwell's last letter to the king makes interesting reading.

Source 9

I beseech your Grace most humbly to pardon this my rude writing and to consider that I am a most woeful prisoner, ready to take the death when it shall please God and your Majesty. Yet the frail flesh incites me constantly to call on your Grace for mercy and pardon for my offences. Written at the Tower this Wednesday the last of June with the heavy heart and trembling hand of your Highness' most heavy and most miserable prisoner and poor slave. Most gracious Prince, I cry for mercy, mercy, mercy.

Adapted from Cromwell's letter to the king in June 1540.

Execution. The letter was signed 'Thomas Crumwell'. On 28 June 1540, Cromwell was led out to Tower Green and executed. Two days later, three Protestants – Barnes, Garrett and Jerome – were burned at the stake. This was further evidence that the Reformation in religion would go no further and that the beliefs of Henry's English Church were to be orthodox Catholic ones.

The King's Book 1543

The final statement on religious matters came three years later with the so-called King's Book. This was a thorough revision of the Bishops' Book, which the king had refused to endorse six years earlier. The importance of the Bible was played down, while the importance of the Mass and transubstantiation and **confession** were re-emphasised. Even images made something of a comeback, provided they were used without superstition. Finally, renewed attention was paid to the importance of obedience and good works in achieving salvation. Justification by faith alone, so central to the Lutheran and other Protestant creeds, was clearly rejected. This rejection of Lutheran doctrine is all the more significant as the King's Book carried much more authority than the Bishops' Book, since it came from the Church's Supreme Head and, like the Six Articles, it was given parliamentary backing.

WAS HENRY VIII THE MASTER OR VICTIM OF FACTION IN THE 1540S?

Motives for faction fighting

After Cromwell's fall, those in close attendance upon the king continued, as was natural, to fight among themselves. The 'prince of faction' may have been destroyed by his own methods, but those who remained

KEY PERSON

Catherine Howard
(1522–42) was Henry VIII's fifth wife. She was the daughter of Norfolk's younger brother, Lord Edmund Howard. They were married in July 1540, but the marriage ended with Catherine's execution for adultery in February 1542, at the age of nineteen.

KEY CONCEPT

Confession was oral confession. The Catholic Church said that people should confess their sins directly to a priest. They usually did penance for their sins and received absolution (forgiveness) from the priest. Protestants were opposed to this, partly because it was contrary to the idea of forgiveness through faith not good works.

inherited a bitter legacy of distrust, intrigue and betrayal. Yet it would be wrong to see the king's servants as divided merely between conservative and reforming groups. Some were, of course, motivated by religious preferences, but many, as always, were out for themselves. The French ambassador's account of the arrest of Cromwell makes this point in relation to the actions of the admiral, Sir William FitzWilliam. He had backed Cromwell up to now, but when he realised that he was doomed, he wanted to be one of the first to denounce him.

Although some people were out mainly for themselves, it is useful to see that there were two loose groupings or factions near the king, which explain the political problems of the 1540s. Disputes were principally over religion but were made worse by the king's last two wives, and there were also disagreements over foreign policy, as the king decided to go to war against the old enemy, France.

The nature of faction fighting

However, in the 1540s, faction fighting was not as deadly as it had been in the hands of Cromwell. Cranmer, Gardiner and even Henry's last wife were accused of capital crimes, but all survived to tell the tale. Partly this was because the king, without the prompting of Cromwell, was not especially vindictive. He liked to balance the factions, showing his ultimate power and control, rather than lurch from one to the other like a frightened puppet. Also, as has been seen, the religious beliefs of the Church had now been settled to the king's liking and he was not about to change his mind again. After Cromwell there was no new chief minister. The king took charge and there was no conflict about who had most influence over him. In addition, there was little real trouble because the factions, reforming and conservative, were so well balanced. One could not destroy the other.

Privy Council and Privy Chamber

In the wake of Cromwell's fall, the conservative group, led by Norfolk and Gardiner, dominated the king's Privy Council. Now with its own secretary, record keeping and regular meetings, it would constantly warn the king about dangers to the realm posed by reformers and reforming ideas. On the other side, the reformers, led by Edward Seymour (Jane's brother) and Sir Anthony Denny, were dominant in the king's Privy Chamber, the group of servants and courtiers who lived with Henry on a daily basis. The groups thus tended to cancel each other out. Both had access to the king, giving him different ideas and lines of policy, but neither could dominate his thinking for any length of time.

Furthermore, it is not clear that either side actually wanted any major changes in political or religious policy. The conservatives were broadly satisfied with the settlement on religion, and as good Erastians they did not wish to go all the way back to papal control over the Church. The king had always controlled the English Church and Henry VIII continued this tradition, so there was no problem. On the other hand, the reformers made no real efforts to make the Church more Protestant. Cranmer, the spiritual leader of the group, had always been a royal servant first and a Christian theologian second. He and the others may have hoped for change, but they decided to wait upon the Lord.

Divide and rule

Throughout the 1540s, until his last few weeks on earth, the king retained control. He had made it clear by 1539–40 that reform would go no further and no amount of faction fighting would budge him from that. He also wanted to rediscover his youth and return to war with France and Scotland, but these were his policies, not those of one or other of the factions. At no time was the king pushed into policies that he otherwise would not have adopted, and frequently he actually seemed to enjoy playing the factions off against each other, to show that he was still the boss. It was the old policy of divide and rule that Henry played so well. Ultimately, both sides feared the king and he knew it – they could not master him until he was cold in his grave.

The marriage and execution of Catherine Howard

The balancing of forces in the 1540s was helped by the spectacular downfall of the king's fifth wife, Catherine Howard, in the second year of her marriage. She was Henry's 'rose without a thorn'. Gardiner and Norfolk had dangled her in front of the king at the time of the unfortunate Cleves marriage and the king was hooked. The marriage to Anne was annulled on the grounds of non-consummation and she was given a pension and a house in the country. Although his wife for the shortest time, she actually came off best. The high point of Cromwell's reforming diplomacy was thus brought low and, even worse for the reformers, the king proceeded to marry Norfolk's niece.

Catherine's lovers. While Catherine was married to Henry, the reformers, without their most able and astute factional leader, seemed doomed to years in the wilderness. However, it was soon discovered that Catherine had one or two skeletons in her closet. First, she was not the virgin that the king had assumed she was when they married. She had had at least two lovers before the king and even that could have been enough to condemn her.

But worse was to follow. One of her ex-lovers, Francis Dereham, used his friendship to become her secretary and she soon took another lover, Thomas Culpepper, a gentleman of the king's Privy Chamber. Catherine was probably bored and possibly disgusted by her husband. He was becoming more repulsive and she was an attractive teenager. It has been

Henry VIII, aged 49, by Hans Holbein the Younger.

suggested that the affair with Culpepper was not as mad as it seems. With her past catching up on her and the king not as virile as he once was, she may have decided that safety lay with a son. Catherine of Aragon and Anne Boleyn had found this out the hard way and Jane Seymour had died to provide one. Perhaps Catherine and her uncle now realised that only with a son on her knee could she quash the rumours about her conduct. If so, it was a desperate strategy and it led to her disgrace and death.

Cranmer reveals the truth about Catherine. The reformers soon found out about Culpepper tripping up the back stairs to Catherine's bedroom. The problem was how to tell the king. He was blissfully happy and might not listen to the accusations. With Anne Boleyn, Cromwell knew what the king wanted to hear and distorted the truth accordingly; in this case, with an unpredictable sovereign, it was trickier. If things went wrong, the reformers might be swept out of court. So it fell to Cranmer, the king's favourite churchman, to tell him. Even he feared telling the king face to face, so he sent him a note instead. At first Henry refused to believe it, then he burst into tears.

Executions. The reformers got their way. Catherine and Culpepper, together with Lady Rochford (widow of George Boleyn), were executed. Dereham was also sent to his death for good measure, but there the killing stopped. The conservatives no doubt endured a few tongue-lashings, but there was to be no punishment for the instigators of the marriage, Norfolk and Gardiner. This was post-Cromwell faction fighting in action – only the guilty were punished.

Charges against Cranmer 1543

Thereafter, there were three main attempts to overthrow three leading figures, all of which failed. The sting was clearly going out of faction fighting. In 1543 the conservatives in the Privy Council persuaded the king to bring heresy charges against Archbishop Cranmer. Without Cranmer the reformers would surely fall apart. Confident that the Archbishop was finished, the conservatives moved in to arrest him. Meanwhile, unknown to them, the king summoned Cranmer and gave him one of his royal rings as a sign of affection. When the conservatives went to arrest him, Cranmer showed them the ring and they realised that Henry had outwitted them. Thwarted of their prey, they raced to apologise to their sovereign lord and reminded themselves about who was in charge of the nation's affairs.

Gardiner's nephew executed 1544

In the next year, the boot was on the other foot. Bishop Gardiner's nephew and secretary, Germaine Gardiner, was executed for denying the Supremacy. This time the conservatives were under attack and it looked as though the Bishop of Winchester would be brought down. He, however, made confession to the king and was spared.

The Anne Askew affair 1546

In 1546 a more complex and deadly conflict erupted, which threatened to bring down the king's last wife, **Catherine Parr**. She was a lady of reforming views, well educated and not afraid of talking theology even with the Supreme Head of the Church. In May 1546, the Privy Council was allowed to investigate the cases of several suspected heretics. Two men from the Privy Chamber were duly executed. One of them, Lascelles, was linked to a Lincolnshire lady, Anne Askew. She was found guilty of denying the real presence and before she was burnt alive, she was tortured on the rack by two of the king's Privy Councillors – Richard

KEY PERSON

Catherine Parr (1512–48) was Henry VIII's sixth and last wife. She was daughter of Sir Thomas Parr, Controller of the Household in the early years of the reign. She was well educated and twice widowed before marrying the king. She was Regent of England in 1544 while her husband was in France. After Henry's death she married Thomas Seymour, brother of Edward and Jane, and she died giving birth to a daughter one year later.

Thomas Wriothesley (d.1550) came to prominence through Cromwell and took over as one of the king's secretaries after his fall. He later became Lord Chancellor and first Earl of Southampton.

Mary, Queen of Scots (1542–87) was six days old when she became queen. Her mother was Marie of Guise, and Mary was later married to Francis, the son of Francis I. She and her mother represented the power of the 'auld alliance' between France and Scotland. She was executed at Fotheringhay during the reign of Henry's daughter Elizabeth.

Rich and **Thomas Wriothesley** – in an attempt to get her to implicate ladies of the queen's Privy Chamber as associates and fellow heretics. The hope was to reach the queen herself.

Once again, however, the king played tricks on his courtiers. He gave Wriothesley permission to arrest and imprison his wife, but he made sure that he himself was on hand when the attempt to take her was made. The king drove the unsuspecting Wriothesley away with insults when he appeared before the queen. Catherine was shaken, but she escaped.

HOW DID FOREIGN POLICY CHANGE IN THE PERIOD 1541–6?

Revival of an aggressive foreign policy

So, throughout the period 1541–6, the two factions remained roughly in balance, with the king continuing to control affairs. There was no new chief minister after Cromwell and the king's control of policy was emphasised by the revival of an aggressive foreign policy. Before 1540, as we have seen, Henry VIII had been seriously concerned about the possibility of England being invaded by either or both of his main rivals on the European stage. After 1541, as Charles and Francis spiralled towards another war, Henry decided to intervene on the European stage. After years of defensive anxiety, it was time to show the world that England could stand up for itself and defy the hostility of the Pope. Henry's chosen enemy would be France, just as in the old days.

Invasion of Scotland 1542

The first task was to ensure that the Scots, usually allied to the French, could not cause problems while Henry attacked King Francis. In 1541, therefore, the king launched a charm offensive and made a splendid progress to York to meet his nephew, James V of Scotland. Unwisely, James failed to turn up. Henry's anger was roused and he sent his ageing military commander, Norfolk, to teach his errant relative a sharp lesson. Norfolk led a huge raid into Scotland and then defeated a Scottish army at Solway Moss in November 1542. This was good news indeed, but matters improved still further when James V promptly died just a few days after the battle. The new sovereign was James' baby daughter, **Mary, Queen of Scots**, and Scotland then became embroiled in factional disputes.

Treaty of Greenwich 1543. With Scotland divided, the king made peace at Greenwich in the summer of 1543. This treaty agreed that the young Prince Edward would be betrothed to Mary, thus holding out the prospect that the same person might soon rule both Scotland and England. In fact the Scots later renounced the treaty as they reverted to their alliance with France. Henry has often been criticised for his undiplomatic handling of the Scots, but in reality there was little more that could be achieved. Henry did not wish to conquer Scotland and Somerset's later attempt to do this ended in fiasco. Furthermore, the age-old rivalry and raiding was unlikely to be replaced by a long period of friendship, however diplomatic Henry was. Henry achieved what he set out to achieve – Scotland was effectively neutralised as he prepared for the invasion of France.

Invasion of France 1544

Despite the enormous expense, which would leave his kingdom virtually bankrupt by the time of his death, Henry was determined to renew his reputation as a warrior king. Encouraged by young courtiers who had not tasted action and were eager for a fight, Henry was winched on to his horse and invaded France for the third time. Although predictably abandoned by his ally Charles, who made a separate peace with the French, the king's men took the port of Boulogne to add to Calais, thus extending England's precarious foothold on the Continent. Henry had hoped for an attack on Paris, but this plan was quickly shelved. Boulogne proved an expensive prize. The walls, badly damaged when the English besieged the town, now had to be repaired at English expense and the English had to provide and pay for garrison troops to hold on to their conquest. Peace was made with France in 1546, by which England would hold the port for just eight years. It was all something of an anti-climax.

HOW DID THE REFORMERS SEIZE POWER IN 1546?

The overthrow of the conservatives

War and peace helped bring to prominence two reformers, Edward Seymour and John Dudley. Seymour, already Earl of Hertford, was Jane Seymour's brother and an effective general in the French war. Dudley, son of the Dudley executed at the start of Henry's reign, led the peace negotiations with France. As the king's health declined in 1546, these men, with the help of William Paget (the king's secretary) and Anthony Denny (second chief gentleman of the Privy Chamber), launched a bold and successful coup against the conservatives. This allowed them to control the king's will and to seize power in the next reign. Being reformers was really a secondary consideration, however. They did not act as they did in order to further the Reformation; their main motive was the pursuit of power.

Gardiner was the first victim. He was encouraged to argue with the king over an exchange of lands, then he was refused access to his sovereign by Denny, who now controlled the king's guest list. Worse was to follow when charges of treason were laid against the swashbuckling **Earl of Surrey**. He was Norfolk's son and generally indiscreet. He and his father

Henry Howard, Earl of Surrey (d.1547) was a poet and the eldest son of the Duke of Norfolk. He was proud and indiscreet and may have harboured hopes of becoming king. He was executed for treason just before the king's death.

had talked of a Howard-dominated minority when the king died. Surrey had rather unwisely had the arms of Edward the Confessor emblazoned on his own, emphasising royal descent on both sides of his family. It was easy to believe that he might be planning to seize the throne himself when the king died. At any event, it was well known that Prince Edward was sickly and might not outlive his father. Perhaps Surrey would prove a more popular heir than Edward's Catholic sister, Mary.

Changing the king's will

Not only did the reformers control access to the king because they dominated the Privy Chamber, but they also controlled the king's will. The king was too ill to write and so his will was authorised using a dry stamp of the king's signature, which could then be inked in. The man who controlled the dry stamp was Denny and the man who had the key to the box that contained the king's will was Seymour.

The reformers were then able to ensure that the king named a Regency Council for his nine-year-old son which had a majority of reformers on it. By this means they could ensure that Seymour himself would assume the title of Protector and with it real power during his nephew's minority. This had not been Henry's intention – he had wanted a balanced Council to rule in his son's name, which would maintain the religious status quo. Thus a violent faction struggle, which coincided with the king's final illness and death, launched England into a brief bout of Protestant Reformation. Henry VIII, who had dominated affairs so overwhelmingly and so dramatically during his lifetime, could not rule from the grave.

SOURCE QUESTIONS

1 To what extent does Source 7 indicate that Cranmer's views on the Mass were unclear? *(4 marks)*

2 How useful is Source 7 as an indication of what happened at the trial of Lambert? *(7 marks)*

3 Using Sources 7–9 and your own knowledge, consider the view that 'In the period 1538–43, the Henrican Reformation was largely undone.' *(20 marks)*

SECTION 3

1547–53: How Protestant did England become in the reign of Edward VI?

REASONS FOR FURTHER RELIGIOUS CHANGE

The next instalment of religious change in England, the Edwardian Reformation, was not meant to happen. It had not been Henry VIII's intention for there to be more changes in religion after his death. His son's tutors may have been reformers or **evangelicals**, but Henry VIII's intention was that **Edward** – only nine years old at the time of his father's death – would rule by means of a **Regency Council**. That Council would balance out conservatives and reformers, and thus the status quo in religion might be preserved. As we have seen, however, the Regency Council never came into being. Instead, the most successful faction fight of the period resulted in **Edward Seymour**, young Edward's uncle, taking charge as Protector.

Seymour was not a committed Protestant, but decided that a further burst of Reformation would be a good idea. First, reform would bring in revenue. New regimes need money and patronage to reward supporters and to buy off important opponents. Henry VIII had left an empty treasury and large debts, so more money was an urgent priority. Second, reform meant change and change is usually encouraged by new regimes – out with the old and in with the new – just like in 1509 when Henry VIII came to power. In addition, Seymour was, in a way, a **usurper** and such men are often anxious not to begin on a defensive note.

On the other hand, more religious change might not be popular – the conservatives were still well entrenched and were potentially vengeful after being tricked by the new Protector. Furthermore, even a Protector could not go round sacking half the bishops. The result then, was a classic compromise – change, but not very much of it. One cannot avoid the conclusion that religious reform during the reign of Edward was guided by political rather than religious considerations.

Foreign problems 1547–9

Before these religious changes could happen, Seymour had to deal with the Scots. Having made himself the Duke of Somerset, he found that French influence had been re-established in Scotland. This was the policy of the new French King, **Henry II**, and Somerset was faced with the prospect of all his good work at Solway Moss being undone by a new and

KEY TERM

Evangelicals.
Protestant men or women who wished to see reform of the doctrine and ceremonies of the Church in England.

KEY PEOPLE

Edward VI was Henry VIII's only son. His mother was Jane Seymour. His tutors in the 1540s, Ascham and Cheke, were reformers.

Edward Seymour was the elder brother of Jane Seymour, Henry VIII's third wife. She had died soon after giving birth to the future Edward VI. Edward Seymour was created Earl of Hertford in 1541 and Duke of Somerset in 1547. During the 1540s Seymour took a reforming line in religion.

KEY TERMS

Regency Council.
The normal way of
carrying on
government when
the monarch was a
child was for the
king's closest male
relative to become
Protector. Henry
VIII, however,
wished to avoid
rule by one man
and so decided that
the Privy Council
would rule in
Edward's name.

A **usurper** is
someone who takes
power or a position
that is not
rightfully theirs. By
going against
Henry VIII's will,
Seymour's taking
of the position of
Protector could be
seen as usurpation.

KEY PERSON

Henry II was the
son of Francis I of
France and
succeeded his
father in 1547. He
was famously killed
in a jousting
accident, while
celebrating peace
between France,
the Emperor and
England in 1559.

**A portrait of
Edward VI, after
William Scrots.**

aggressive French sovereign. In addition, of course, the French were
zealous Catholics on the whole, so zealous Scots reformers, including
John Knox, had been forced to flee. The chances of a Protestant Scotland
being established as a close ally of Protestant England looked remote.

Seymour was a better soldier than he was a politician and a quick military
victory against the auld adversary might help to secure his dubious title.
In August 1547, he invaded Scotland and duly defeated the Scots at the
Battle of Pinkie in September. However, his victory backfired. The
French sent 10,000 troops to Edinburgh and Seymour's attempts to
establish English garrisons in Scotland proved an expensive failure. One
estimate puts the cost of the Scottish campaign at £600,000. Even worse
followed as Mary Stuart, the young Queen of Scotland, was taken to
France where she soon married the **Dauphin** Francis. With four hostile
Catholic powers – Scotland, France, the Low Countries and Spain – now
surrounding England, Seymour realised that Protestant reform would
have to be cautious.

HOW IMPORTANT WERE SEYMOUR'S RELIGIOUS REFORMS?

Royal proclamations

The first moves were made by royal proclamations rather than the more
official and durable channel of parliamentary statute. All churches were
now to have a copy of Erasmus' *Paraphrases on the Gospels* to go alongside
their English Bible. Erasmus, despite being a fierce critic of the Church in
his day, had remained a staunch Catholic in terms of doctrine, so these

Paraphrases were uncontroversial. More upsetting to the conservatives was the declaration that parts of the ceremony of the Mass were to be performed in English.

The clergy were told to preach sermons at least four times a year. Those unable or unwilling to preach were to read from the *Book of Homilies*, a recently published volume that contained sermons written by Cranmer, among others. Alternatively, vicars might take advantage of **licensed preachers**. However, the employment of such men might prove unpopular, as Source 10, written in 1547, shows:

Source 10
The first year of the reign of King Edward VI, I the said Thomas, having licence of Bishop Cranmer, preached at Christchurch Twinham [Hampshire] where I was born. Mr Smythe the vicar of Christchurch and bachelor of divinity was present and I took my text from St John, chapter 16, verse 8, where our Saviour Christ says that he goes to the Father and that we shall see him no more. The priest being then at Mass, I declared to the people that they could see the consecrated bread and wine which the priest did hold over his head with their bodily eyes. Yet, in this text, our Saviour Christ says plainly that we shall see him no more. So you who do kneel unto it, pray unto it and honour it as God, do make an idol of it, and you commit most horrible idolatry. At this the vicar, Mr Smythe, sitting in his chair in front of the pulpit, said these words, 'Mr Hancock, you have done well until now and now you have played an ill cow's part, which when she has given a good mess of milk, overthroweth all with her foot, and so all is lost', and with these words he got me out of the church.

Written by Thomas Hancock in 1547.

The source reminds us clearly that Protestant ideas about the Mass were not always popular, even when the preachers were in their native parish! One also doubts whether Mr Smythe was the kind of vicar who would have volunteered to say parts of the Mass in English. Government proclamations might prove something of a dead letter in the **localities**, especially when such proclamations cut across traditional religious belief and practice.

Destruction of the Henrician Settlement in religion
Parliament was eventually called in November 1547. The Act of Revilers allowed the laity to receive wine as well as bread at the Mass, but reaffirmed the real presence of Christ in both. This was a move to discourage more radical Protestants, such as Mr Hancock, as well as one

Dauphin was the title given to the heir to the French throne, rather like the British Prince of Wales.

Licensed preachers were wandering priests who had obtained a licence or permission from a bishop or archbishop to preach in churches. A major problem for the reformers was that most of the clergy remained conservative or Catholic and unwilling or unable to preach. Preaching the Word of God was a key Protestant idea.

Localities are areas outside the capital and centre of government, London. It is often thought that reforming ideas had much more impact in large cities than they did in rural areas.

Main religious changes in Edward's reign

- Repeal of Act of Six Articles
- Destruction of chantries
- Attacks on ceremonies and images
- First Prayer Book and Act of Uniformity, 1549
- Priests allowed to marry
- New Ordinal
- Prayer Book and Act of Uniformity, 1552
- The 42 Articles, 1553

KEY TERMS

Treason Acts.
Henry VIII passed
Treason Acts in
1534, 1536 and
1541. Somerset
repealed these, but
immediately
enacted a new law
saying that denial
of the Supremacy,
in deed, writing or
words, would be
treason and
therefore a capital
offence.

Chantries were
religious
foundations, often
quite small, which
had religious,
charitable or
educational
purposes. The
main religious
function of the
chantries and of
chantry priests was
to say Masses for
the souls of dead
benefactors to
reduce their time
in Purgatory.

that might appease the conservatives. However, by tampering with the religious settlement of Henry VIII at all, Seymour brought about disaster.

He swept away the **Treason Acts** and all existing heresy laws. These moves destroyed the Act of Six Articles, the cornerstone of the state's religious policy, and seemed to open the floodgates to reform. The old was swept away, but the new had not yet arrived. Gardiner was later imprisoned and continental reformers like Peter Martyr and Martin Bucer turned up in London, but Somerset did not have a new religious settlement to hand. The result was chaotic, with reformers fighting among themselves (which reformers are wont to do) as well as against the conservatives.

Destruction of the chantries

Somerset's policy of destruction did, however, bring in some much-needed cash, as Parliament agreed to the Chantries Act, which destroyed the **chantries**. Pious hopes of diverting money to educational ends were expressed in the Act, but these were largely ignored once it was passed. The 2400 chantries, 90 colleges and 110 hospitals that were dissolved represented rich pickings for the regime, just as the monasteries had done before them. Unlike the monasteries, however, many of the chantries and colleges were in towns and represented a more visible and tangible sign of Protestant destructive tendencies, which was not popular in some quarters. The fact that the destruction of the chantries represented a major attack on the doctrine of Purgatory (see key term on page 182) was very much an afterthought.

Abolition of ceremonies and removal of images

Meanwhile, the Privy Council abolished a series of familiar Catholic ceremonies – Candles at Candlemas (2 February), Palms on Palm Sunday (Sunday before Easter), Ashes on Ash Wednesday (first day of Lent) and Creeping to the Cross on Good Friday. Just for good measure, the Privy Council also ordered the removal of all images remaining in any church

A portrait of Edward Seymour, Duke of Somerset, by an unknown artist.

or chapel. This included stained-glass windows depicting saints and wall paintings.

The Prayer Book of 1549

Among the significant changes introduced into religion during Edward's reign were the two English Prayer Books. The first was introduced by parliamentary statute as part of an Act of Uniformity. This Act demanded that all priests use the new Prayer Book. A committee of bishops headed by Cranmer devised this volume, which sought to introduce English services that would be used throughout the land. This uniformity in itself was a major change, as Catholic ceremonies and wording had varied from parish to parish, according to which of the five rites – Bangor, Lincoln, Hereford, York or Sarum (Salisbury) – was in use. Now there would be one standard English Book of Prayer, which would be in use everywhere.

Changes to the Mass. In order to get the book accepted, Cranmer shied away from anything radical or clearly Protestant in terms of doctrine. The book was, in fact, largely a translation of the Sarum Rite. The main point of contention was, not unexpectedly, the wording of the Mass. The final wording, which was adopted to get the book through the conservative House of Lords, was quite acceptable to those who held traditional beliefs. On receiving the bread, communicants heard the words, 'The Body of our Lord Jesus Christ which was given for thee, preserve thy body and soul unto everlasting life.' Even Stephen Gardiner approved of this. The Prayer Book encountered only limited overt opposition outside the south-west, but we know that many priests avoided the full impact of

Elevation of the Host. The priest raised the bread (Host) as he consecrated the bread and wine. It symbolised the miracle of transubstantiation.

Puritans were described as 'the hotter sort of Protestants' – those who thought that all Catholic ceremonial and doctrine should be swept away. They were always critics of the religious settlement in England.

Godly Reformation was the objective of Puritans. They saw themselves as the 'Godly' and wanted a thorough change in morality and behaviour in accordance with the Word of God.

the book by mumbling the English words, so that they might as well have been in Latin. Priests were now forbidden to **elevate the Host**, but many used some other gesture instead.

Penalties for non-compliance. The penalties for not using the new Prayer Book were fairly mild and there were few prosecutions as a result of non-compliance. The key thing was that conservatives realised that they could use the book without abandoning their Catholic beliefs. In other words, the Prayer Book had not moved the nation into full-blown Protestantism – Somerset could not risk that.

John Hooper, the radical Bishop of Gloucester, was furious. He declared that the book was 'very absurd' and 'full of popish errors and superstition'. Hooper was one of the first **Puritans**. He thought that **Godly Reformation** should mean a complete break with the Catholic past. Translating a Catholic Prayer Book was thus unacceptable. For him a truly Protestant Prayer Book would have to be a complete rewrite.

Priests allowed to marry

In the same session of Parliament, early in 1549, an Act was passed that would allow priests to marry. This may have had more impact than the Prayer Book in announcing Reformation of the Church. However, the Act did not *encourage* priests to marry; it merely removed the rules forbidding it.

Source 11

It is not only better for the estimation of priests and other ministers in the Church of God that they should live chaste, sole and separate from the company of women and the bond of marriage … and it is most to be wished that they would willingly commit themselves to a perpetual chastity and abstinence from the use of women. However, as this is not always the case, be it enacted that all and every law which does prohibit or forbid marriage to any ecclesiastical or spiritual person shall be utterly void and of none effect.

Adapted from the Act allowing priests to marry, 1549 (2&3 Edward VI, c.21)

THE REBELLIONS OF 1549 – CAUSES AND CONSEQUENCES

During 1549 there were two full-scale regional rebellions as well as large-scale rioting in at least nine other counties. The disorders were centred around local economic problems, which were blamed on the government. There was also discontent in some areas with Somerset's religious changes.

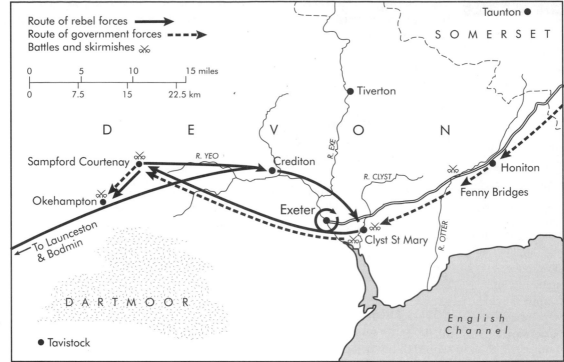

The Western Rebellion

Events of the rebellion. Most people accepted the new Prayer Book and
all the other changes in religion, perhaps with reservations and
apprehension for the future. In the south-west of England, in Devon and
Cornwall, however, there was resistance and rebellion, which helped to
bring down Protector Somerset. In Cornwall, the upheaval was associated
with the careerist archdeacon of Cornwall, William Body. He was clearly
very unpopular as he strove to enforce the Edwardian edicts and the Act
dissolving the chantries. In April 1548 he was set upon by a mob in
Helston and killed. The next year, there was even more trouble when the
Prayer Book was introduced on Whit Sunday. Led by men of gentry
status, the rebels drew up articles against the religious changes and
advanced into Devon.

Meanwhile, a separate uprising based on the same grievances had begun
in that county around Sampford Courtenay, and the rebels there
advanced to the regional capital, Exeter, and besieged the city. For a
period of some two months, the government – central and local – lost
control of the area. Somerset sent in **Lord Russell** and eventually, after
several skirmishes, the rebels were dispersed. Somerset was acutely aware
of the Cornish Rising of 1497, which had seen thousands of disgruntled
Cornishmen advance all the way to London to demand lower taxes.

Lord Russell was
John Russell, who
was later elevated
to the peerage as
Earl of Bedford.
His family largely
filled the gap left
by the destruction
of the Courtenay
family in 1538.

KEY TERM

Economic grievances are complaints about financial hardship. This may be caused by bad harvests and thus rising food prices, or by unusual demands for tax from local or central government.

KEY PERSON

John Dudley was the son of Edmund Dudley, executed in 1510. He was made Viscount Lisle in 1541 and became Earl of Warwick in 1547 as a reforming ally of Somerset. He helped to overthrow Somerset in 1549 and made himself Duke of Northumberland in 1551.

A portrait of John Dudley, Duke of Northumberland.

Causes of the rebellion. There is no doubt that the rebels of 1549 were fired up not by taxes but by religious changes. They disliked the Bible as well as the Prayer Book being in English. They demanded a Prayer Book in Cornish (the language was still widely spoken) and a return, in religion, to the last years of Henry VIII and especially the reinstatement of the Act of Six Articles. They believed that the new changes in religious practice were being introduced by a faction and that no such changes could be made until the new king reached maturity. The rebels put this at age twenty-four: in other words, some twelve years hence.

Economic grievances, of course, made an appearance in the rebels' articles once the rebellion had started. Somerset had introduced new taxes on goods, including a tax on sheep and a tax on the sale of woollen cloth. These would hit the common people hard, especially in Devon where there was much sheep farming. Rumours were soon fanning the flames, with claims that there would soon be taxes on pigs and geese and other animals. In some of the rebel articles, there are references to the lack of food and rising prices. Nonetheless, there is no doubt that the mainspring for the rising was religious conservatism.

Kett's Rebellion

Events of the rebellion. Kett's Rebellion broke out in East Anglia at the same time as the Western Rising. Like the far south-west, East Anglia had recently lost its aristocratic regional power-broker, who might have nipped conspiracy and rebellion in the bud. In East Anglia the Howard family had ruled supreme until the disaster of 1546. Now their power was largely eclipsed and no other great family had taken their place.

The rebellion was organised by Robert Kett and began with a few riots and some fence breaking in the Norfolk villages of Attleborough and Wymondham before spreading across the rest of Norfolk. Kett soon had a considerable force of well-organised men under his command just outside Norwich. This time the regional capital (unlike Exeter) fell to the rebels, apparently without violence. A government force under the Earl of Northampton was beaten back and the rebellion seemed to have been won the day.

However, Kett's initial success meant that a stronger army would soon be sent and a force some 6000 strong duly appeared, led by **John Dudley**, the recently ennobled Earl of Warwick. He was something of a soldier and, although he seemed willing to negotiate, his men were spoiling for a fight. Kett's forces were destroyed at Mousehold Heath just outside Norwich. The rebellion came to a traumatic end.

Causes of the rebellion. Concerns about religious change which were so important in the Western Rebellion were absent from Kett's complaint.

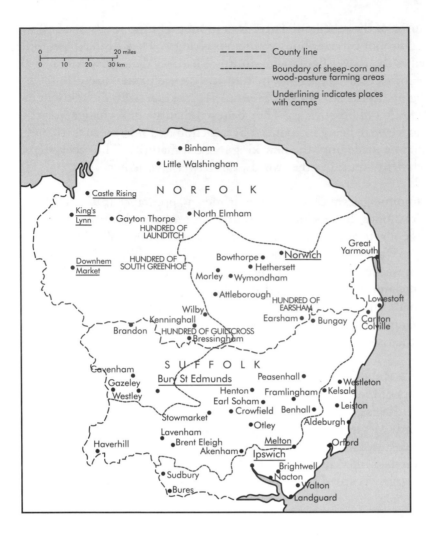

Kett's Rebellion.

Robert Kett was of minor gentry status and the rebellion that he led was directed partly against the **enclosure of common land** on the part of improving landowners.

The overthrow of Somerset

By the autumn of 1549, the Protector's power seemed to be waning. The man who had seized power by a *coup d'état* (by force) two years earlier was now brought down by the same means. Henrician-style faction fighting was back with a vengeance, but there was no King Henry to moderate the outcome. The rebellions in the summer had done much to undermine confidence in Somerset and many of the Councillors had always resented his assumption of the title of Protector. They were not really consulted about matters of policy and the more conservative ones resented the destruction of Henry VIII's national Catholicism.

KEY ISSUE

Enclosure of common land. Landlords who decided to introduce sheep on to their land needed extensive fields for grazing. Thus they often took over common land. Wolsey had taken measures against such enclosures, but the practice continued.

The **Tower of London** or White Tower was originally built by William the Conqueror. It was a royal residence as well as the most secure gaol in the country.

Princess Mary (1516–58) was the daughter of Henry VIII and Catherine of Aragon. According to Henry VIII's last Succession Act, she was Edward VI's heir. She became queen after his death.

Somerset sent to the Tower. It was a group of these same conservatives, led by the Earls of Arundel and Southampton, who now saw their chance to reverse the recent changes by overthrowing Somerset. However, they needed to win over the Earl of Warwick, who had now emerged as the 'strong man' of the regime. Although his religious sympathies lay with the reformers, he was persuaded that the Protector was doomed. The marvellous thing about the coup was that it was bloodless. Somerset negotiated with his enemies and, realising that he had forfeited the confidence of the leading Councillors, agreed to go, provided that his life and lands were spared. He was lodged in the **Tower** on 14 October 1549 and the office of Protector was abolished. The overthrow of Somerset shows that the forces opposed to religious reform were still powerful.

Princess Mary. Many of the plotters hoped that Edward's elder sister, **Princess Mary**, might now be persuaded to become regent. She was in her early thirties and, true to her mother, Catherine of Aragon, a devoted Catholic. With her as regent, the Henrician Settlement of the 1540s could be revived and consolidated. More importantly for the future, this arrangement, which might last for six years until Edward came of age, would allow the king to be 're-educated' in more conservative religious opinions. Sadly for the conservatives, their hopes were dashed when Mary refused the offer.

The emergence of Warwick

Execution of Somerset. After the removal of Somerset, the faction fighting continued. The victors were jealous of each other and worried about the former Protector. As a result of a variety of plots, Somerset was actually released and appeared at court, only to be arrested again a few months later. He was put on trial late in 1551 and executed early in 1552. The trial had all the hallmarks of a Cromwell-style rigged trial, engineered by Warwick as a pre-emptive strike against his former ally.

Warwick becomes Lord President of the Council. Warwick, like Somerset before him, now elevated himself to the top rank of the peerage with the title Duke of Northumberland. By early 1552 his power was secure, even though he wisely resisted the temptation to make himself Protector. Instead, he settled for the title of Lord President of the Council, which sounded rather more humble and democratic. During the faction fighting of late 1549 to early 1552, the conservatives had lost out, and Northumberland had been able to ditch them while filling the Council with men of more reforming spirit. At the same time, young King Edward began to appear at Council meetings, perhaps to reinforce the reforming stance of the re-formed Council.

HOW IMPORTANT WERE THE RELIGIOUS CHANGES UNDER NORTHUMBERLAND?

In the period 1550–3, further reforming moves were made which established the English Church, officially at least, as more firmly Protestant than ever before. The influence of Cranmer was of paramount importance here. He was a valued ally of Northumberland and a man trusted by the young king, just as he had been trusted by the old king. He was a great survivor because he tended to remain aloof from faction fighting at court and in the Council. This also meant that both Somerset and Northumberland saw him as a man who could be relied on to toe the line. As a reformer, however, he was cautious and slow-moving.

Ordination of priests

In 1550, Cranmer brought in a new Ordinal. This document set out the order of service for the ordination of new priests. The actual ceremony was traditional enough, but the new Ordinal stressed the ordinand's preaching function instead of his function in carrying out rituals and ceremonies. In the past, budding priests had been asked to 'receive authority to offer sacrifice and to celebrate Mass both for the living and the dead'. Now, by contrast, the new minister was given a Bible and told, 'Take thou authority to preach the Word of God and to minister the holy sacraments in the congregation.' The sacraments had not disappeared, of course, but they had been relegated in importance, and the dead, along with the idea of **Purgatory**, were not mentioned.

Reform among the clergy

Removal of conservative bishops. At the same time, a number of conservative bishops were deprived of their sees. Nicholas Heath of Worcester lost his for opposing the new Ordinal. Gardiner, who approved of the Prayer Book of 1549 and hoped for early release from the Tower, was deprived of his see of Winchester in February 1551. Day of Chichester and Tunstall of Durham were the other casualties of the purge.

Communion tables. Meanwhile, more evangelical bishops were introducing their own reforms in their own sees. Most notable was the work of Nicholas Ridley, Bishop of London, who ordered that all altars should now become Communion tables. The altars were moved from the east end of the church, rotated through 90 degrees and placed lengthways in the nave (or main body) of the church. In some cases, the stone altar was destroyed and a new wooden table used.

The doctrinal implications of this move were clear. An altar signified sacrifice and thus implied transubstantiation. In the traditional Mass, the Body of Christ was really present and was being sacrificed afresh on the

KEY TERM

Purgatory, according to the Catholic Church, was a place reserved for the souls of the dead while their sins were washed away to prepare them for Heaven.

altar, under the forms of bread and wine. This was underscored by the position of the altar at the east end of the church. Here it was removed from the congregation in an area reserved for the clergy. By placing it in the nave of the church and calling it a table, reforming clergy were showing support for Protestant ideas about a purely spiritual presence or, indeed, among more radical Protestants, no presence of Christ at all.

Relations with European Protestants

The period of Northumberland's ascendancy also saw more Protestant propaganda and the arrival of a leading continental reformer, Martin Bucer from Strasbourg, who was given the Regius Professorship of Divinity at Cambridge. So England was becoming more friendly towards Europe and more clearly part of a European Protestant movement.

The Prayer Book of 1552

The culmination of the Protestant Reformation of Edward's reign came with the Prayer Book of 1552 and the 42 Articles of Religion of 1553. The new Prayer Book made the moving of altars official policy. Traditional colourful **vestments** worn by priests were now replaced with a plain surplice (white church gown). Doctrinally, the most important change was, once again, in the Eucharist. Instead of being given 'the Body of our Lord Jesus Christ', which had annoyed so many reformers and reassured conservatives in 1549, by 1552 the congregation was invited to 'take and eat this in remembrance that Christ died for thee and feed on him in thy heart with thanksgiving'. While still ambiguous, this was a clear move away from transubstantiation towards a memorialist view, where Christ's body was not actually present, but was represented by the bread and wine. The renaming of the ceremony as the Lord's Supper also heartened reformers.

Limitations of the new Prayer Book. The new Prayer Book did not repeal its predecessor. It did not come into force until November 1552, so it is not clear how many parishes actually made use of it before Edward's death seven months later. Despite the links established with continental reformers, the Prayer Book was decidedly insular – it proclaimed that it was a Prayer Book for England only. Finally, it was introduced via Parliament and was never put before **Convocation**.

There was then a major row between the reformers while the book was at the printers. Knox and Hooper put pressure on Northumberland and the Council to abolish kneeling for communicants during the Lord's Supper. As a result, Cranmer was forced, very reluctantly, to insert the now famous 'Black Rubric' into the book, which enforced kneeling, but proclaimed that this was done for seemly order and did not imply superstitious reverence for the bread and wine.

KEY TERMS

Vestments were the official clothes worn by the clergy as they performed their sacred duties. Traditional vestments were colourful, stressing the priest's special power and position. Many Protestant clergy preferred to dress in plain black and white garments. John Hooper annoyed Cranmer by refusing to wear the traditional vestments for his enthronement as Bishop of Gloucester.

Convocation was the Church's Parliament. It consisted of Southern and Northern Convocation, led by the Archbishops of Canterbury and York respectively.

The 42 Articles

After the Ten Articles of 1536 and the Six Articles of 1539, the English Church now adopted a set of 42 Articles of Religion. Cranmer drew them up possibly because of concern that the maverick Bishop of Gloucester, Hooper, was drawing up his own set for use in his diocese. If no national set appeared, each see might have its own set according to the local bishop's taste. So Cranmer drew up his Articles and sent the final version for approval to the Council in November 1552.

Then nothing happened and the Articles were not submitted to Parliament in March 1553. Had Northumberland had enough of religious controversy or was he already concerned about Edward's health? In the end, the Articles were issued in June just a few weeks before the king's untimely death. In three key areas, the Articles were clearly Protestant.

Centrality of the Bible. Article 5 proclaimed the centrality of the Bible to matters of doctrine, ceremony and salvation:

Source 12

Holy Scripture containeth all things necessary to Salvation; for whatsoever is not read therein, nor may be proved thereby, although sometimes it may be admitted by God's faithful People as pious, and conducing unto order and decency; yet is not to be required of any Man that it should be believed as an article of Faith, or be thought requisite or necessary to salvation.

Justification. In terms of justification (the attaining of salvation), Article 11 gave a clearly Lutheran definition:

Source 13

Justification by Faith only in Jesus Christ, in that sense wherein it is set forth in the Homily of Justification, is the most certain and wholesome Doctrine for a Christian Man.

Just to make the point even more clearly, Article 12 told the faithful that works done 'before the Grace of Christ' were 'not pleasant to God'. Although this phrasing was not very clear, the gist was unmistakable – good works were no more.

Predestination. Article 17 gave the English people their first official encounter with the terrifying doctrine of Predestination:

Source 14

Predestination unto Life, is the everlasting purpose of God, whereby (before the foundations of the world were laid) he hath constantly decreed by his Counsel, secret unto us, to deliver from Curse and Damnation, those whom he hath chosen out of Man-kind, and to bring them by Christ to everlasting salvation.

Belief in Predestination was implicit in Luther and was more clearly expounded by Calvin in Geneva. Not only could mankind not hope to achieve salvation by doing good works, but God had already chosen those who would be saved. By extension, of course, God had also chosen the many who would be damned for all eternity and for whom there was, apparently, no escape.

Lay control of the Church

One of the main features of the religious changes after 1532 was the increasing power of the laity in Church affairs which mirrored the king's position as Supreme Head. The Church was now to be more firmly under lay or secular control. The taking of wine as well as bread by the laity was a symbol of the Protestant view that laymen and clergy were not separate orders of men. Article 20 of the 42 Articles reinforced the point: 'The Visible Church of Christ, is a congregation of faithful Men, in which the pure Word of God is preached.'

The same concern that the Church should not be independent of the State and laymen may explain the refusal of the Council to sanction Cranmer's attempt to revise canon law (the laws drawn up and enforced by the Church). Much of canon law had become outdated when Henry VIII established his Supremacy. Now the Council was unwilling to promote a new set of canon law that would give the Church greater freedom from lay control. After all, one of the most important reasons for lay support of the Reformation was that changes to religious belief and practice might line lay pockets.

Confiscation of Church property

In Edward's reign, the government moved to confiscate much of the remaining Church plate and jewels, and a large part of the proceeds ended up in the pockets of the commissioners, rather than supporting spiritual causes such as education or preaching. It was a similar story with the bishoprics. When John Ponet, a reformer, succeeded Gardiner as Bishop of Winchester, he was given a salary of £1300 per annum. His predecessor, by contrast, had enjoyed £3000 a year from the lands and other sources of revenue attached to the see. Well might the historian W. G. Hoskins entitle his book on the economic and social impact of the English Reformation *The Age of Plunder*.

FOREIGN POLICY 1549–53 AND THE DEATH OF THE KING

Relations with the Emperor

Religious policy during Edward's reign, as in his father's reign, was influenced by the situation abroad which, from a Protestant point of view, appeared rather threatening. Somerset counted on hostility from France and Scotland, so he had sought friendship with the Holy Roman Emperor. But the Catholic Emperor was not likely to be England's ally, especially as he had finally managed to crush the German Protestant League at the Battle of Muhlberg in the spring of 1547, just a few months into Edward's reign.

The cautious note in Somerset's religious policy was due partly to his fear of war with France and his fear of losing the Emperor's friendship. The Emperor was still Princess Mary's cousin and saw himself as her protector in difficult times. If he became really annoyed, he might encourage Mary to lead a coup perhaps to establish herself as regent or Protector in order to bring back the true religion.

Relations with France

Meanwhile, Somerset had trouble with the French. They declared war on England in August 1549, hoping to take advantage of internal unrest and dissension. Coligny, the French commander, quickly took the pale (area) around the city of Boulogne and laid siege to the port itself. By 1550, the English had had enough and negotiated the handover of Boulogne to the French in return for £100,000. Once this was done, the way was clear for an improvement in Anglo-French relations. King Edward was betrothed (engaged but not married) to a French princess and relations further improved when the English withdrew Somerset's expensive and unpopular garrisons from Scotland.

Isolationism

Overall, Northumberland's policy, unlike Somerset's, became **isolationist**. He was on reasonable terms with both Henry II of France and the German Emperor. When war broke out between them in September 1551, England refused to help either side, despite the Emperor's demands that it should honour the treaty made between the Emperor and England in the later part of Henry VIII's reign.

Armed with renewed conflict between the Emperor and France, Northumberland could afford to pursue a more radical religious policy. Nevertheless, he and the Council were realistic enough to see that, when the two great powers made peace, England might be the object of joint invasion. As we have seen, religious reforms did not proceed as quickly as Cranmer and Hooper would have liked and the uncertain situation abroad contributed to that caution.

Death of King Edward

In fact, it was internal developments that would blow the Edwardian Reformation off course. That Reformation had survived the death of Somerset and conservative attempts to take control, but it could not survive the death of Edward VI. The boy had never enjoyed robust good health and in 1552 he contracted measles and smallpox. By January 1553 he was in a serious condition, probably caused by acute pulmonary tuberculosis. By the end of May a young medical student wrote that 'the sputum which he brings up is livid, black, fetid and full of carbon; it smells beyond measure. His feet are swollen all over. To the doctors these things portend death.'

England's Protestant Reformation depended entirely on the life of the king, but his power to bring about decisive moves towards doctrinal Protestantism was hampered by his age, the limited authority of Somerset and Northumberland as well as the divisions within English Protestantism. His sister Mary would destroy that Reformation and bring England back to full papal obedience. The faltering and cautious Protestant Reformation would now be undone and England would experience Catholic Reformation instead.

HOW PROTESTANT WAS ENGLAND WHEN EDWARD VI DIED?

Factors indicating that England was not fully Protestant

- In 1547 the English Church was essentially Catholic in doctrine and ceremonies, although it was governed by the king not the Pope.
- By 1547 one estimate suggests that only 20 per cent of Londoners were Protestant.
- Religious changes under Edward were gradual – Cranmer was cautious.
- Hostility to reform from Catholic powers abroad encouraged limited reform.
- More radical changes – the Second Prayer Book and 42 Articles – were not in force for very long.
- Opposition to religious change in the Western Rebellion has implications for religious allegiance outside London and the south-east.
- Conservatives were still powerful – Princess Mary was heir to the throne and conservatives helped to overthrow Somerset.
- Somerset and Northumberland were not as powerful as Henry VIII. Both were overthrown. Neither was a committed Protestant.

Factors indicating that England was Protestant

- Edward VI, Cranmer, Somerset and Northumberland were all Protestants.
- England was not fully Catholic because of the break with Rome.

- There were many changes in religion during the reign of Edward, making England officially Protestant in terms of doctrine.
- Religious changes in Edward's reign were building on foundations of reform stretching back to 1533.
- There were English Bibles in every parish church.
- After 1540, in many parishes, less money was being spent on Church goods.
- Chantries had been abolished.

SECTION 4

1553–8: How effectively did Queen Mary restore the Catholic Church in England?

ARGUMENT

The Jesuits (or Society of Jesus) were founded by a Spaniard, Ignatius Loyola. The Society's initial aim was to work with the poor and needy, but with its military-style organization and dedicated personnel, it came to spearhead the Catholic fightback against the spread of Protestant heresy.

The Inquisition. The first Catholic Inquisition was developed in Spain in the late fifteenth century to ensure that Muslims who had been forcibly converted to Christianity did not revert to their old faith. Later the Papacy established a Roman Inquisition. These institutions achieved a reputation for brutality.

In the past, historians like Elton and Dickens have tended to dismiss Mary's brief reign as a failure – a hopeless and destructive reactionary twist, in a tale that would see the inevitable triumph of Protestantism during the reign of her half-sister and successor Elizabeth. The argument runs that Protestantism was so well established by the time of Mary's accession that it was impossible (and therefore foolish) for her to try to turn the clock back. All over Europe, Catholicism was being trampled underfoot, so why did Mary try to stop the march of Protestant triumph?

In fact, this view is very much a distortion of events – the product of Protestant hindsight. Seen from the viewpoint of her own day, Mary's reign was a triumph. She easily quashed an attempt to prevent her accession; she easily restored Catholic beliefs and Catholic rituals to English churches; and she even brought back the papal headship of the English Church, rejected by Henry VIII nineteen years earlier. Reginald Pole, who might have led the rebels in the Pilgrimage of Grace, now arrived in triumph as the new Archbishop of Canterbury to oversee the revolution.

In addition, Mary's Catholic Reformation was genuinely popular in many quarters and encountered very little open opposition. Leading Protestants saw Mary's accession as God's judgment on their failures and either acquiesced in the new religious settlement or fled abroad. Only four bishops – Cranmer, Latimer, Ridley and Hooper, who refused to give way – were eventually burnt at the stake. Furthermore, the Marian regime avoided some of the harsher methods adopted by its continental counterparts. The **Jesuits**, for example, were not invited to the party even though they offered their services, and there was no **Inquisition** on the Spanish or Roman models.

There was, it is true, increasing persecution of persistent heretics, especially in the south-east, but these were often lesser men (and women) and, with more time, this persecution might have achieved its objective of largely stamping out heresy and heretical groups. After Luther's protest, no country in northern Europe could hope to achieve complete religious uniformity, so we should not criticise Mary's regime for failing to wipe out Protestantism. It could not achieve the unobtainable.

OVERVIEW OF THE REIGN

Overall, this was a very English Counter-Reformation accompanied by very little violence. Other parts of Europe would suffer years of religious wars during the second half of the sixteenth century – not so England. The people of England knew that Mary would bring back the old ways and the vast majority acquiesced with varying degrees of enthusiasm.

Mary's marriage to Prince Philip of Spain was not wildly popular, but a small-scale rebellion against it (Wyatt's Rebellion of 1554) was crushed and the marriage contract made it clear that Philip and his servants would not be able to exercise power in England. One major potential benefit of the marriage was the stipulation that any child born to Mary and Philip would inherit the Low Countries (owned by Spain at this time) as well as England.

In the end, and in the longer term, Mary's triumph was short-lived because she reigned for only five years, she had no child and she was succeeded by Anne Boleyn's daughter. To blame her for any of these eventualities is to read history backwards and would clearly be unfair, although this didn't stop one historian from claiming, rather unkindly, that 'sterility was the hall mark of the reign'. In truth, success outweighed failure and that success shows us a great deal about the limited impact of Protestantism on the English people and the English Church by the time of Mary's accession.

This lack of progress was entirely consistent with a Church of England that had been born out of the Aragonese divorce and sustained or constrained by the government in power rather than by a great religious leader. Thomas Cranmer was a royal servant not an English version of Luther, **Zwingli** or **Calvin**. Mary's triumph shows that the term 'English Reformation' is rather misleading. It was certainly English, but not much of a Reformation.

Zwingli and **Calvin** were more radical than Luther and spread their different versions of the Protestant Reformation from Zurich and Geneva respectively. In estimating the success of the Catholic Counter-Reformation, it is important to remember the weaknesses of divided Protestantism.

MARY'S ACCESSION 1553

The attempt to stop Mary's accession

By the summer of 1553, it was clear to all, not least to the Duke of Northumberland, that young King Edward – only sixteen years old – was not long for this world. Faced with the prospect of the accession of Catherine of Aragon's very Catholic daughter, who was living in East

Anglia at the time, Northumberland could either open negotiations to try to salvage something of his power or offer the realm a radical but Protestant alternative.

Lady Jane Grey proclaimed queen. Northumberland chose the latter course and, when Edward died, proclaimed Lady Jane Grey as the new queen. She was Henry VIII's great-niece, being the granddaughter of his younger sister Mary and, as luck would have it, a Protestant (see the family tree below). Also in her favour was that she had been married to Northumberland's son, young Guildford Dudley, and had been adopted by Edward VI as his heir in 1553.

Henry VIII's Succession Act. Given Henry VIII's complicated matrimonial life, it had become accepted that a king could clarify the succession to the throne via parliamentary statute. Henry's last Succession Act was passed in 1543. This Act declared that, if Edward died childless, his elder half-sister Mary should succeed him. The Act also allowed Henry to state in his will who would succeed to the throne if all of his children died childless – as, in fact, they did. He chose the heirs of his younger sister Mary, rather than those of his elder sister Margaret. This provision was famously ignored when Queen Elizabeth died in 1603. She should have been succeeded not by James VI of Scotland – great-grandson of Margaret Tudor – but by the heirs of Lady Jane Grey.

Why did Lady Jane Grey fail to hold on to the Crown?
Arguments in her favour. Northumberland's attempt to speed up the Grey succession did not have parliamentary backing, but it did have the undoubted support of the current monarch and one might have thought that his will would overcome that of his father. In addition, Edward and Northumberland were offering the nation a continuation of Protestantism, rather than a return to Catholicism – surely this would prove popular with the political nation. By contrast, the accession of Mary would undoubtedly stop Protestantism in its tracks and bring back the old ways. Many an old score might now be settled and the realm might dissolve into religious civil war, with the Protestant south and east fighting a Catholic north and west.

The Tudor family tree.

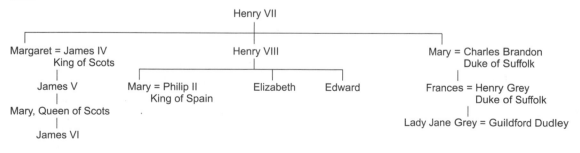

A portrait of Mary, aged 28, painted in 1544 by Master John.

Arguments against her. In the event, very few people supported the Grey option. Mary declared herself queen when Edward died, marshalled her supporters and moved in triumph towards London. The unfortunate Lady Jane Grey lasted only nine days as queen, while the majority of the nobility and gentry, sensing the way things were going, flocked to Mary to pronounce their loyalty to the new regime. Faced with the choice between Catholic and Protestant and between legitimate heir and unwitting pretender, the English **political nation** chose Catholic and legitimate.

Executions. Northumberland, Lady Jane and Guildford Dudley were all executed, but the killing stopped there. Mary hoped to spare Lady Jane but realised that, despite her youth and innocence, she would always represent a threat to the regime. The innocent victim of political intrigue might become an innocent victim of intrigue once again. Mary's

KEY CONCEPT

The **political nation** is a term often used by historians to describe those people who exercised political power in central and local government.

accession was a triumph. Leading Protestants scattered in disarray at the sign of divine displeasure.

What were Mary's aims?

The complete restoration of the Old Church, Catholic ritual and the papal headship was Mary's most cherished desire. Her father had broken with Rome in order to divorce her mother; now Mary would bring back the old order. Mary had remained defiantly Catholic throughout her years of torment. During her father's reign, she had suffered imprisonment and been kept away from her mother. She had even been forced to attend on Anne Boleyn's daughter Elizabeth when the latter was a baby. Although brought back to court in the later years of her father's reign, she was seen as too much of a threat to be married at home or abroad, and she was probably involved in clandestine correspondence with her cousin, the **Emperor Charles V**.

KEY PERSON

Emperor Charles V was Catherine of Aragon's nephew and therefore Queen Mary's cousin.

During Edward's reign, she was imprisoned or placed under house arrest and had to witness the Protestant (she would have said heretical) direction of religious legislation. The early death of Edward and the lamentable fiasco of the Lady Jane Grey affair convinced her, as it convinced the Protestants, that God was once again intervening decisively in the affairs of men. After so much suffering, illness and emotional trauma, all of which might explain her subsequent infertility, Mary was given the chance, as she saw it, to put things to rights and this she proceeded to do.

HOW DID MARY CARRY THROUGH HER RELIGIOUS CHANGES SO SUCCESSFULLY?

Three key features of the change back to Catholicism explain the success of the Marian Restoration: first, she acted without undue speed; second, she acted with the freely given consent of Parliament; and third, especially in the first few years, the regime was not unduly vengeful towards its Protestant enemies.

Repeal of Protestant laws

Mary entered London to take the throne in July 1553, the same month as Edward's demise. In October of that year, Parliament met and duly passed a Statute of Repeal. This statute repealed the Act of Uniformity of the previous year and proclaimed that all divine services and administration of sacraments should be as they had been in the last year of Henry VIII's reign, less than seven years before. This again underlines the Catholic nature of the Church of England after the Act of Six Articles of 1539.

Several reforming bishops had been arrested before the parliamentary session began, which helped to remove potential opposition from the House of Lords. Hence the Act was passed easily. However, an attempt to impose penalties upon those who did not attend church services was defeated and there was no early return of laws against heresy.

England reunited with Rome

The next phase, the return of the papal headship over the Church in England, was potentially more controversial, but it was successfully carried through by Mary. Cardinal Reginald Pole, declared a traitor at the time of the Exeter Conspiracy and then coming within two votes of becoming Pope, was empowered by Pope Julius III to bring England back to Rome. The Reformation had begun with the fall of Cardinal Wolsey; it was ended with the triumph of Cardinal Pole. He arrived in November 1554, over a year after Mary's accession, and pronounced a solemn absolution upon the realm. Amid a public reaction that appears to have been euphoric and enthusiastic, England was brought back to papal obedience after twenty years in the wilderness of heresy.

Although Mary's counsellors were divided on the timing of the reconciliation with Rome, they were not divided on the fact of restoration. So by 1555, Mary had successfully brought back the Church of 1529. However, she was forced to recognise that monasteries and monastic lands would not return. As with laws to enforce church attendance, Mary moderated her demands in the face of opposition.

England's Erastian Church

Although Mary had thus given up the Royal Supremacy established by her father, in fact the monarch and Parliament retained extensive powers over the Church. The Pope remained a distant and essentially spiritual head of the English Church. In 1557, for example, the new violently anti-Spanish Pope, Paul IV, stripped Pole of his legateship and demanded that he return to Rome to answer charges of heresy. Pole ignored this request and continued his work as Archbishop of Canterbury. The Pope sent a new legate to England, but Mary refused to allow him into the country. The Pope accused Pole of heresy; Mary replied that as an Englishman he could not face charges in Rome. The powerlessness of the Papacy over the Church in England had once again been demonstrated. In this sense, Mary did restore the old English Church, not a new Papal Church.

Bishops and other clergy were still appointed by the Crown, and the destruction of the monasteries meant that the laity continued to control many aspects of Church life at the local level. The Reformation had not invented the process of lay control, but it had speeded it up and the Marian restoration did little to halt the process. The Marian Counter-Reformation was successful because the gentry and landowners, represented in Parliament – the political nation, if you like – approved of it.

Index of prohibited books

The Counter-Reformation was also successful because, despite the burning of nearly 300 Protestant heretics, it was not, on the whole, extreme or unduly Spanish-looking. An **Index** of prohibited books was introduced in June 1555 and three years later the Council proclaimed the death penalty for those who possessed forbidden books, but few people were prosecuted and many of those convicted were treated leniently.

Persecution of Protestant clergy

The existing Protestant clergy were not pursued or persecuted with undue vigour. The twenty-one English and Welsh bishops at the outset of the Reformation had grown to twenty-six by 1553. Of these bishops, only seven had been deprived by March of 1554, four of them on the pretext that they had married. Cranmer, the Archbishop of Canterbury, was put in the Tower in September 1553 for offering publicly to defend the Mass as established in the second Edwardian Prayer Book.

Only four bishops suffered martyrdom for their faith – Hooper of Gloucester, Latimer of Worcester, Ridley of London and Cranmer himself. They were not all executed at the same time, however. Hooper went in February 1555, in Gloucester, Latimer and Ridley died together in Oxford in October of that year, while Cranmer was not executed until March 1556, having been deprived of his position in December 1555, when he was replaced by Pole.

The clergy conform

It is crucial to realise that the majority of the Edwardian bishops – men who had supported the Protestant innovations of Edward's last months – conformed to the new regime. In March 1554, the bishops were told to enforce all religious legislation of the last year of Henry VIII. This meant the return of Latin in services. The reaction, once again, was one of conformity.

What was true of most bishops was equally true of the lesser clergy. In all, about 800 beneficed clergy were deprived of their livings. The sees of London and Norwich saw some 25 per cent of their clergy deprived. However, the vast majority of such deprivations occurred because the clergy concerned were married, not because they objected to the return of the old ways. Many of them got their livings back by promising to put away their wives. In Norwich, all but 40 of the 243 lesser clergy initially deprived got their livings back.

KEY TERM

The **Index** was a list of heretical books, introduced by the Pope to warn Catholics against reading them. Catholics found in possession of such works could be accused of heresy.

Return of Catholic ornaments

Furthermore, there is clear evidence of enthusiasm for the return of the old order. In some parishes, church ornaments that had disappeared at the time of the Henrician and Edwardian reforms now reappeared. In many cases, this was because good Catholics had decided to hide them away and wait for better times, rather than lose them to grasping reformers. There were some Protestant iconoclasts, of course, who wished to destroy images and idolatry, but there were also many good Catholics who sought to preserve the time-honoured accoutrements of their faith. Often men who had bought church ornaments now sold them back to the church. Thomas Season in Ludlow and John Ray in Warwick are examples of such men.

The reforms of Pole

As Catholic decoration returned, Pole also set up seminaries in every diocese to educate and train new clergy. The numbers who came forward to be trained were rather greater under Mary than in the early years of Elizabeth I, when Protestantism returned. Pole and Mary usefully ignored offers of help from the Jesuits, showing that they did not want to be associated with a violent and foreign brand of Catholicism.

In the same way, there were hopes of sponsoring a Catholic translation of the Bible and a Catholic version of the English Prayer Book. However, the ending of Pole's legatine commission interrupted such hopes. Pole was not perhaps an inspiring leader of the Church in England, but he was a dying man and was Archbishop for less than three years. He was also an English gentleman and a moderate Catholic reformer.

WHY DID OPPOSITION TO THE MARIAN REFORMS FAIL TO CHANGE HER POLICIES?

The burning of Protestants

The area of religious policy under Mary that has received most criticism is the burning of some 224 Protestants, most of them laymen, during the period February 1555 to November 1558. This was certainly un-English. Religious persecution on this scale had not been seen before. Nonetheless the persecution must be kept in perspective. It represents five executions per month in a 44-month period, mainly of lesser men or 'mechanics' and concentrated very much in the sees of Norwich and London. Much of England would have seen no burnings at all.

Certainly the executions eventually became counterproductive, but this is partly because the next regime (Mary was succeeded by her Protestant half-sister, Elizabeth) was Protestant and **John Foxe**'s *Book of Martyrs*, giving detailed and often exaggerated accounts of the burnings, became a

bestseller. At the time of the burnings, there was no indication that the persecution would produce a Protestant rebellion. Most of the leading English Protestants, like Foxe himself, had fled abroad, and in England those who opposed the return of the old ways remained silent and submissive.

The Spanish marriage

Arguments in favour. Mary has often been criticised for her marriage to the future Philip II of Spain, but such criticism is unfair for several reasons.

- It was perfectly natural, indeed desirable, for her to marry a Spaniard. Her mother was Spanish, her cousin Charles V, a constant support in times of trouble, was King of Spain, and Philip was his son.
- Spain, which controlled the Low Countries, England's vital trading partners across the Channel, had been England's normal ally against France since the Treaty of Medina del Campo during the reign of Henry VII. Even during the reign of Mary's father, when Catherine of Aragon and Spain had been out of favour, there had been only a brief period of friendship with France.
- Mary's advisers ensured that Philip, even as Mary's husband, would exercise no real power in England. In the marriage treaty, Philip was bound to uphold the laws of England, could promote no aliens to English office, could not remove the queen from the realm and had no executive powers in his own right.
- Most attractively for the English, the Spanish conceded that any child born to Mary and Philip would inherit the Low Countries as well as England, thus creating a secure and extensive land empire on the Continent.

The marriage problem. The problem with the marriage was not that it happened, but that it produced no heir. Philip was in England for thirteen months and although Mary believed herself to be pregnant on more than one occasion, she was wrong. The dream of a Catholic heir, and with it the dream of a long-term Catholic restoration in England, was dashed, probably as a result of the prolonged ill-health that Mary had endured since her parents' protracted divorce rocked Europe. In these circumstances, it is to Mary's credit that she resisted attempts to put her half-sister and heir Elizabeth to death, even though she was a known Protestant sympathiser. When Mary died there would be no Catholic version of Lady Jane Grey.

Wyatt's Rebellion 1554

The Spanish marriage did, however, help to spark off the only rebellion of the reign, led by the Kentish gentleman Sir Thomas Wyatt. The marriage of a reigning English queen was a new problem, of course, and

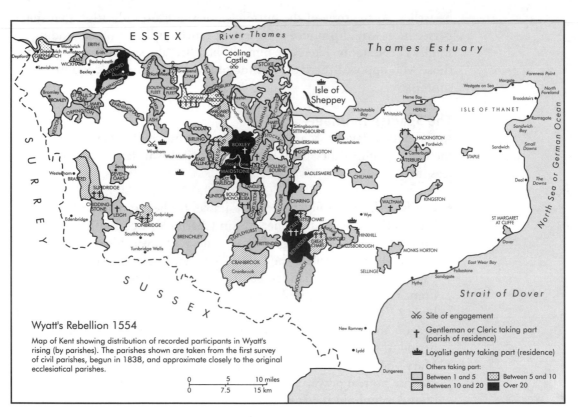

Wyatt's Rebellion 1554

Map of Kent showing distribution of recorded participants in Wyatt's rising (by parishes). The parishes shown are taken from the first survey of civil parishes, begun in 1838, and approximate closely to the original ecclesiastical parishes.

✗ Site of engagement

† Gentleman or Cleric taking part (parish of residence)

♔ Loyalist gentry taking part (residence)

Others taking part:
Between 1 and 5
Between 5 and 10
Between 10 and 20
Over 20

there were bound to be many who were fearful of a Spanish takeover. The House of Commons had petitioned against the match, urging Mary to marry within the realm. Mary was outraged at this interference and she and her Council then announced her determination to marry Philip. Sir Thomas Wyatt, Sir James Croft, Sir Peter Carew and the Duke of Suffolk (Lady Jane Grey's father), with others, then conspired to co-ordinate a rising from different parts of the country, which would converge on London and depose Mary.

A new king? The idea was to depose Mary in favour of Edward Courtenay – son of the Marquis of Exeter, who had been executed after the so-called Exeter Conspiracy of 1538. As a candidate for the throne and, incidentally, an alternative candidate for Mary's hand in marriage, Courtenay had clear drawbacks. Aged only twenty-five, he had spent most of his life in the Tower and rumour had it that he was mentally unstable. His only claim to fame was that he was a great-grandson of Edward IV, who had died some seventy-one years before.

Of course, to rally support, Wyatt could not claim officially that he was attempting to depose the queen. Instead, he had to say that he was really trying to protect Mary from unwise counsel, and that he was not rebelling against the restoration of Catholicism, merely against the Spanish marriage. Thus the rebellion hinged on him playing the patriotic card against a supposed evil plot to allow the Spanish to rule England. Soon there were stories of shiploads of Spaniards arriving in early 1554 ahead of their prince and being secretly smuggled through Kent to the capital.

The failure of the rebellion. However, such anti-Spanish rumours did not bring about widespread support. The Spanish were not yet the national enemy that they would become by 1588 when Philip II sent the great Spanish Armada to invade England. Away from the south coast, the Spaniards excited very little hostility. Three of the four prongs of the rebellion were complete fiascos and Wyatt's march on London little better. News of the conspiracy leaked out in January 1554, so the conspirators had to act before they were ready and in the middle of winter. Croft failed to raise any troops in Herefordshire. The Duke of Suffolk found little support in Leicester, encountered outright hostility in Coventry and gave up without a fight. Carew in Devon soon realised he had no hope of taking Exeter and fled to Normandy. Wyatt alone managed to raise some troops in Kent and began a threatening march on London.

Mary had no standing army and found it hard to raise many troops on the spur of the moment. Nonetheless, her persuasive and defiant speech to Londoners, combined with loyal forces led by the **Earl of Pembroke** and the apparent indifference of the Londoners in the face of Wyatt's propaganda, led to Wyatt's retreat and capture. The rebellion was hardly worthy of the name: it had nothing of the power and scale of the Pilgrimage of Grace and its abject failure indicates that the Spanish marriage and the return of Catholicism were not widely unpopular.

The punishment of the rebels. Mary's Councillors decided to treat the rebellion as the débâcle it was, by meting out only limited punishment on the rebels. In all, 350 Kentish men were convicted of conspiracy and treason, but only thirty were executed, Wyatt himself going to the block in April 1554. The conspiracy spelt the end for Lady Jane Grey and Guildford Dudley as well as for Jane's father, the Duke of Suffolk. Courtenay and Princess Elizabeth were imprisoned briefly, but then allowed to go free. Future conspiracies, favoured by the French, would involve plans for their marriage and joint accession to the throne.

The limited appeal of the rising indicated that hard-line Protestantism or Puritanism, which in future would be such a desperate enemy of Catholicism, had not made any headway in England by 1554. Even Kent and London, later the storm centres of Puritan opinion, showed very little enthusiasm for the overthrow of the Catholic queen.

HOW SERIOUS A FAILURE WAS MARIAN FOREIGN POLICY?

The loss of Calais to France in 1558 is often seen as a fitting climax to a misguided and disastrous Marian foreign policy. 'From that day her regime was doomed' opined Geoffrey Elton. However, such a view is clearly exaggerated.

Reasons for war against France

After the fiasco of Wyatt's Rebellion, Mary proceeded to marry Philip of Spain. The marriage was celebrated in July 1554 amid great splendour and festivities. As a result of the marriage, English foreign policy was once again dominated by friendship with Spain and hostility to France. In January 1557, war broke out between France and Spain, and by this time, Mary's husband Philip was King of Spain and ruler of the Low Countries. The marriage treaty did not oblige England to help Spain in this conflict with France and the Privy Council was, at first, opposed to the idea of England's involvement in the war.

However, evidence of French plots to overthrow Mary tipped the balance. In April 1557 the French backed a rising against Mary led by Thomas Stafford. He landed in Scarborough with a few troops, declared Mary deposed and was easily captured. As a result, England declared war on Henry II. The Earl of Pembroke was sent to France with 7000 men. Unfortunately, they were too late for the main battle between the French and the Spanish, which saw the French routed outside the French town of St Quentin. But they arrived soon afterwards and played an important part in capturing the French town for Spain.

So far, so good. The English were on the winning side and the declaration of war on France had seen many disaffected Englishmen renew their loyalty to the government. Sir James Croft and Sir Peter Carew, pardoned after Wyatt's Rebellion, joined the war effort. The three surviving sons of the Duke of Northumberland, despite the execution of their father and brother, all fought at St Quentin. Meanwhile, the English made useful preparations to protect against an invasion from Scotland. As things turned out, feuding and heavy downpours of rain in Kelso wrecked the Scots' hopes of invasion.

Fall of Calais 1558

English celebrations at this successful foreign policy were seriously marred by the loss of Calais in January 1558. Attacking unexpectedly in mid-winter, the French force under the Duke of Guise gained some measure of revenge for the loss of St Quentin. This revenge was at the expense not of Spain, but of England, which lost its last foothold on the Continent. The Calais defences were in reasonable condition, but the English commander, Lord Wentworth, may not have taken the threat from the

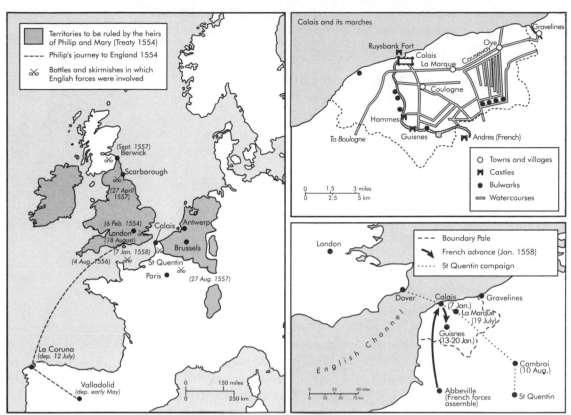

England and the Calais Pale during Mary's reign.

French too seriously and was unprepared for such an unexpected and unseasonal attack.

Although English pride was seriously dented, the loss of Calais was not a national disaster. In the event, English luck ran out, but English trade with the Continent was not seriously affected. Indeed, the loss of Calais may have stimulated trade by encouraging English merchants to trade with other continental ports. Nor was national security threatened by the loss, and the Exchequer was relieved of the enormous cost of financing three fortresses in the Calais Pale.

THE MARIAN ACHIEVEMENT – REFORMATION DEFEATED

The Catholic English Church restored

Despite the loss of Calais early in 1558, the Marian Settlement remained unchallenged. In many ways, the queen had restored, to a not unwilling nation, the Church of their ancestors and the traditional Catholic English Church. The papal headship was restored, but the power of the monarchy over the Church remained. Catholic ceremonies, rituals and ornaments all returned along with sensible Catholic reforms. Opposition to all of this was minimal and in many ways the Church in England had come full circle back to the days of the 1520s. As many good Catholics had hoped all along, God had returned the English Church to its true obedience.

The limited progress of English Protestantism

As we have seen, Protestantism had made only limited progress in England during the Reformation period and then only when allowed to by English governments. Henry VIII had introduced reforms reluctantly because of his divorce problem and only after a prolonged period of hoping for a papal solution. From 1539 to 1547, reforms were put on hold and Catholic doctrine was restored to the Church. Protestant reforms under Edward had been imposed only briefly, before they succumbed to the Marian reaction. In addition, English Protestantism had produced no great reforming leader like Luther in Germany or Calvin in Geneva.

Changed circumstances

On the other hand, of course, things could never be the same again. Although 1558 looks a lot like 1525, circumstances had greatly changed. Europe was now permanently divided by Protestant Reformations and would see religious wars on a terrifying scale over the next 100 years. Protestantism and Catholicism would develop radical wings that would denounce their religious opponents as unchristian and even demonic. In England, the monasteries would not return and the English Bible had now reached many more people, giving rise to serious disagreements over religion and allowing Protestantism to take root in some areas and among many of the nobility and gentry.

Nonetheless, the English people at all levels in society seemed unwilling or unable to countenance serious religious violence. Respect for government and a growing sense of English unity meant that the Church in England was the Church of England, run and directed by the monarch, aided by a reasonably compliant bench of bishops. Faced with religious controversy, most important people agreed with the government's policies.

Catholic reform

So it is clear that if Mary had lived longer, or had produced a Catholic heir, then the English Church would have remained Catholic for the foreseeable future. The various forms of English Protestantism would have remained, but English Protestants would have been powerless to mount a serious challenge to the English Catholic Church because it was and had always been English Catholic not Roman Catholic. Even in Mary's reign, it had proved impossible to denounce the Church Settlement as Spanish. As such, Mary triumphed in 1558 as she had in

1553 because she represented a Church that was still widely popular and that had not lost the ability to reform itself.

One of the greatest disservices of Protestant historiography to our understanding of the Reformation has been to link Protestants, and not Catholics, with the idea of reform. One of the greatest disservices of sixteenth-century Protestantism to European society was that it ensured that Catholic reform, when it came, would often become violent and reactionary, leading to the horrors of religious warfare. In England, however, Catholicism remained moderate and traditional, its clergy conservative and its appeal widespread and popular. One telling example of the strength of the Marian settlement was that when Elizabeth's Protestant religious settlement was passed in 1559, all but one of the Marian bishops resigned in protest. The Protestant Edwardian bishops did not do the same in 1553.

Queen Mary and Reginald Pole died within hours of each other in November 1558. Mary was only 42 years old. She and Pole had reinvented and reinvigorated the traditional Church of England. In the long term, England became a Protestant nation not because Catholicism was corrupt and unpopular, not because Protestantism was more truly Christian and appealing, but because Mary reigned for only five years, while Anne Boleyn's daughter reigned for nearly fifty.

SECTION 5

1547–58: Was there a mid-Tudor crisis during the reigns of Edward and Mary?

ARGUMENT FOR

Having looked at the reigns of Edward and Mary in previous chapters, it is easy to see why some historians have seen this period as constituting a crisis. W. R. D. Jones, writing in 1973, was the first to really outline a specific theory proposing the existence of such a crisis. In his book, *The Mid-Tudor Crisis, 1539–1563*, he extended the chronological limits of the proposed crisis beyond the reigns of Edward and Mary. He claimed that the reforming work of Cromwell in the 1530s, which had seen the creation of a stronger central government as a result of the Reformation under Henry VIII, had been undone in the 1540s and 1550s and this led to a 'crisis of governance'. At first glance the theory seems attractive:

- In the last years of Henry VIII, the country was ruled by an ageing and vindictive bully and faction fighting was rife.
- The crisis deepened during the extended royal minority which came after him.
- Faction got out of hand and there were five *coups d'état* in just six years: Somerset's accession in 1547; his fall in 1549; the accession of Northumberland in 1550; the accession of Lady Jane in 1553; and the accession of Mary just a few days later.
- Edward's reign had also seen extensive rioting and disorder and two full-scale rebellions in different parts of the country in the same year (1549).
- Added to this there was religious conflict as the unpopular Edwardian governments strove to impose radical Protestantism on the nation.
- Under Mary the situation was hardly any better. The first female ruler in English history turned out to be a misguided 'Spanish' queen, devoted to the Papacy in Rome. She married a Spanish prince (who would later send an Armada to invade England) and attempted to overthrow the new religious order which had just been established, an enterprise which was by this time clearly hopeless.
- There was a very serious and very patriotic rebellion in 1554 in Kent, when the regime teetered on the brink of destruction and subsequently, there was an inhuman and self-defeating policy of burning Protestants which only confirmed the alien nature of the regime.

- English foreign policy was dictated by Spain and Calais, the last English outpost on the Continent, was lost in a disastrous war with France.
- In addition, the whole period was overlaid by a series of bad harvests during 1549–51 and 1555–6 (the last being the worst in living memory) and there were terrible bouts of sickness and disease which may have carried off 20 per cent of the entire population between 1555 and 1560.
- On Mary's death, there was further religious confusion – and another female ruler – as Elizabeth struggled to impose yet another Protestant Settlement.

Taken together, heaped one upon another, this list of coups, changes and crises would seem to justify the use of the term mid-Tudor crisis.

While Jones has thus painted a bleak but quite compelling picture, one feels that he has achieved this by taking a long time-span and by focusing exclusively on the problems and conflicts and missing out the more positive aspects of the period. If one takes this approach to history, then many of the periods studied in this book could be seen as crises. There is no doubt too that Jones has been influenced by a longer historical tradition that has tended to be highly critical of government and governors of the realm between the death of one great Tudor, Henry VIII and the accession of another, Elizabeth I.

The work of earlier historians such as A. F. Pollard, who wrote *A History of England from the Accession of Edward VI to the death of Elizabeth*, and S. T. Bindoff in his *Tudor England* of 1950, saw the period as one of a series of crises set in a sea of sterility. Bindoff saw Somerset as a Good Duke, an unworldly and idealistic liberal who ended the tyranny of Henry VIII, conducted 'an experiment in liberty' and was brought down by wicked and grasping men, led by that 'bold, bad man' Northumberland. During what Bindoff describes as the 'Tudor Interregnum', the Duke was able to, 'indulge his ambition and practise his villainies at the expense of the kingdom'. His concluding remarks on Mary's reign are scarcely less gloomy. 'Politically bankrupt, spiritually impoverished, economically anarchic, and intellectually enervated, Marian England awaited the day of its deliverance.' Geoffrey Elton in his *England under the Tudors* (1955) and *Reform and Reformation* (1977) later joined the fray with ringing condemnations of Mary and all she stood for. So the idea of crisis and sterile interlude has had a long history.

More recently, however, revisionists have been at work who have dismantled and largely killed off the notion of the mid-Tudor crisis. Alan G. R. Smith in *The Emergence of a Nation State* (1984) claimed that the idea of applying the term to a twenty-year period 'obscures as much as it illuminates'. David Loades played down the idea of a crisis in his *The Mid-Tudor Crisis, 1545–65* (1992) and began to qualify the disapproval of Mary by claiming – in his book, *The Reign of Mary Tudor* (1979) – that although she failed in the long term, her regime had provided, 'a legacy of sound administration, financial reform and strengthened episcopacy'. Going rather further in pointing to the achievements of the mid-Tudor period, have been Jennifer Loach, Robert Tittler and Dale Hoak in *The Mid-Tudor Polity* (1980) and a number of other works.

It now seems clear that there was no mid-Tudor crisis. There was no civil war, no breakdown of central or local government, no threat of foreign invasion or take-over and no large-scale mortality crisis. Even if one opts for a less extreme definition of crisis, mid-Tudor England does not fit the bill. Ronald Hutton was surely right when he commented that, while historians of the middle decades can debate whether the people of England were Protestant or were Catholic, the fact of the matter was that they were governed. The reaction of most English people, most of the time, to the Reformations that they witnessed was acquiescence and conformity. The Tudor monarchy continued to be revered during this period. Central and local government remained strong and local government strove to implement the will of central government. Of course there was conflict at a variety of levels, as there always is in any society. The clear proof that mid-Tudor society was essentially strong and united is that there was no mid-Tudor crisis when there should have been one.

WHY THERE WAS NO MID-TUDOR CRISIS

THE SUCCESS OF CONCILIAR GOVERNMENT

Under Edward. During the reigns of Edward and Mary, monarchical government of the type exercised by Henry VII and Henry VIII seemed to be in abeyance. Edward was only a boy, who was not involved in the important decisions of his reign, while Mary is seen as rather remote from government, except for her clear objectives in religious policy. In this situation, the Royal Council, nurtured by Cromwell in the 1530s and tempered by the faction fighting of the 1540s became the centrepiece of effective government in mid-Tudor England.

The overthrow of Somerset, who tried to rule without the Council demonstrates its collective power. Paget's letter to Somerset in July 1549 made the point but his advice was ignored. Paget claimed that, 'every man of the Council mislikes your proceedings and wishes it otherwise.' Somerset had tried to rule autocratically as Lord Protector but when the failure of his policies at home and abroad became obvious in the autumn of 1549, it was the Council, for so long ignored, which stepped in to overthrow him.

Northumberland's decision to rule as Lord President of the Council, shows that he had learnt this lesson well. Whereas Somerset had pushed through only modest religious reform because the Council still contained powerful conservatives like Arundel, Tunstall, Rich and Brown, Northumberland could enact more radical reforms and secure his position, because he brought more reformers into the Council. During the period of intense faction fighting after Somerset's fall, Northumberland was under attack from Wriothesley and other conservatives. He secured his pre-eminence by getting friends appointed to Edward's Privy Chamber and, with their support, got Edward to agree to the appointment of four more reforming Councillors. These men then tipped the balance in favour of the reformers and Northumberland emerged as Lord President. Once in power, he realised that he could retain that power only by controlling the Council. He then assumed the King's power to appoint new Councillors and appointed twelve of his own men to the Council after February 1550.

Now secure, Northumberland revived conciliar government. As most of the Councillors were in favour of religious reform and as Northumberland realised that this would win favour with Edward, reform was duly delivered. Backed by the King and Council, the more radical reforms of the Second Prayer Book and the 42 Articles excited little opposition, unlike the more modest reforms under the autocratic Somerset.

Under Mary. It is often claimed that Mary's Council of some 43 members was unwieldy. However, at the instigation of the experienced Paget, the number of Councillors was cut in 1554 and a 'select Council' was established in 1555. Even when there were 43 Councillors, an inner circle of important men soon developed which made decisions and directed the others. Meanwhile the 'surplus' Councillors were often employed to link the Council to the shires. Each Councillor was expected to govern in his shire using the added prestige of his office and to report back to the Council in London. Improved communication between the centre and the shires had also been achieved under Northumberland. The Lord Lieutenants, appointed temporarily in certain shires during the troubled months of 1549, were now made permanent and given statutory authority in November of that year. One was appointed in every county and told to give political oversight and report back any matters of importance to the Council.

Improvements in royal finances. Another area of success for conciliar government under Northumberland and Mary was in rescuing royal finances from the mess created by Somerset. Between 1547 and 1549, the Protector had spent some £580,000 on warfare, together with £30,000 a year for the upkeep of Boulogne and the navy. He is also believed to have transferred some £20,000 worth of the Crown's landed income into private hands, some 40 per cent of it as gifts to win political support.

This extravagant expenditure came on top of the huge sums spent on warfare during the last five years of Henry VIII's reign, estimated at some £2,000,000. When Northumberland emerged triumphant in 1550, royal finances were almost in crisis and were not helped by another round of gifts and transfers as a result of Northumberland's coup. Royal debt now stood at some £300,000 with royal income only some £150,000 a year.

At first the new regime followed the bad old ways of the 'quick fix' by debasing the coinage in 1551, which did help to bring down the debt. At the same time, expenditure was cut by the ending of war with France and Scotland and more effective and successful strategies for the management of the royal finances were put into place. First, Northumberland established an excellent team of administrators to institute financial reform including William Cecil, Sir Walter Mildmay, Sir Thomas Gresham and William Paulet (Lord Treasurer 1550–72). They abandoned debasement and brought in a new coin issue in 1552, paving the way for the restoration of the coinage under Elizabeth. These men also brought in severe retrenchment on government expenditure, which was accompanied by stricter accounting methods and commissions to investigate negligently uncollected revenues. An attempt was also made to tackle the huge increase in fees and administrative costs paid by the government. One estimate suggests that the cost of running the Crown's financial departments alone ran to £17,500 a year in 1551, compared to half that in 1547 and there had been major financial scandals in the Exchequer, Mint and Court of Wards. One further measure indicating a more serious financial policy under Northumberland, was an emergency fund of £40,000 which was established within the royal Household. By these means, the Council acquired its own 'privy coffer' or private treasury and the whole overseas debt (mainly money borrowed on the Antwerp money market) was liquidated.

Finally, the Council established a Royal Commission which completed a survey of royal revenues, analysing faults in the five financial departments (Exchequer, Augmentations, First Fruits and Tenths, Court of Wards, and the Duchy of Lancaster). The end result was the amalgamation of Augmentations and First Fruits into the Exchequer and the emergence of an Exchequer which was much more responsive to government needs than its predecessor under Henry VII. Geoffrey Elton claimed that the Royal Commission was 'one of the more remarkable achievements of Tudor administration'. By the end of Edward's reign, royal debt had not been eliminated but was down from £3,000,000 to the more manageable figure of £180,000.

Under Mary, financial reform continued under the guiding hand of the Council. C. E. Challis has shown that the Council made good preparations for reforming the currency and shelved the plans only because of the serious economic and social problems of 1556–7, including the worst harvest of the century. This was prudent, as re-coinage might have added to short-term economic problems. Nonetheless, the planned re-coinage was successfully put into operation under Elizabeth. Meanwhile, Sir Francis Englefield was made Surveyor General of the Customs and in May 1558 issued a new Book of Rates. These increased import and export duties on goods and may have increased royal revenue from this source from £29,000 in 1557 to £83,000 in 1559. This was an excellent and far-sighted addition to royal revenues and customs duties would come to be the most important single source of royal income. Furthermore the healthy state of royal finances was enhanced by an increase in income from Crown lands. One estimate puts the increase at £400,000 a year. Among other things, the improving state of royal finances allowed Mary to wage war on the Continent, sending out one of the best-prepared expeditionary forces of the century. Improving revenue also meant a major rebuilding of the navy, starting in 1555. In the years 1558–9, as much new tonnage was built as in the five years prior to the Spanish Armada in 1558 and, for the first time, the Council made available a regular peacetime allocation of money for the upkeep of the nation's ships.

All of this serious and sensible financial reform had been executed by the Council and shows that, while the government of the realm remained underfunded, the Crown's financial position improved. There was certainly no mid-Tudor crisis in royal finances.

Limited impact of faction fighting. Despite the success of the Council in financial matters, it has been all too easy to exaggerate the importance of faction fighting and disagreements amongst Councillors, to show that there was a dangerous level of political instability at the centre of government in the mid-Tudor period. The conflict between Somerset and Northumberland during Edward's reign and that between Paget and Gardiner under Mary have been viewed as serious evidence of crisis and confusion. However, such a view is clearly exaggerated and fails to appreciate the limited impact that faction fighting had on the effective conduct of government.

In any conciliar system there is bound to be conflict. Men jostle for power and influence at all times and during this period there was the added problem of serious ideological conflict about religion. Compared to the last eleven years of Henry VIII's reign, faction fighting under Edward and Mary probably resulted in fewer and more justified executions. Despite his manifest failings, Somerset was not executed when he was overthrown in 1549 and indeed was restored to the Council. He was only eventually executed in 1552 as he persisted in his attempts to undermine Northumberland's leadership. Northumberland himself was rightly executed for treason as he had sought to pervert the succession. Lady Jane and

Guildford Dudley were executed not because Jane had been proclaimed queen but because Wyatt's Rebellion showed that they might be the focus of future rebellion. Despite serious lobbying from some of Mary's Councillors terrified about the succession, Princess Elizabeth was not executed. On the whole then, faction fighting was not very deadly in this period.

While there were a number of coups, attempts to seize ultimate power in this period were not particularly long drawn out. Only the sustained struggle between Wriothesley and Northumberland during the period of October 1549–February 1550 lasted more than a few weeks. Once power was seized by Somerset, Northumberland and Mary, the result was accepted and government continued. Once established, Somerset was allowed to rule unhindered for 30 months, Northumberland for somewhat longer and Mary for longer still, all without serious challenges to their power.

Furthermore, Ann Weikel has demonstrated that the impact of faction fighting within the Council has been seriously exaggerated. The Council at the time of Wyatt's Rebellion has been seen as indecisive and divided. Partly, this is because historians have given too much weight to the excitable temperament of Charles V's Ambassador, Simon Renard. At the time of the rebellion in 1554, it was Renard who over-reacted to the crisis in his reports to the Emperor, as he wanted Charles V to send troops to stifle the revolt. In doing so he created a picture of a regime in crisis and a Council crippled by divisions and panic. In fact, the Council handled the crisis well, acting with purpose and energy. First it used its intelligence network to discover the plot, forcing the rebels into action before the various groups were ready. Then it quickly arrested suspected persons and secured the person of Princess Elizabeth. Government propaganda, explaining the benefits of the Spanish marriage, was quickly distributed and the government played for time, as Henry VIII had in 1536, by attempting to negotiate with the rebel leader. The real crisis occurred, not because the Council failed to rise to the challenge, but because the first military force sent against the rebels, under Norfolk, was disorganised and withdrew.

The other incident of faction fighting under Mary which has been exaggerated, is the conflict between Paget and Gardiner played out in Parliament in April and May 1554. Gardiner and Paget had first clashed over the queen's marriage. Gardiner favoured Edward Courtenay, the son of the executed Marquis of Exeter, while Paget was in favour of the Spanish match. When the queen made her wishes known, Gardiner, of course, fell into line but in the wake of Wyatt's Rebellion, which was opposed to the match, he feared that he was losing favour with the queen. He tried to reassert his position by pushing for a fast-track approach to Catholic restoration and introduced a Bill to revive the old heresy laws. Paget, fearing loss of influence, and with the administrator's more cautious approach to religious change, managed to get the Bill defeated in the House of Lords on the grounds that it might undermine property rights. Six months later, with Paget more in control, the Bill was passed without opposition. The disagreements between Paget and Gardiner thus had no real impact on the direction of government policy. Gardiner agreed to the marriage and Catholicism was restored. Although the two men apparently disliked each other, they composed their differences before Gardiner's death. One must also remember that disagreements in the Council were entirely natural. It was (and is) one of the strengths of conciliar government that alternative approaches and ideas could be explored and discussed before decisions were taken.

THE INCREASING IMPORTANCE OF PARLIAMENT

Disagreements over religion. The disagreement between Paget and Gardiner played out in the House of Lords, highlights another crucial reason why there was no mid-Tudor crisis – Parliament. After 1529 Parliament played a more significant role in government and was instrumental in all the great changes (reforming and conservative) in religion, as well as in a host of other areas of central and local government. The House of Lords consisted of the great men of the realm and the purging of the 29 abbots after the dissolution of the monasteries meant that the House now had a lay majority. The Commons, usually the junior partner was now seen as an equal partner with the Lords in the passing of new laws, due to procedural changes. The volume of legislation and the frequency with which Parliament now met also increased its importance. Between 1215 and 1509, a period of 294 years, the statutes passed by Parliament occupy 1092 pages, in Henry VIII's reign of 37 years new statutes take up 1032 pages and most of these were passed after 1529! Due to the many changes of regime and the changing religious complexion of the mid-Tudor period, Parliament continued to be called frequently and to enact vast quantities of legislation. It is clear that Parliament's authority, combined with the authority of the Council, ensured that there was only limited opposition to the many changes introduced. The tradition of acquiescence and conformity, noted in relation to the many and contradictory religious reforms under Edward and Mary, stemmed from the fact that most had statutory authority. Under Henry VIII, Parliament had always been overshadowed by the king. Then, during a royal minority and afterwards under a female ruler, Parliament came into its own. Somerset's Rule by Proclamation had failed and subsequent changes would need parliamentary sanction. With that sanction, the realm was freed from domestic upheaval.

Traditionally, it has been thought that there was a Protestant ascendancy in Parliament which meant harmony under Edward and conflict under

Mary. In fact both reigns saw opposition to government measures in Parliament. The Chantries Bill in 1547 ran into difficulties, while the attempt to use Parliament to deprive Tunstall of his bishopric was defeated. The repeal of Edward VI's religious laws was, of course, opposed by 23 per cent of the House of Commons – some 80 MPs – which is not surprising as the House, in terms of membership, was not dissimilar to the one which had passed the legislation just a few years earlier. In the light of this it is surely more notable that 75 per cent of the MPs did agree!

Also under Edward there was serious opposition to most of the religious changes in the House of Lords. Here, Catholic bishops and peers had the special right to formally register their opposition to a new Act. In 1547 the Bishops of London, Norwich, Hereford, Worcester and Chichester registered their disapproval of a bill allowing the Sacrament in both kinds to the laity. The Earls of Derby and Shrewsbury as well as Lords Dacre, Wharton, Windsor and Mounteagle also made use of this lordly privilege, to register their disapproval. Meanwhile the Bill allowing the marriage of priests took two months to pass the House of Lords.

It was a similar picture under Mary. In 1555, the Bill to restore First Fruits and Tenths to the Pope was passed after disagreements in the House, while a Bill to confiscate the property of Protestant exiles failed, not because Parliament was pro-Protestant but because, once again, it saw itself as the defender of property rights. Henry VIII of course would probably just have confiscated the property and it is a measure of more settled times that Parliament's consent was sought and that, when it was not forthcoming, the government accepted the decision. Finally the Act to re-unite England with Rome took two weeks to get through Parliament, not because the MPs were opposed in principle but because they insisted that the Papal dispensation allowing men to retain ex-monastic lands should be part of the new law. Only parliamentary statute could give security of tenure.

Given the apparent importance of all the changes in religion during this period, it is surprising that there was not more opposition. Parliament acted as a kind of safety valve. It allowed for arguments and disagreements among the ruling class to be aired but it also ensured that decisions then arrived at in Parliament would be respected and conformed with in the shires. On the other hand, Parliament's importance should not be exaggerated. It did not initiate the changes in religion but its support added real authority and legitimacy to the new order.

Non-religious Acts. Too much attention paid to religious change has obscured Parliament's role in the day-to-day government of the realm and, in particular, its importance as a mediator between the centre and the peripheries. For many MPs and even members of the Lords, practical local issues and problems might be more absorbing than religious, national ones. They assumed that Edward's reign would bring changes in religion and they knew that Mary's would. Instead of arguments over religion, there was a myriad of other problems which Parliament did its best to deal with. In this regard, Tittler has argued that in response to the possibility of crisis and rebellion, the government, especially under Mary, worked hard to support urban communities, giving them new powers to regulate their own social and economic affairs and further powers over defence with the Militia Act and Arms Act, both passed in 1558. The Retail Trade Act (1554), Weavers Act (1555) and Woollen Cloth Act (1557) were all designed to bolster cloth-making in towns, and punish unregulated cloth manufacture outside urban areas. In addition, the mid-Tudor period saw a large number of towns receiving corporate status which allowed them more self-government and the right to send MPs to Westminster. Under Mary they averaged four per year, rather higher than before or after. Such grants in such numbers hardly smack of a regime in crisis. Rather they serve as an antidote to the realm of high politics, demonstrating how the regime used Parliament and the incorporation of boroughs to create a stronger and more united polity. The mayor and corporation had their rights and privileges confirmed and the town of Wycombe was pleased to take its seats in the increasingly influential mid-Tudor Parliaments.

WHY RELIGIOUS CHANGE DID NOT LEAD TO CRISIS

Acceptance of religious reforms

In April 1557, Ralph Allerton, a Protestant of Much Bentley in Essex was confronted by the Catholic Bishop Bonner. With a typical show of assurance, he told the bishop that there were currently three religions in England: 'The first is that which you hold, the second is clear contrary to the same and the third is neuter, being indifferent, that is to say observing all things that are commanded outwardly as though they were of your party, his heart being set against the same.' Allerton clearly exaggerated the number of Protestants to suit his purpose but he may have hit the nail pretty much on the head. There was little opposition to the religious changes and no signs of a long-term crisis because so many English men and women became neutral and conformist. John Jewel a leading Protestant, writing at the beginning of Elizabeth's reign, made much the same point in more direct fashion: 'Many will believe neither side, whatsoever they allege. Bring they truth, bring they falsehood, teach they Christ, teach they Antichrist: they will believe neither, they have so hardened their hearts.'

Protestant howls of woe are familiar enough to any student of the period but Jewel's analysis rings true of the English situation. Faced with contradictory and increasingly opposed religious messages, many people slumped into apathy or indifference. How could they decide what was right if their governors and betters disagreed among themselves? Others who were less clearly apathetic, decided it was best to go along with whatever changes were being suggested. Opposition was dangerous and conformity might bring reward.

In reality, from the moment of Henry VIII's death, the religious future looked uncertain and this encouraged conformism rather than opposition. While Edward was inclined to reform, his heir, everyone knew, was a Catholic. While Mary brought back the old Church, her heir was Anne Boleyn's daughter. Elizabeth herself never married and for nearly thirty years, her heir seemed to be the Catholic Mary, Queen of Scots. For an unprecedented 40 years all was uncertainty and people soon appreciated that religious settlements could soon be changed in ways which were legally binding upon subjects, with severe penalties for non-conformity.

Even before Edward was crowned, the English people were aware that religious change was not permanent. In the late 1530s, after all, Henry VIII had moved decisively away from Protestant reform and used Parliament to frame and enforce the change of direction. What Parliament had enacted by way of settlement, one day, could easily, it seemed, be repealed by a later Parliament. To identify too closely with one side or the other would be dangerous.

Thus the changes in religion in the mid-Tudor period did not lead to crisis and confusion but to apathy and conformism. Robert Whiting, at the end of his highly illuminating study of the south-west during the Reformation, concludes that the Reformation process was 'less a transition from Catholic to Protestant than a decline from religious commitment into conformism or indifference'.

Problems of Protestantism

The lack of crisis over religion during this period was also caused by problems and weaknesses within Protestantism. Since Protestantism was weak it could not launch an effective and rapid assault on traditional Catholicism which in turn might have led to crisis and confusion. Many leading Protestants gave up in the face of hostility from the State, rather than fighting to establish their faith, so religious confrontation was kept to a minimum. Rex Pogson has noted that there was little serious conflict over religion at parish level. Leading Protestants went into exile after 1553 rather than face persecution. In addition, Protestants who stayed in England had not developed convincing theories of resistance to a God-given Catholic monarch, so the Marian Counter-Reformation was accepted by the Protestant community.

Meanwhile, the Protestant leadership proved unwilling to mount serious opposition to the re-introduction of Catholic ceremonies and services.

Cranmer, after all, was a loyalist. His reforming ideas had always developed slowly in the 1530s and 1540s and he always conformed to the wishes of Henry VIII. He stayed on after the passing of the Catholic Act of Six Articles in 1539, while keener Protestant bishops resigned their sees. Given more room to manoeuvre under Somerset and Northumberland, his ideas still developed slowly and in deference to his political masters. When Mary came to the throne, his reaction was typical of his deferential attitude: 'O good Lord be merciful unto us for we have been too remiss in punishing offenders, and many things we have winked at.' He would have agreed with Hooper that Mary had been sent, 'by reason of our sins'. While John Knox denounced the monstrous regiment (rule) of women, Cranmer was confused and upset, trying to make sense of God's purpose. He was desperately torn between loyalty to his God-given Sovereign and loyalty to his faith. He recanted six times before his execution in 1555. Neither he nor Hooper, nor any of the other Protestant Bishops gave the Protestant community a clear and dynamic lead in times of trouble. No wonder most conformed!

The limitations of Cranmer as a Protestant leader mirrored the divisions of Protestantism in mid-century as at all other times in the sixteenth century. Above all, Protestants were men of the Book, they relied on the Bible as the inspired Word of God and the ideas which they drew from it could be very varied and contradictory. Protestantism was far from being a clearly defined set of theological beliefs and thus it could neither impose a coherent creed in favourable circumstances, nor provide a secure refuge in unfavourable circumstances. John Foxe, in his *Book of Martyrs* tended to lump together all dissenters as good Protestants in order to lengthen the role call of the Godly. In fact, Hooper and Ridley disagreed with Cranmer's notions of 'things indifferent'. Hugh Latimer was a more radical Protestant than Cranmer and refused to take up the duties of bishop a second time as he preferred to preach. Preachers licensed and unlicensed always made governments nervous. In 1549 Protector Somerset issued clear warnings to unlicensed preachers:

Source 16

In order that the King's subjects should not, by evil and unlearned preachers, be brought into superstition, error, or evil doctrine, and be made stubborn and disobedient to the King's Godly Proceedings; the King, by our advice, has thought it right to inhibit all manner of unlicensed preachers. They shall not be allowed to preach or stir the people . . . the people being tossed to and fro with seditious and contentious preaching, with every man going about to set out his own fantasy and to draw the people into his own opinion.

Adapted from Somerset's proclamation against unlicensed preachers, 1549.

But how could the authorities be sure about who was a Godly preacher and who ungodly? John Knox, the fiery Scots minister who had drunk deep of the Gospel in Calvin's Geneva, was established in Newcastle by late 1550 and was even preaching at Court in 1552.

While looking at the problems of preaching from the authorities' point of view, it is worth remembering that preaching and a number of other Protestant traits did not necessarily have widespread appeal. For the mass of people who were still illiterate, Protestantism's more intellectual approach to matters of faith did not have universal appeal. Many people disliked sermons and preaching and preferred the comforting and traditional ceremonies of the old Church. Many Protestant preachers commented on the unwillingness of people to listen to the message and their willingness to 'harden their hearts'.

Emergence of Protestant separatists

English Protestantism was also weakened in mid-century, by the emergence of Protestant separatists, who would break away from the Protestant mainstream. This was a pre-echo of the separatism which would develop further during the reign of Elizabeth. In 1550, for example, Henry Hart and his group of followers were arrested in Bocking in Essex. Hart had his own version of Protestant theology which included opposition to the idea of predestination. Disagreement over this would divide Protestants for the next century and beyond. Hart had also drawn up certain articles of faith which were to be observed by his 'company', suggesting that the group had cut itself off from the Church of England. During Edward's reign there were also many foreign dissenters who came to England to seek asylum from persecution at home. We know of several congregations of Zwinglians and Calvinists established in and around London in this way and we know that there were a number of Anabaptists in England. Joan Boucher was burnt as an Anabaptist in 1551 and claimed that there were a thousand of her sect in London. Bishop Hooper became embarrassed by the fact that foreign and English Anabaptists (separatist groups who did not believe in infant baptism) were often called Protestants and thus gave the movement a bad name. For the same reason, several of Cranmer's 42 Articles of 1553 were designed to distance the Godly from the errors of Anabaptism. English Protestants were fighting to establish their identity and fighting a war on two fronts, against Catholics on the one side and against Protestant Radicals on the other.

One other feature of English Protestantism helped to keep religious conflict and confrontation to a minimum during the mid-Tudor period. This was that official English Protestantism did not tend to persecute its opponents. Clearly, a wave of persecution by Protestants might have set off long-running and escalating violence. Instead, English Protestantism, when it had government support, executed very few people for their religious beliefs. No one was executed on such a basis under Somerset and only two Anabaptists – George van Paris and Joan Boucher – under Northumberland: Paris for denying that Christ was human and Boucher for denying that Christ was God!

Moderation of Catholicism

Although Mary had her doubts about the policy, the large numbers of Protestants burnt during her reign was very unpopular and seen as un-English because it appeared in stark contrast to the occasional execution of religious dissidents in previous reigns. Nonetheless, not everything done by Catholics and the Catholic authorities was quite so drastic and it is the more moderate aspects of the Catholic reaction that also explain the absence of religious crisis at this time. Catholic devotional publications of the time, such as *A profitable and necessary doctrine* or *A plain and Godly treatise concerning the Mass and the Blessed Sacrament of the Altar*, were often moderate rather than confrontational in tone. They showed that the Protestants did not have a monopoly on the word Godly or on the Word of God. They quoted from the Scriptures in English and stressed the need for informed and pious Catholics to participate in the sacraments. Saints and images, so loathed by more extreme Protestants, were mentioned but not made central, while references to the Pope were fairly minimal. In other words, the Catholicism on offer during Mary's reign was not militant and papalist but moderate and English, based on the Erasmian Catholicism of the 1520s which was so much part of Pole's Catholic upbringing and on the time-honoured traditions of the old English Church.

Nor was there a crisis in the number of ordinations to the Catholic clergy. In the Diocese of Chester, there were no new Ordinands during Edward's reign but there were 12 in 1555, 17 in 1557 and no less than 70 in 1558. The number of new priests in the diocese of London makes the same point – the average figure per year under Edward was between 25 and 30; under Mary it was 48. Meanwhile the Universities of Oxford and Cambridge – crucial centres for the education of clergy – were cleaned up for Catholicism, and Protestantism withered.

When considering Catholic and Protestant together, it would be well not to make too much of the division between the two. Radicals on both sides stressed the differences in theology and religious practice, but the more moderate elements, of which there were many, would be hard to identify as distinctly one or the other. The political and dynastic causes of Henry VIII's Reformation meant that there were large numbers of reformers, both Catholic and Protestant.

Historians have too often allowed the Protestants to monopolise terms such as 'Godly' and 'Reformer' to imply that Catholics were 'un-Godly' and 'non-reforming'. The reality was that Catholicism was learning from the continental Reformation. Men like Pole wanted a dynamic, caring and spiritually uplifting Catholicism which mediated with compassion between men and women and the Almighty. The likes of Gardiner, who had accommodated Henry VIII's Supremacy with some ease, wished to see a revived Catholicism established within the framework of an English, rather than a Papal, Church. In other words the notions of Christian religious revival appealed to both Protestants and Catholics and we should see many of them as engaged in a common struggle against materialism and apathy.

LIMITATIONS OF SOCIAL AND ECONOMIC DISTRESS

Social and economic problems have often been used in an analysis of the mid-Tudor crisis. The basic line of argument is that a rising population after about 1520 caused social and economic distress. The inability of primitive agricultural techniques to keep pace with population increase led to recurrent shortages of food which were exacerbated during the mid-Tudor period by runs of bad harvests in 1549–51 and 1556–7. A Suffolk rector writing about conditions in 1556, claimed that, 'the scarcity of bread that year was so great, in so much that the plain poor people did make much of acorns and a sickness of strong fever did sore molest them'. As this source points out, bad harvests were often accompanied by virulent and deadly diseases. In the mid-Tudor period, there were visitations of sickness and plague which seem to have been more widespread than usual. The year 1551 saw one of the worst outbreaks of sweating sickness with tens of thousands of deaths and the psychological impact was worsened by the fact that the disease killed very quickly. Some historians have suggested that possibly 20 per cent of the population may have died during the period 1555–60 as influenza and sweating sickness carried off many people already weakened by malnutrition.

There is likewise much evidence for rising food prices and declining real wages, for those in the lower reaches of society. Bad harvests and growing competition for jobs (because of population increase) meant that food prices went up, while average wages went down. The gloomy picture then becomes even murkier when one adds in the impact of enclosures during the mid-Tudor period, with small men and their families being driven off the land by rapacious landlords.

However, such interpretations need to be treated with caution. There is no way to quantify the extent of disease and malnutrition during this period, nor can the impact of such mortality crises be compared effectively to other 'mortality crises' before and after. Whatever the real levels of suffering, contemporary accounts do not speak of famine, or of large numbers dying merely for lack of food. While there were bad harvests, there were also good ones during this period in the usual cyclical pattern. The years 1553 and 1557 are seen as 'good', while 1558 was 'abundant'. While prices fluctuated, it is hard to avoid the conclusion that a rising population, during the Tudor period as a whole, which all historians seem to agree with, is a sign of increasing prosperity not dearth.

Meanwhile, enclosure should not be seen as necessarily evil. Many men profited through a less wasteful system of enclosed fields rather than the old 'open field' system of strip farming. More sheep on the land led to prosperity in the wool and cloth industries and more meat. The real problem of the period lay not so much with enclosures as such but with landlords attempting to increase rents because of inflation. During Kett's Rebellion, some hedges were thrown down, as a way of demonstrating frustration and hostility towards landowners but the real grievance among the rebels was the level of rents. They wanted rents back at 1485 levels and they thought that Somerset agreed with them.

Other complaints were not about enclosure of common land by landlords but about their overstocking such land with sheep. Problems on the land may have been made worse by the redistribution of land associated with the Reformation. As the Crown sold on confiscated lands to new landlords, it is easy to imagine the rise of a new class of grasping and unscrupulous landlords; new men who paid no heed to established local practices. While the great transfer of land after 1536 did allow some families to rise more quickly than before into the ranks of the landed gentry, most of the land was bought by men who already owned land and were used to agrarian customs.

While the reigns of Edward and Mary may, overall, have witnessed serious social and economic problems, they were probably not much worse than what had gone before and what would come afterwards. There is also some evidence of increasing poor relief. In the normal way, the wealthy did respond to the problems of the poor. W. K. Jordan's study of bequests for hospitals and similar institutions for relief of the poor and needy, shows that in the ten counties he studied, such bequests increased from around £26,000 in the 1540s to £104,000 in the 1550s.

Many Edwardian propagandists seem rather gloomy about conditions at this time but most were Protestants inspired and misled by rising expectations. They thought that in Edward's reign, the Gospel would shine forth and a more just society would be created. When the Gospel merely glimmered, when rebellion broke out and when Catholicism then returned, they knew that covetousness was not yet at an end.

REBELLION AND THE ARISTOCRACY

Rebellion during the mid-Tudor period may have been more frequent than at other times in the sixteenth century, but this does not mean that there was a deep-rooted and intractable crisis or malaise in society. Rebellion did not mean civil war between governors and governed nor did it imply serious conflict within the governing classes. The rebellions of 1549 were both short-lived and too far from the capital to cause a real crisis. Neither wished to overthrow the King or the government. The Western rebels, unlike their counterparts in 1497, did not march on London nor did they rise again when Northumberland introduced religious reforms more radical than those of 1549 which had sparked off the protest. Nor were the two rebellions about the same things. In the west it was religious conservatism and Catholic clergy that sparked off revolt, in the east it was, for the most part, economic grievances. Neither rebellion was on the scale of the great Northern revolts of 1536 and 1569.

Wyatt's Rebellion too, did not portend a society in crisis. It had rather unclear aims. Was it merely a protest against the proposed Spanish marriage, was it an attempt to stop the re-introduction of Catholicism or was it an attempt to overthrow Mary in favour of Elizabeth? This protest was more serious than the others in that it was closer to London and had wider gentry support than the outbursts of 1549. However, it was defeated. Furthermore, by mid-century, propaganda against rebellion was well rehearsed and entirely convincing. Philip Nichols, a Devon Protestant wrote this against the western rebels of 1549:

Source 17

What other fruit or end may hereof ensue unto you but the devouring one another and an universal desolation of your own selves, besides the extreme peril of God's high wrath and indignation, besides the undoubted plague of mortality which, unless you call for mercy in season, must needs light upon you by the severe rod of princely justice in our realm. You, in the meantime, do neglect your husbandry by which you live, your houses fall to ruin, your wives are ravished, your daughters deflowered before your faces, your goods spent upon vagabonds and idle loiterers. What will happen to your own children when your own living is thus, through your own folly, brought to penury and famine . . ?

Adapted from a version written by Philip Nichols in 1549.

Most ordinary people would have agreed with him. Open rebellion by the common people never succeeded and only made matters worse.

What all three rebellions also lacked was support from the aristocracy. Only with full-blooded aristocratic support could a rebellion be successful or lead to sustained crisis. The French Wars of Religion, which continued for two generations in the second half of the sixteenth century, were fuelled by great aristocratic families that had broken free of monarchical control. These magnates had large accumulations of land and men in regional power bases and could fight each other and the Crown apparently indefinitely. In France, religious conflict took advantage of a weakened Crown to produce a serious political and social crisis punctuated by civil war and slaughter.

In England, by contrast, the Crown remained strong during the mid-Tudor period. The aristocracy had been tamed and had shown no signs of concerted opposition to the Reformation, Catholic or Protestant. Even if they had, they would have been unable to sustain that protest. None of the titled magnates had great regional power bases or the ability to raise large numbers of troops. Those who were seen as threats to the regime were picked off with ease by a watchful and suspicious government. The government's paranoia is seen in the fact that none of the great men executed in the 1520s and afterwards, were actually plotting rebellion. In 1521, the last of the great English magnates, the Duke of Buckingham, was executed. The Courtenays and Poles were dispatched by Henry VIII for having Yorkist blood and a Cardinal in the family, while the Earl of Surrey, went to the block for foolish and arrogant language that seemed to threaten Edward VI's minority. Somerset and Northumberland were guilty of treason but they were new men, who were awarded their dukedoms at their own instigation and had limited political power of their own. These executions served to encourage the rest and most aristocrats settled for service at court as a means of achieving political advancement, rather than the dangerous game of protest and opposition. Thomas Howard, the Duke of Norfolk, probably the most powerful magnate of his generation, opted for loyal service to the Crown. Even so, he only just escaped execution because of Henry VIII's death.

By the mid-Tudor period and indeed ever since 1483, the aristocracy could no longer mount a serious challenge to the Crown's authority. The three Yorkists, who had sustained the crisis of the late fifteenth century – Richard of York, Edward IV and Richard III – had been backed by large regional estates, aristocratic allies and a plausible claim to the throne. None of their Tudor successors among the aristocracy could match these advantages. None of the Tudor monarchs had powerful male heirs, who were usually the source of serious political or religious conflict, and the English aristocracy, after 1485, was largely emasculated by the increasing power of the Crown. None of the Tudor magnates had a great regional power base; indeed, it was the absence of aristocratic control, not its presence, that allowed the rebellions of 1549 to get out of control.

The changing fortunes of the great magnates can be seen by reviewing and contrasting the power of the Dukes of Suffolk. Michael de la Pole, who held the title under Henry VI, was a hugely powerful and corrupt chief minister to the King. His bloody overthrow in 1450, by other magnates, helped to spark off the Wars of the Roses. Under Henry VIII, the title was held by Charles Brandon, a significant figure, always a loyal servant to the Crown during the Reformation, who had been elevated to the dukedom by Henry himself. During the mid-Tudor period the new holder was Henry Grey, father of Lady Jane. He exercised only limited power, played an ignominious part in Wyatt's Rebellion and was executed for treason. Grey's relative anonymity also came about because he was, like Somerset and Northumberland, a recent creation. He acquired the title because he married Henry VIII's niece Frances Brandon. Other aristocrats of the period were likewise relatively new, acquiring titles through royal service.

Furthermore, most aristocrats, far from wishing to oppose the Reformation, realised soon enough that they could profit from it. If the Church was under attack and its assets were about to be stripped, then the aristocracy, along with the Crown, would be the main beneficiaries. The political subservience and religious passivity of the aristocracy in the face of the Reformations of the Tudor period is well illustrated by the words of Henry Pole, Lord Montague. In 1538, in a pre-emptive strike, so typical of Cromwell at his most ruthless, Pole and his mother and his cousin, Henry Courtenay, Marquis of Exeter were accused of treason. Pole, like many of his class and generation, did not approve of the English Reformation and wished to see the abbeys up again. Although the charges against him were clearly exaggerated, some of the words imputed to him, probably on the testimony of servants, ring true. Pole reportedly said that 'Cardinal Wolsey would have been an honest man if he had had an honest master.' Yet while Pole blamed the King for the nation's woes, he made no attempt to stop him. Even more revealing, in terms of the passivity and weakness of the English aristocracy, is Pole's comment, that 'I like well the doings of my brother the Cardinal [Reginald Pole] and I wish we were both overseas for this world will one day come to blows.' In other words he knew that he hated the Reformation and he approved of his brother the Cardinal, who was in Rome, but he was not prepared to make a stand against the changes. Faced with the prospect of a world which would come to blows, he wished that he could be abroad to keep clear of trouble, rather than at home to rally the forces of the old order. Sadly for him, and for so many of those who thought like him, the world of Tudor England did not come to blows. Despite the apparently seismic upheavals of the period, the State remained strong and the Reformations remained Erastian. The aristocracy proved weak and pusillanimous.

OVERVIEW

Alan G. R. Smith claimed that while there was no mid-Tudor crisis for the English State, there was one for the English people. The State showed unexpected resilience in the face of political intrigue and religious upheaval, while the people of England suffered the consequences. Even this notion can now be questioned. In the face of the evidence provided throughout this book, it is hard to believe that the people of England suffered to any great extent as a result of the Tudor Reformations.

If anyone or anything was the victim of crisis, a sustained attack on its power and wealth, during this period, it was surely the Church itself. The Reformations, both Protestant and Catholic, that had hoped to revive the Church in England and to improve its ability to minister to the spiritual needs of the people, were undermined by the combined attacks of Crown, aristocracy and Protestantism. Despite the short-lived restoration under Mary, in which the Church remained shorn of much of its wealth and was still controlled by the laity, religion in England would continue to be a divisive issue – one which divided rather than united the people. In the longer term, these divisions, stirred up by Henry VIII, would undermine, rather than strengthen, the power of the monarchy which had been so obviously enhanced by Henry VII and his son. These religious divisions would lead, in time, to a serious and sustained crisis. This was not the mid-Tudor crisis but the mid-Stuart crisis – the crisis of Civil War. In the short term, however, the impact of the English Reformations was muted, resulting in a more ordered society, not one beset by crisis and confrontation. All in all they were very English Reformations.

A2 ASSESSMENT: ENGLISH REFORMATIONS 1533–58

THE REFORMATION IN ENGLAND, 1529–47

Source questions in the style of AQA
You will need to read Chapters 4 and 5 to answer them.

1 Read the extracts below and then answer the questions which follow.

Source A
Without question the English Reformation belonged to that far larger breakaway which detached half of Europe from the Papacy. In essentials the early English Protestants of the 1520s and 1530s were Lutherans, led by Tyndale, Barnes and Cranmer, by the young Cambridge scholars of the early twenties, by Coverdale and the lesser Bible translators, and by a host of other publicists and pamphleteers with strong continental affinities . . . Even Thomas Cromwell, the first great executive of the state reformation, displayed a cool but unmistakable affinity with the Lutherans. He despised antiquated superstitions and what he regarded as clerical hypocrisy; he boldly printed and distributed the Bible in English and he strove to link English policy with that of the German Lutheran princes. Eventually, his conservative English enemies denounced him not merely on a totally false charge of treason, but also as a heretic, which seems distinctly more appropriate.

From *The English Reformation*, by A. G. Dickens, 1989

Source B
When Henry VIII began his attack on the papacy, he had in his favour the strong dislike of the clergy and of foreign interference in English affairs which animated certainly the politically effective part of the nation and was represented in parliament. He did not by superhuman power and coercion drag a faithful people from the fold; rather he unleashed those passions which for years only the government's frown had been able to stem. Attacks on the church, on its way of life and its great wealth (rumoured to be even greater than it was) were some 150 years old at least; and so was dislike of papal usurpations and encroachments. But . . . the crown had stood good ally to Rome; the anti-papal legislation remained a dead letter, and England's mediaeval history culminated in

a royal minister who was also papal legate and who adapted his country's foreign policy to the needs of the Pope. Until Henry fixed his eye on Anne Boleyn, . . . there was nothing to disturb the harmony of king and Pope; and until their alliance was broken all the latent feelings which Henry VIII was to harness remained powerless. That is the place which the divorce occupies. It did not alone cause the Reformation; it did not, even if we like, play any large part in bringing about a movement which rested on national sentiment and the scandal of a corrupt church; but without it, there would have been no Reformation because the powerful intercession of the crown would have been against it and not for it.

From *England under the Tudors*, by G. R. Elton, 1974

Questions

1 Consult Sources A and B. To what extent and for what reasons, do the authors of these two extracts disagree about the causes of the 'Break with Rome' in the 1530s? *(10 marks)*

How you should answer this question. At the higher levels of response, candidates will focus on the extent of disagreement about the causes of the Break with Rome in the 1530s, as revealed in these two sources. In Source A, Dickens seems to claim that the Break occurred because of the increasing influence of English Lutherans in general and of Thomas Cromwell in particular. Elton, in Source B, underscores the importance of the divorce since this meant that Henry VIII was no longer concerned to protect the English Church from the reformers. While the authors emphasize different factors in these short extracts, their ideas are not mutually exclusive and so the disagreement between them might not be as serious as it seems.

To answer the 'for what reasons' part of the question, you will need to comment a little more widely on the different views of these two historians. Dickens has usually emphasised the importance of the spread of reforming ideas from the continent which created the essential springboard for the Reformation. In his view the Church in England was very unpopular during the 1520s and therefore ripe for Reformation during the 1530s. The divorce, in his view, was the occasion not the cause of the Reformation. Elton, by contrast, puts more emphasis on the role of the king. He wanted to take charge of the Church and his Supremacy was the real key to the Reformation process. In this process, he made use of Cromwell and Cranmer.

The vital point to notice is that a top-level answer will require own knowledge as well as source use. The instruction at the start of the question is to 'consult Sources A and B' not 'using Sources A and B . . .' In other words the sources are being used as stimulus material, to act as a point of reference in an historical debate with which the candidate is already familiar. A descriptor for top-level responses might say that candidates, 'will use appropriate material from sources and their own knowledge to argue that the causes of the Break with Rome owed much to both external and internal factors.'

> **2** Consult Sources A and B and use your own knowledge.
> 'The Divorce was the occasion not the cause of the English Reformation.'
> Discuss this statement in relation to the Reformation in England under
> Henry VIII.
> *(20 marks)*

How you should answer this question. In this question you are asked to make a judgement on how likely it was that the Reformation would have occurred if there had been no divorce. The quotation claims that the divorce merely determined the timing of the Reformation rather than acting as the main cause. You will be rewarded according to the range of factors that you cover and your ability to sustain a judgement, for or against the quotation, throughout the essay. Once again, thoughtful planning, based around relevant ideas, will be vital so as to order your thoughts in a logical way and to arrive at a clear conclusion. Once you have planned, it would be very useful to announce your overall answer at the start of the essay. At the higher levels of response, you might be expected to challenge the quotation or at least to be able to counter those who would challenge it. A favourite device might be to look at why some people might agree with the quotation but then go on to explain why you think they are misguided. Did England seem on the brink of Reformation before 1525? If so, then the divorce only affected the timing. If, by contrast, the Church seemed secure before 1525, the divorce was probably the most important factor. You should also cover a wide range of factors both long-term and short-term which brought the Reformation about and evaluate the importance of each factor.

Remember, too, that the question gives a specific instruction to use own knowledge *and* the sources in your answer, so it will be important to include a few quotations from the sources to back up your line of argument.

THE CRISIS OF THE TUDOR STATE, 1547–58

Source questions in the style of Edexcel
You will need to read Chapter 7 and sections 3, 4 and 5 to answer them.

1 Study Sources A to E below and then answer questions which follow:

Source A

The reign of Mary lasted only five years but it left an indelible impression. Positive achievements there were none : Pollard declared that sterility was its conclusive note, and this is a verdict with which the dispassionate observer must agree. Even the financial and administrative recovery which has been noted, owed nothing to the queen or her policy; planned in the previous reign, it was the work of Winchester who played no part in Marian politics. The decline of good government was accentuated by Mary's preference for a large Council of nearly fifty members and her encouragement of cliques and cabals, not to mention the influence of Charles V's ambassador Simon Renard and of Mary's husband, Philip of Spain. For the first time in English history, a queen regnant occupied the throne, an event which, on this occasion, only served to prove right the fears which had gripped Henry VIII in the 1520s. After the rule of factions in the reign of a child, the accession of the wrong type of queen nearly completed the ruin of dynasty and country . . . Two things dominated her mind – her religion and her Spanish descent. In place of the Tudor secular temper, cool political sense, and firm identification with England and the English, she put a passionate devotion to the Catholic religion and to Rome, absence of political guile, and pride in being Spanish.

From G. R. Elton, *England under the Tudors*, 1974

Source B

On at least two important occasions Mary seems to have shown political skills of a high order. The first was when negotiating with Pope Julius III at the beginning of her reign over the terms of England's return to obedience to Rome. The Pope clearly assumed that, before he agreed to absolve the English from the 'schism' of Edward's reign, the wealth of the church, confiscated over the previous 20 years and in particular the ex-monastic lands, would be returned. But Mary knew that, politically this was quite impossible. Hence her task was to bargain with the Pope until he gave his legate, Cardinal Pole, the power to dispense the present owners of these lands from having to give them back. During the bargaining, Mary showed that she was quite prepared to stand up to papal pressure.

The second occasion when Mary showed her political acumen was over her marriage negotiations. Whom to marry? Just as Elizabeth was to discover a few years later, this was a major problem. Everyone expected her to marry, but equally there was bound to be widespread protest against whichever candidate she picked. Mary's choice fell on Philip, son of Charles V and heir to Spain and the Netherlands . . . By stressing the weakness of her own position in the face of an overwhelmingly nationalistic Council and House of Commons, Mary was able to obtain astonishingly generous terms for the marriage from Charles. Philip was to be King of England during Mary's lifetime but to have no rights in the country after her death . . . The terms were so favourable that the government took the unusual step of publishing the articles for public consumption.

From R. Lockyer and D. O'Sullivan, *Tudor Britain 1485–1603*, 1997

Source C

Almost everywhere there were phased and realistic programmes of restoration, reflecting the developing flow of instructions and the practicalities of getting Catholic worship going again. In 1553 parishes generally set up the high altar, and bought vestments, books and a cross. In 1554 most paid for plate, candlesticks, side altars, a sepulchre, cloths and banners. In 1555–6 they bought a rood and images, and then many began fabric repairs. Some churches simply kept pace with the prescriptions of Mary and her bishops; but that in itself is surprising, for this was an expensive reconstruction paid for by the whole parish, not cheap Edwardian destruction which could be done by a pair of nervous churchwardens.

From Christopher Haigh, *English Reformations*, 1993

Source D

Dr. Taylor said with a loud voice, 'Good people, I have taught you nothing but God's holy word and those lessons that I have taken out of God's blessed book, the Holy Bible, and I am come hither this day to seal it with my blood.'

With that word Holmes, yeoman of the guard, who used Dr. Taylor very cruelly all the way, gave him a heavy stroke upon the head, and said, 'Is that the keeping of thy promise of silence, thou heretic?' Then the doctor knelt down and prayed, and a poor woman that was among the people stepped in and prayed with him. When he had prayed he went to the stake and kissed it. Then they bound him with chains, and having set up the faggots, one Warwick cruelly cast a faggot at him, which struck him on his head and cut his face, so that the blood ran down.

At last they kindled the fire, and Dr. Taylor, holding up both his hands called upon God and said, 'Merciful Father of Heaven! . . . receive my soul into Thy hands! So he stood still without either crying or moving, with his hands folded together till Soyce with a halberd struck him on the head.

Adapted from John Foxe's *Book of Martyrs*, 1563

Source E

She spoke to the people, and said that the objects she had ever had in view since coming to the throne were to administer justice, keep order and protect the people's peace and tranquillity. The rebel, Wyatt, had taken up arms under the pretext that she had married his Highness [Philip], but his reply showed clearly that he aimed at the Crown and meant to tyrannise and molest the people. So elegant and eloquent was her speech, that all the people cried out loudly that they would live and die in her service, and that Wyatt was a traitor; and they all threw up their caps to show their goodwill.

From a despatch from Simon Renard,
ambassador to the Emperor Charles V, 1554

Questions

> 1 Using your own knowledge, and the evidence of Sources A, B and E, explain the strengths and weaknesses of Mary I as Queen. *(10 marks)*

How to answer this question. It is important here for candidates to start out with a clear and well-thought-out view about the strengths and weaknesses of Mary as Queen of England. Less effective answers might provide only a couple of points on strengths and weaknesses, with limited explanation. Better answers will show an appreciation of the problems that faced Mary in attempting to rule a divided kingdom. To be really effective answers should not be too well balanced. If you can, try to argue that strengths outweighed weaknesses or vice versa. The better answers will argue quite firmly in terms of either strengths or weaknesses but will be able to argue against the opposite viewpoint expressed in some of the Sources. So if you think that, on the whole, Queen Mary ruled well, you will use Sources B and E to back up your view and then argue against the gloomy view put forward by Professor Elton in Source A. Make sure that you make use of all the sources by incorporating short quotations from them with explanation, in your own words, about how this backs up your line of argument.

At the same time you must remember to include your own knowledge, both to back up points from the sources and to develop relevant ideas that are not mentioned in Sources A, B and E.

> 2 'In effecting her Catholic Reformation, Mary I moved with caution, and understood the religious turmoil created by the Protestant reforms of Edward's reign.'
> Using your own knowledge, and the evidence of all five sources, explain how far you agree with this interpretation. *(20 marks)*

How to answer this question. This should be a longer answer than the answer to the first question as it is rather broader and worth more marks. Once again you need to approach the question with a clear view about how well, or how badly, Mary reintroduced Catholicism into England. Did she try to do too much too quickly? How powerful and entrenched were Protestant and anti-Catholic views by 1553? You will then need to plan out your answer clearly and aim to include each of the five sources at some point in your essay. Sources A and D give a hostile view, while Sources B, C and E are more favourable. Notice that the question forces you to look at the extent of religious reform under Edward as well as the speed and severity of the changes under Mary.

If you broadly agree with the statement in the question, you might start by looking at Sources A and D, explaining why you think that their conclusions are overdrawn. How much evidence does Elton produce to back up his views in Source A? Use your own knowledge to explain why his ideas seem unacceptable. Is there evidence of Protestant propaganda in Foxe's account of Taylor's death in Source D? Use this as a springboard to discuss the problem of the burning of Protestants during Mary's reign. Then continue by using (via brief quotations) the other three sources to explore ideas which back up the statement in the question. Again, integrate own knowledge to expand these ideas as you deal with each of them. In this way you should find that sources such as these do help you to structure your answer. They each raise different issues and ideas which can act as convenient hooks upon which to hang your arguments. As always, the best answers will provide the reader with a convincing and well-supported line of argument.

Essay question in the style of AQA
You will need to read Chapter 6 and Section 2 to answer this question

1 'Between 1530 and 1540, Henry VIII's foreign policy was driven by the need for security. After 1540 it was driven by the King's desire to conquer Scotland.'
How far do you agree with this view ?   (20 marks)

How you should answer this question. You are being asked to discuss the factors affecting the formulation of foreign policy between 1530 and 1547, including the political and religious developments of the period. Having considered these you will need to decide how far you agree with this quotation. Clearly, questions of security were important in the 1530s when the Reformation isolated England from the two great and Catholic powers of Europe. However, the real concerns about security were largely confined to the later 1530s, especially after Charles V and Francis I made peace in 1538. In the 1540s the defeat of the Scots and attempt to marry Prince Edward to Mary, Queen of Scots might be seen as evidence of the desire to conquer Scotland. On the other hand the invasion of Scotland was seen as the normal prelude to war against France, rather than an act of conquest. The war against France, in alliance with Charles V, saw a return to the patterns of foreign policy seen in the early part of Henry's reign, when his personal desire for military glory seemed to be the mainspring of English foreign policy.

In the mark scheme, it may well say that, for the highest bands of achievement, candidates should demonstrate sound conceptual awareness of the demands of the question by providing a wide range of well-selected evidence to assess the objectives of Henry's foreign policy in this period. There will be evidence of sound knowledge of the 1530s and 1540s allied to sound judgement of the motives behind the twists and turns of English foreign policy in this period. Once again, the quality of the argument and the quality of the supporting evidence are vital in the assessment of your essay. You will need to plan carefully to ensure that your essay does not lapse into a description of foreign policy.

Essay question in the style of OCR

You will need to read Sections 3, 4 and 5 to answer this question.

> 1 To what extent do the rebellions and political instability during the reigns of Edward VI and Mary I show that there was 'a mid-Tudor crisis' during this period? *(35 marks)*

How to answer this question. Overall, you are being asked whether you think there was a mid-Tudor crisis or not. You need to focus your answer squarely on the rebellions and political instability of the reigns but you need not confine yourself entirely to those factors or indeed just to these two reigns. If you think that political instability of 1547–58 was not much worse than that of the period 1536–47, then this could clearly be an important and relevant part of your answer.

This is also an example of a 'definition' type of question. You need to clarify at the outset what you think a 'crisis' involves and your definition of the term can then act as a yardstick for measuring the events of these two reigns and providing a sustained answer to the question.

This can also be seen as a 'change over time' type of answer. In other words do you think that there was a crisis but only for one reign or part of one reign? Could 1549–52 be seen as a crisis because of the two rebellions of 1549 and the protracted overthrow of Somerset, while the periods before and after were relatively untroubled?

As always, this question demands a lot of thought and planning because there is no ready-made answer. To achieve high marks you will need to make a judgement, preferably at the start of your essay, and then sustain that judgement throughout your answer. One useful device, if you disagree with the title, is to spend some time explaining why people/historians might have thought there was a crisis and then show why such views are misguided.

BIBLIOGRAPHY

AS section: Politics and religion 1485–1558

Claire Cross, *Church and People 1450–1660*, Fontana (1976)
C. S. L. Davies, *Peace, Print and Protestantism*, Paladin (1977)
Susan Doran, *England and Europe 1485–1603*, Longman (1996)
G. R. Elton, *Reform and Reformation*, Arnold (1977)
Alexander Grant, *Henry VII*, Methuen, Lancaster Pamphlets (1985)
John Guy, *Tudor England*, Oxford University Press (1988)
W. J. Shiels, *The English Reformation*, Longman (1989)
Alan G. R. Smith, *The Emergence of a Nation State*, Longman (1984)
David Starkey, *The Reign of Henry VIII*, Collins and Brown (1991)
Robert Tittler, *The Reign of Mary I*, Longman (1983)

A2 section: English Reformations 1533–58

S. Brigden, *London and the Reformation*, Oxford University Press (1989)
A. G. Dickens, *The English Reformation*, Fontana (1964)
Eamon Duffy, *The Stripping of the Altars*, New Haven (1992)
Anthony Fletcher and Diarmaid MacCulloch, *Tudor Rebellions*, Longman (1997)
Peter Gwyn, *The King's Cardinal: The Rise and Fall of Thomas Wolsey*, Barrie and Jenkins (1991)
Christopher Haigh, *The English Reformation Revised*, Cambridge University Press (1987)
Christopher Haigh, *Reformation and Resistance in Tudor Lancashire*, Cambridge University Press (1975)
Christopher Haigh, *English Reformations*, Oxford University Press (1993)
Jennifer Loach and Robert Tittler (eds), *The Mid-Tudor Polity circa 1540–1560*, Macmillan (1980)
Jennifer Loach, *Parliament under the Tudors*, Oxford University Press (1991)
David Loades, *The Reign of Mary Tudor*, Ernest Benn (1979)
David Loades, *Revolution in Religion: The English Reformation 1530–1570*, University of Wales Press (1992)
David Loades, *Essays in the Reign of Edward VI*, Headstart History (1994)
Diarmaid MacCulloch, *The Later Reformation in England, 1547–1603*, Macmillan (1990)
Diarmaid MacCulloch (ed.), *The Reign of Henry VIII*, Macmillan (1995)
Diarmaid MacCulloch, *Thomas Cranmer*, Yale University Press (1996)
Diarmaid MacCulloch, *Tudor Church Militant: Edward VI and the Protestant Reformation*, Allen Lane (1999)
Richard Rex, *Henry VIII and the English Reformation*, Macmillan (1993)
J. J. Scarisbrick, *Henry VIII*, Penguin (1968)
J. J. Scarisbrick, *The Reformation and the English People*, Blackwell (1984)
Peter Servini, *The English Reformation* (based on primary sources), Hodder and Stoughton (1997)
Retha M. Warnicke, *The Rise and Fall of Anne Boleyn*, Cambridge University Press (1989)
Alison Weir, *The Six Wives of Henry VIII*, Pimlico (1991)
Robert Whiting, *The Blind Devotion of the People*, Cambridge University Press (1989)
Joyce Youings, *The Dissolution of the Monasteries*, Allen and Unwin (1971)

Warwick Video/J. J. Scarisbrick, *The Dissolution of the Monasteries*
Two film versions of Robert Bolt's play *A Man for All Seasons* with 1) Paul Scofield and 2) Charlton Heston as Sir Thomas More
BBC Videos, *The Six Wives of Henry VIII*, starring Keith Michell as Henry

INDEX